Dark Days

Tales of Disaster, Murder and Mystery
in the East Liverpool Area

Copyright © 2015 Gary Cornell

All Rights Reserved.

ISBN # 1517586267

No part of this book may be reproduced
in any form by any electronic or mechanical
means including photocopying, recording, or information
storage and retrieval without permission in writing from the author.

To my wonderful wife

Laure

You always love, support and believe in me
and you always listen.

To my children

Rebecca and Michael

Thank you for your love and faith in me.

To all my friends and supporters I could not
have done it without you

Table of Contents

Preface..i

1. **Fire or Water**
   The Winchester Disaster, February 23, 1866..........13

2. **Holocaust!**
   The Destruction of the Sloan Family, February 23, 1881......23

3. **Siren's Song**
   The Mysterious Murder of Joseph Martin,
   December 7, 1918..39

4. **Hurtling to Destruction!**
   Accidents on Streetcars, 1893-1915......................43

5. **Taken for a Ride!**
   The Roy Marino Murder, September 10, 1937.......67

6. **Ninety Minutes of Terror!**
   The "Dry Goods District" Fire, March 3, 1892.......91

7. **Something Terrible Has Happened!**
   The Tweed-Morris Murders, July 30, 1973...........101

8. **Wrong Place at the Wrong Time**
   The Tragic Death of Herbert Sayre, October 8, 1925..........109

9. **Death of a Firefighter**
   The Henry Avenue Tragedy, August 2, 1962.......113

10. **Shootout in Little Italy!**
    The Jim Kenney Murder, May 17, 1926................123

11. **Chlorine Gas!**
    The Water Filtration Plant Fire, April 3, 1958......139

12. **The Deadly Chain**
    The Accidental Death of George Morley, June 5, 1898.........141

13. **Tragedies on the Mainline**
    Railroad DisastersAccidents, 1893-1948..............147

14. **Conflagration!**
    The Great "Diamond" Fire, February 28, 1905 159

15. **In-Flu-Enza**
    The Spanish Influenza Pandemic of 1918 183

16. **Morning of Mayhem!**
    Samuel Mann's Insane Rampage, November 16, 1902 191

17. **I'm not Drunk; I'm Crazy**
    The Murder of Letha Barrett, May 23, 1946 195

18. **Fields of Flame**
    Oil Well Accidents, 1877-1899 205

19. **The Old Mill is on Fire!**
    The Rock Springs Park Tragedy, June 5, 1915 211

20. **Poison for Medicine**
    The Strange Life of Laura Christy, 1879-1937 221

21. **East Liverpool is Burning!**
    Major Downtown Fires 237

22. **A Wild and Treacherous Man**
    The Life and Death of "Crip" Cain, 1895-1905 253

23. **The Exploding Lamp!**
    The Hazlett House Fire, June 3, 1905 263

24. **The Wrong Man**
    The Murder of William Hyatt, February-March 1923 269

25. **Pursued by Misfortune**
    The Laird Family, 1903-1911 275

26. **A Mighty Deluge!**
    The Reservoir Collapse, October 13, 1901 283

27. **The Death Badge**
    The Death of James McCullough, May 13, 1913 293

28. **A Degenerate**
    The Adamant Porcelain Murders and Arson,
    February 7, 1918 303

Postscript 317

Chapter Sources 319

Photo Credits 337

Bibliography 339

Preface

All my life I have been interested in history. In my youth it was the Civil War and military history. As an adult these topics still remain a passion. Now other topics such as true crime and local history have become an interest as well.

In 1975 I was appointed to the East Liverpool Fire Department, and soon I was introduced to the darker side of my home town. It does not take long in an occupation such as a firefighter, before you see and take part in disasters, large and small. Every fire or accident is a disaster to those who are involved with it.

In 1980, I married the love of my life, my beautiful wife Laure. She has always supported my career as a firefighter and an amateur historian. We have two wonderful children, Rebecca and Michael.

During my free time at the fire station, I began to look through the old daily log books. The department has been keeping a daily log for more than one hundred years. I was drawn to the stories of the fires and the men who fought them so long ago. Consequently, I began to write down the events, and share them with my fellow firefighters. Soon the guys began talking about my "book."

In 1984, East Liverpool was celebrating its 150th anniversary. The Firefighters Union Local #24 wanted to put a museum together at Central Fire Station. Many of the guys worked hard to bring this about, and I became the unofficial department historian. My first experience with public writing came when the *East Liverpool Review* asked me to write about the fire department's history. The newspaper was putting out a historical edition for the 150th anniversary. They asked other people to write on other subjects, so I was not so special.

The "book" continued to grow. After a few years it began to look like a book and not just a bunch of random papers. I thought about publishing it; however, I did not. During the next twenty plus years, I was given the opportunity to speak to a number of organizations and clubs. People seemed to enjoy my stories about long forgotten fires and disasters. At least I hope they did, because I really enjoyed the opportunity to tell them.

In 1990, I was promoted to Lieutenant, and received my first experience of being in command at scenes where life and death sometimes hung in the balance. In 1995, I was promoted to Assistant Chief, which meant now I was responsible for the fire protection of East Liverpool during my 24 hour work shift. Potential disasters were always on my mind. The people of East Liverpool are fortunate that there are a great group of dedicated firefighters on the department. They kept the disasters to a minimum and always made me look good.

In the spring of 2007, Laure and I decided it was time for us to retire. The life of a professional firefighter also involves your family. They watch you go off to work, not knowing what danger lies ahead. My family was my support team, and I am sure they lifted more than a few prayers to our Lord Jesus, for my safe return. So after more than 32 years, I retired from a job that I really enjoyed. Our retirement has been a blessing, filled with travel and work at our church. Laure and I are growing closer to each other as well as to God.

However, my love of history remains a passion. I still have opportunities to speak and tell my stories every so often. At Christmas of 2011, my son Michael gave me a present of a series of books by John Stark Bellamy II. They are about crimes and disasters in the Cleveland area. I enjoyed reading them and told Michael, *"I could write a book like that."* He said, *"Well, why don't you?"* I could not think of a reason not to.

I started by putting together a selection of stories that I consider interesting. The stories are of fires, accidents, and also a few murders. They are the kind of tales that stir something dark in our spirit. We love a good murder mystery or an exciting catastrophe. We eagerly await the morning newspaper so we can read about the latest trial or that big fire. We slow down to gawk at the accident on the highway; it is in our nature. At the same time, we lament over the fact that good uplifting stories all seem to fall by the wayside. The reason for that is simple; they are just not fun.

Most of my stories took place nearly 100 years ago. All of them are at least 25 years old. I believe that newer stories should be left for a future time. Several of these stories have been told by other authors. Each writer tried to make his version of the story a little better and a little more interesting than the last. I have tried to do the same. My goal is to be as accurate as possible. I did this by using as many primary sources as possible, and leaving out all the old legends that cannot be authenticated. However, I believe some of my stories are fresh despite the fact that they have been long forgotten and untold since the event happened so many years ago.

This is not a novel. The people are real, and the events truly happened. The stories stand alone, covering various types of misery and mayhem, and just maybe a little mystery. I hope you enjoy them.

Gary J. Cornell

Chapter 1
Fire or Water!
The *Winchester* Disaster, February 23, 1866

Accidents on America's rivers were almost commonplace in the 1800's, for the riverboat business was dangerous; even in the best of times. Steam powered riverboats caught on fire, blew up and sank far too often. It could be said that death and destruction has always been the riverman's unwanted partner. So it was that East Liverpool was visited by that unwanted partner on a cold winter night in 1866.

The end of the Civil War had ushered in a new era of river commerce. The threat of war was now past and the "Golden Age" of the riverboats had begun. The entire inland river system was open once again for trade and there was a lot of money to be made.

The past four years of war had been hard on the river trade. Many boats had been sunk or burned in the fighting, and those that survived were worn out. It was into this environment that a group of experienced rivermen joined together to build a new riverboat. The group consisted of Captain Daniel Moore, Captain George D. Moore, James Hamilton, and John Ackley, all of Pittsburgh, Pennsylvania. A. M. Sheets and S. Sheets of Washington County, Ohio rounded out the ownership group. The plan was to build a first class packet style riverboat to work the Ohio River between Pittsburgh and Parkersburg, West Virginia. The group quickly raised the necessary funds and construction began in the fall of 1865.

Throughout the winter of 1865-66 the sound of construction was heard as the new boat took shape. It was built at the shipyard of Crissinger & Son of McKeesport, Pennsylvania, near Pittsburgh on the Monongahela River. The new boat was large at 560 tons. She was 220 feet long, 32 feet wide and drafted a little over six feet of water. She was a side-wheel packet type boat, whose two paddle wheels were 28 feet in diameter.

Four twenty-one foot long, 40 inch diameter steam boilers, built by the Watson & Munroe Company, powered this wooden monster. Her cost came in at $81,000, and she was given the name *Winchester*. She was an elegant looking boat, expensively fitted out. Even before her first trip the owners turned down an offer to buy the boat for $91,000.

The *Pittsburgh Commercial,* a daily newspaper reported on January 19, 1866 the following;

The Parkersburg to Pittsburgh packet line will receive a valuable addition upon the opening of navigation. The new and splendid side wheel steamer Winchester has been fitting out at the Allegheny wharf, by Capt. A.S. Shepherd will take her place as a Tuesday packet. The boat is entirely new and is one of the handsomest crafts yet built. She will be named after one of the most popular boats that ever left Pittsburgh.

Advertising in the *Pittsburgh Commercial* for the Winchester began a full month prior to her first trip. An advertisement read as follows;

Marietta and Parkersburg Packet Line

Speed   Safety   Comfort Combined

Pittsburgh-Wheeling-Marietta-Parkersburg

Daily Packet Line

Comprising the First Class Side Wheel Passenger Steamers Bayard, Winchester, Forest City

Down Trip

Leaves Pittsburgh every Tuesday & Friday at 11:00 am

Leaves Wheeling every Tuesday & Friday at 9:30 p.m.

Return Trip

Leaves Parkersburg every Wednesday and Saturday at 2:00 p.m.

Leaves Wheeling every Thursday and Sunday at 7:00 a.m.

James Collins & Co. Agents,

Wharf boat at the foot of Wood Street, Pittsburgh, Pennsylvania

---

A packet boat is one that carries the mail. These boats also carried passengers and freight between towns along the river. The *Winchester* would make her run from Pittsburgh to Parkersburg and back in three days.

The *Pittsburgh Gazette* reported on February 15th that the beds were equipped with box springs. The bar was handsomely fitted out and connected to both the wash room and the barber shop. Bartender George Young and Steward James Diven were in charge of this part of the boat.

The February 20th edition of the *Pittsburgh Commercial* carried this news:

> *The new and magnificent packet Winchester, Captain A.S. Shepherd leaves today on her first trip to the Virginia oil region. This boat has been built regardless of expense, being entirely new. She is destined to create a sensation along the river. Captain A.S. Shepherd is an officer of large experience and gentlemanly deportment, and understands his duty in all its departments. The First Clerk is our old friend Captain D. Moore formerly of the Bayard. As an officer and a gentleman he stands at the head of his profession.*

The Winchester arrived in Parkersburg, West Virginia without incident. She left for Pittsburgh on Wednesday, February 22nd. No more was heard from her until the early morning hours of Friday, February 23rd. She was heavily loaded, with at least 100 passengers and crew aboard. The freight load was heavy as well; it included 211 barrels of crude oil, 1200 empty oil barrels, 1000 empty nail kegs, 65 bales of batting, 150 bales of hay, and fifteen head of horses and cattle owned by the passengers. There was also other freight, such as the personal belongings of the passengers.

The night was bitterly cold with some ice floating in the water. At around 3:30 a.m. as she was passing the head of Babb's Island just above the sleepy village of East Liverpool, Ohio, disaster struck. When one of the firemen threw a shovel full of hot coals from the boiler overboard, the wind caught it, blowing the coals back onto the boat. The hot embers landed in the hay about ten feet forward of the boilers. The crew raised the alarm and began to fight the fire, but within moments it was beyond control. The flames spread in a flash to the empty oil soaked barrels and then to the full ones. Within minutes, all attempts to extinguish the blaze were abandoned.

Captain Asa Shepherd, upon hearing the alarm and seeing the blaze, ordered the boat's pilots, William Gordon and William Abrams to run the boat aground on the West Virginia shore. The engineer, G. Washington Dunbar, gave the boat a full head of steam as the boat sped toward the dark shore. Dunbar was driven from his post by the heat and flames before the boat grounded. He was forced to make a dash through the fire to escape.

Unfortunately, the *Winchester* slammed bow first into a sandbar just short of the shoreline, and shuddered to a stop. Captain Shepherd and Watchman Bill Hendley leaped from the bow and dragged a chain ashore to tie the boat to a tree so it could not drift back out into the channel. Pilots Gordon and Abrams narrowly escaped death as a burning stairway collapsed just behind them. The *Winchester* was now horizontal across the river, with the stern extending out into deep water.

The passengers who had been roused from their slumber by crewmembers now came out onto the burning deck. Quickly they were driven toward the stern by intense heat and flame, away from the safety of solid ground and out toward the deep icy water. As the flames grew in intensity, people began to climb onto the railings. Within moments they were forced to choose their destiny; the flames or the icy, black river. Most jumped at the same time although a few held on until the flames drove them too into the river. Witnesses later reported that one woman was seen as if in prayer as the flames swept over her. In the water there was utter panic as people struggled to get to shore. People clung to whatever they could find that would float. It did not matter how well one could swim, for after just a few minutes in the icy water, hypothermia would occur.

As the survivors struggled ashore, they could see the *Winchester* completely engulfed in flames. It was reported that at the height of the blaze, it was as light as day. No one on board was left alive. What no doubt had been a merry evening cruising majestically upon the river, had turned into an indescribable horror.

The Winchester burning

The place where the *Winchester* was grounded is the extreme eastern end of Chester, West Virginia. No town existed there in 1866. Hugh Newell did live nearby, and he immediately opened up his home to comfort the frozen survivors. R.R. Gardiner, who also lived nearby, arrived in his skiff and took a boat load of people to East Liverpool. However, most of the frightened and exhausted victims had to walk along the shore to a site opposite of the town. There they huddled together in disbelief, waiting to be ferried across the wide frigid river.

By this time East Liverpool had been aroused, and its citizens sprang into action. Several people opened their homes to the survivors, giving them warm food and drinks. Several store owners provided clothing and shoes since most were in their night clothes and bare feet. In the coming days, several hundred dollars were raised in both East Liverpool and Wellsville to aid those unfortunate souls. A letter to the editor of the *Wellsville Union* appeared from some of the survivors in the March 8th edition, thanking the ladies of East Liverpool for their relief efforts.

Daylight brought a sense of the loss. The boat had burnt to the water's edge, and was a shattered, smoldering hulk, a total loss. The boat's owners had only carried $50,000 of insurance. Also lost were all the records, including the passenger manifest. Consequently, no completely accurate account of the death toll can be made. The first reports estimated between twenty and thirty lives had been lost. Later this was lowered to around fifteen, but no one was really quite sure.

Those known to have perished included:

Mr. & Mrs. James Algeo of Matamoras, Ohio.

Ebenezer Martin of Sistersville, West Virginia.

Mr. George Walters and son. His wife survived by floating on her back with her infant son on her chest.

Michael Fragret (or Faggott or Gazzet). He was thought to be a German from Sewickley, Pennsylvania.

Mr. John Van Meter drowned along with three sons. He had tied them to himself and then jumped into the river. His wife, his older daughter and infant child survived.

Mr. George Young, the boat's bartender, from Rochester, Pennsylvania.

Mrs. Ridgley, the boat's chambermaid.

Mrs. A.M. Sheets, wife of one of the owners.

William Johnson, one of the firemen of the boat.

Mr. Armstrong, a member of the crew.

That makes the fifteen known victims; however, there may well have been others. No record exists of just who was aboard. Most of the passengers did not know each other, so they would not have known who was missing. Around one hundred people jumped into the dark, icy water that night. It is a testament to God's mercy that a great many more did not perish.

Over the next few days, stories telling of escapes and the fixing of blame began to appear. One story was that several crewmen got into the boat's yawl and floated downstream away from the people struggling in the freezing water. They said they had no oars and could not control the boat. Others said if they had just done their duty, then maybe no one would have drowned.

One of the boat owners, Mr. A.M. Sheets, said he had put a life preserver on his wife and told her to follow him as he jumped into the river. A lady jumped in right behind him and thinking it was his wife, Sheets pulled her to safety. The lady he rescued was not his wife. Mrs. Sheets was not so fortunate. Her arms became entangled with her clothing and she was unable to swim. The heavy wet clothes dragged her under, life preserver notwithstanding. Mr. Sheets swam out three more times after hearing what he thought was his wife calling for help. Each time he brought someone to shore with him. However, his wife of just six months was gone.

The worst story came from an unnamed officer of the *Winchester* which was reported by the *Wheeling Intelligencer* on February 26th. As the story goes, the officer says the fire was started due to negligence by the black crewmen. He said they were angry because Captain Shepherd had made them do double duty. They vowed to get even with the captain, saying they would certainly quit the boat in Pittsburgh. It was said that the watchman had warned one of the firemen to be careful in disposing of the hot coals, before the fire broke out. The paper speculated as to why these men would have carelessly risked their lives. The newspaper answered their own question, saying who could tell what their desperation and anger could produce. Also, they speculated that the crewmen may have been under the influence of liquor. The story went on to say that most of the black crewmen had escaped death and had simply disappeared into the woods, after doing some looting.

This story illustrates the racist feeling that was so prevalent at that time. The Civil War had ended less than a year earlier, and blacks, though free, were still treated little better than slaves. Unfortunately, in the quest to place or possibly shift blame away from others, the black crewmen became an easy target. The fact that hot coals started the fire is most likely true. There is no evidence, however, that it was anything but accident.

Over the weekend, the bodies began to surface. Several were taken to the home of Mr. & Mrs. William Davidson of East Liverpool to be prepared for burial. John Van Meter and his three sons were buried in East Liverpool on Sunday, February 25th. The remains of George Young, the bartender, and Mr. Fragret (sic) were sent home to their families when they were found. The bodies of fireman William Johnson and Mr. Armstrong were also recovered. The search for the others would continue, although dragging operations had to be suspended on Sunday due to the large amount of ice and the high water.

East Liverpool did not have a newspaper in operation at the time of the accident. The *Wellsville Union,* the nearest newspaper, published weekly, as did most of the other local papers. This meant news was slow in being reported. Hence, as each week passed the story grew colder. Soon the story of this tragedy became nothing more than a local legend.

The packet boat line continued operations using just two boats instead of three. The partners took this disaster in stride knowing that accidents were an unfortunate part of the business. The loss of life was of course never an acceptable part of the business.

As a postscript for this tragic accident, the *Pittsburgh Commercial* ran an editorial on February 28th. In it they declared that the transportation of passengers and hazardous freight on the same boat should be stopped. They declared that a load of oil barrels and hay was no less dangerous than gunpowder when exposed to fire. However, they understood that the carrying of passengers and freight was a necessary part of the business and it probably would not stop. They did, however, call for separate boats to be used. The practice finally did stop after many years. Today, towboats pushing barges filled with thousands of tons of freight glide past the site of the *Winchester* disaster. Today, passenger-carrying excursion boats pass by East Liverpool and even stop on rare occasions. The dangerous days of river disasters are past, although accidents do still occur. Fortunately, it has been a long time since women and children have stood on the railing of a burning boat and been forced to choose between *Fire or Water*.

Chapter 2
Holocaust!
The Destruction of the Sloan Family
February 23, 1881

The census of 1860 listed 1,600 people who called East Liverpool home. Ten years later the population was set at 2,077. The next census in 1880 listed the population at 5,567. East Liverpool was booming and it was already the largest city in Columbiana County.

Along with this population explosion came a building boom. New and larger potteries were being built, and many new business buildings were filling in the vacant lots on city streets.

East Liverpool seemed to have everything that a growing community could want; everything, that is, except protection from fire. Up until now the timely use of a "bucket brigade" was all that was necessary. However, with the buildings continuing to be built higher and to be more costly, it was apparent the old system would have to change.

As the 1870s were drawing to a close, several fires occurred that scared city officials. Although none caused serious damage, the potential loss was frightening. City Council began taking the necessary steps toward forming an organized fire department.

In September of 1877, Council passed an ordinance to provide for the building of a room attached to the new City Hall located on the corner of Market Street and 3rd Street. The room would be the headquarters of the future fire company. For the next several months nothing more happened.

Council voted in May of 1878 to set aside a half mill of taxation money to fund the fire company. They also appointed a fire committee of three Councilmen to get prices on a hook & ladder wagon.

The committee decided to go with the bid from the Caswell Improved Coupling Company of Chicago, Illinois. The wagon was ordered on July 4th at a cost of $475.00, and the wagon was delivered by rail in early August.

It was a hand drawn wagon which contained several ladders of various sizes. Other equipment included axes, pike poles, lanterns, rubber buckets and other hand tools. It also included a winch with ropes and chain attached to a grappling hook. This was used to pull down walls left standing following a fire. That is why even today some fire trucks are called hook & ladder trucks.

Advertisements were placed in all the city newspapers calling for good men to volunteer for the fire company. The ads included the warning "Drunkards need not apply."

On August 13th council named Robert Hague to be the chief or captain of the fire department. Little is known about Hague except that he was a house painter who lived on 4th Street. It was not reported if there were other applicants. He went right to work organizing the volunteers.

At the first meeting of the Crockery City Fire Company on August 19th the volunteers confirmed Hague as their captain. Other officers were elected, rules adopted and the company was organized. Following the meeting the men set about learning their new duties.

By October 30th the company was trained and ready to serve. The city accepted the company under the direction of Captain Hague. One newspaper described the Captain as being *"a live man."*

The Tribune reported on July 5, 1879 that the fire company had made good time in responding to the June 25th fire at Rinehart's Livery Stable on 2nd Street. The had arrived in about five minutes. It was their first fire.

As the city continued to grow and spread up the hill away from the river, the need for a steady water supply became imperative. During the summer of 1879 a water pumping station was built on the River Road, and a reservoir on Thompson's Hill. Water lines were laid to connect the system, and on November 5th water began to flow into the city. This was a great boon to the fire protection of East Liverpool, but some people still had their reservations.

Commenting on a recent fire, *The Tribune* ran an editorial on January 31, 1880. They said in part, *"that a "bucket brigade" was worth six fire engines at the start of any fire, if you have the water. To hook hose up to the fire hydrants and spray water would have destroyed the building and its contents."*

City Council, however, did not agree since they had already purchased a second hand hose reel from the Cincinnati Fire Department. Several potteries also bought hose and other equipment for their protection.

The fire company was put to the test again, when fire destroyed the grocery store of Mr. A.M. Davidson on May 25, 1880. The business was located on 2nd Street and the loss was $5,000. City Council praised the work of Captain Hague and his men following the blaze. However, there was an undercurrent of dissatisfaction with the fire company.

Events at this blaze prompted the *Potter's Gazette* to editorialize on May 27th that, *"The Fire Company should turn their hoses onto the people that are trying to tell them what to do at fires."* The paper went on to say, *"If the Fire Department is incompetent then replace them but do not interfere with them."*

East Liverpool's building boom continued through the summer of 1880 with several business buildings springing up around town. One of the new buildings belonged to Mr. Frank Stewart. Stewart was from Hancock County, West Virginia, and he had come to East Liverpool in 1879 to get in on the boom.

During the summer of 1880, he constructed a large three story wood frame building at the corner of 6th Street and Washington Street, where they intersect with Broadway. The building was located on the southwest corner and faced onto 6th Street. It was divided into three sections.

Mr. Stewart occupied the eastern section, operating a feed store on the first floor. Part of the second floor and the entire third floor was used as a warehouse for his feed store. A vast amount of combustible material was present within the building. An elevator connected all three floors in this section of the building. It was operated by an engine located in the basement.

At about 2 a.m. on October 13, 1880, fire broke out on 2nd Street. L.R. Farmer owned the two story wood frame business building, which was known as the Farmer's Block. The fire started in the shoe store operated by H.C. Schlimme and it quickly spread throughout the structure.

The fire company responded quickly and soon had three good streams of water in service. For a while the large crowd was in fear that the fire would spread to adjoining properties, but the fire was eventually brought under control. The building was a total loss, and the cause was never determined. Five businesses were ruined and one family was left homeless. The dollar loss was put at about $10,000 or about two hundred thousand today. Again, the city newspapers praised the work of the fire company. It was the worst fire they had yet faced.

In mid-November, two brothers arrived from New Matamoras, Ohio to seek their fortune in this fast growing city. The brothers were originally from Harrisville, Ohio in Harrison County. William and James Sloan rented the center section of Stewart's building. The brothers opened a drug store under the name of Sloan & Brother. They were on a busy corner of a fast growing area, and things were looking up.

William Sloan was described as an honest looking man of medium height and build. He was thirty-five years old, and wore a full beard. In January of 1867, he had married Hannah Ann Yost of Short Creek Township, in Harrison County. She was now thirty-one years old, with a fair complexion and light colored hair. Together they had seven children; the oldest was thirteen and the baby only twenty two months.

The Sloans moved into a second floor apartment over their storefront. James Sloan was living with them until they got the business up and running. Then he would bring his family to East Liverpool from Harrison County.

By now the western section of the building had been rented to George Kaufman. He ran a grocery store out of his storefront and lived upstairs with his large family.

Business had been good these few months, and Sloan & Brother was building a good customer base. The Sloan children were attending school, which was a major part of the family's decision to move to East Liverpool. They were settling in, and James was getting ready to bring his family to town.

Tuesday, February 22, 1881, was like most days. William and Hannah operated the drugstore while the older children attended school. The younger children played on the floor of the store. James had gone back to Harrisville to prepare his family for the move to town.

Something out of the ordinary happened that afternoon. A horse had stepped onto the cellar door, covering the stairway on Kaufman's part of the basement. The horse broke through and got stuck, so William went out to help free the animal. While he was in the basement, he noticed that a barrel of carbon oil in Kaufman's cellar was leaking. The oil had saturated the floor around the barrel. He would have to tell Kaufman. He also had an oil barrel on his side of the basement petition wall. He checked his basement area and determined all was well. He went upstairs, but he forgot to lock his cellar door. He also forgot to tell Kaufman. Kaufman went down and secured his cellar door, but did not notice the leaking oil.

That evening James returned bringing with him Wilmer Skeels their brother-in-law. Skeels was married to James and William's sister Amanda. He was a mechanic and had come to East Liverpool hoping to find work. After catching up on the family news, everyone settled down for a good night sleep. William extinguished all the lanterns and banked the stove in the kitchen. There were no gas lights in his section of the building.

The apartment had two exits both were located in the kitchen, which was in the rear of the apartment. One exit was a stairway leading into the first floor store room; it was covered by a trap door. Another door led to an outside stairway. The other two sections of the building were designed the same way.

At about 2 a.m. on February 23rd, a loud noise woke William Sloan from a deep sleep. To him it sounded as if someone or something had struck the house. He ran to the window and saw smoke and flame which seemed to be coming from his basement.

By now James and Wilmer were up. The men could see flames racing up the side of the building. William had now awakened Hannah and the children. They were hurrying to get everyone dressed. William and James ran into the kitchen and opened the trap door. Smoke quickly began to fill the kitchen. Downstairs was filled with smoke and fire.

They ran back to the family and told them they had to leave now, regardless of their state of dress. The apartment was now filling with thick black smoke. James called out, *"We have to get out now! Follow me!"* Little Katie cried out, *"Take me, Uncle Jim!"* James grabbed up the child and headed through the dense smoke into the kitchen. The smoke was nearly suffocating as James struggled to find the outside door. Finally he found it and burst it open. Still carrying Katie, he rushed down the staircase, which was now starting to burn. He could hear the pounding feet and voices of people coming behind him. He was relieved to think the others were right behind him. When he got to the bottom he looked back and saw that it was not his family that had followed him. He had heard the Kaufman family escaping from their apartment. After getting Katie to safety James tried to go back up the stairs to help the others, but the stairs were now impassable.

Meanwhile, William had seen the difficulty James had in getting out through the kitchen. Also, now that the door was open, the fire had gained oxygen and had grown in intensity. With the children baulking, he had to find another way out. He led the family into Stewart's section of the building. This area was also filled with heavy smoke. As they crossed the room Hannah called out, *"Don't fall down that hole, Will!"* They had nearly fallen down the elevator opening.

Reaching the Washington Street side of the building, William flung open the window. Outside a crowd of people had gathered. They saw William in the window and began to yell, *"Jump, Jump!"* Seeing no other course, he yelled to Hannah to jump, but she refused. The thick smoke was blocking their vision and sapping their strength, and the children were crying loudly. Wilmer Skeels told William, *"Jump and you can catch the children,"* or at least break their fall. Wilmer said, *"I will help the others to get out."* Quickly, William climbed onto the windowsill and jumped. The distance was about twenty feet and he was barefooted, wearing only his long johns. He hit the pavement hard, nearly breaking his left ankle. Struggling to his feet, he expected to start catching the children. However, looking up, there was no one at the window, just heavy black smoke pouring from the opening. He began calling out to them to come back to the window, but there was no answer.

William made his way around to the burning staircase and tried to make his way back into the apartment. After just a couple of steps, two men grabbed him from behind and pulled him away. Just then a loud crashing sound was heard. Everyone knew it was the sound of an upper floor crashing down onto the floor below. William knew his family was gone. He collapsed, crying uncontrollably and calling their names.

What had happened after William jumped can only be guessed. Were they overcome by the smoke? Did the children refuse to jump, and Hannah and Wilmer decided to face death with them? Maybe one of the children had gotten separated from the group and the other tried to find them? We do not know. What we do know is that eight lives were snuffed out that terrible night.

Chief Hague and the Fire Company were on the scene in good time, but there was little they could do to save either life or property. They went to work quickly and soon had several hose streams in action. Local potteries loaned their private hose and equipment to the struggle. The building however, was a firetrap. It was built without any fire stops, with every room connecting to the other. The stock in the feed store was all flammable, and the oil barrels in the basement exploded early, feeding the massive blaze. The elevator openings through the floors allowed the fire to spread quickly as did the several stairways.

The building burned freely. The heat was nearly unbearable. Men took off their coats and soaked them in the water. They then held them up to shield the men working the nozzles.

Within no more than thirty minutes the building was reduced to a huge pile of burning rubble, resembling a huge bonfire. The residence of Frank Stewart adjoined the building, and although moderately damaged, it was saved.

Firemen continued to pour water on the blaze throughout the night. It was dawn before the ruins were cool enough to permit a search for the victims. The building had been reduced to little more than ashes, so there was little difficulty in finding the bodies. However, because of the intensity of the blaze the victims had been nearly cremated. The bodies were hardly recognizable as human beings. One by one, the pitiful remains were wrapped in sheets and laid side by side in a temporary morgue. By ten o'clock that morning, seven bodies had been recovered. They had been found close together near where the elevator would have been. The bodies were surrounded by piles of half cooked grain.

Officials surmised that they may have fallen through the elevator opening because there was not much debris under the bodies. What little debris that was not reduced to ashes was on top of the victims. This leaves the question, did they fall through the opening, or did they jump? Perhaps they sought a quicker death as the flames approached.

Late into the afternoon the eighth and final victim was found. It was thought to be that of four-year-old Paul. The victims were identified only by the size of the remains. Hannah was the only one they were sure of, since what remained of the baby's body was attached to the larger victim's body. It was thought Hannah had been holding the child at the end.

As it is with people in any era, the desire to see the macabre side of life is powerful. All day long a steady flow of people entered the unguarded morgue to look at the horrific spectacle. They were not disappointed, since all that was left of the victims were headless, limbless trunks.

The victims included Mrs. Hannah Sloan and six of her seven children. The children were Edna Luella 13; Clyde 12; Libbie 10; Alexander 8; Paul 4; and the baby, Mary Jane, "May," only 22 months old. The final victim was Wilmer Skeels, thirty-four, who had picked a very bad time to visit his family.

Within days this terrible story had been carried in newspapers around the country. Editors called for an end to the "firetraps," for they existed in every town. Fire officials knew that disaster could happen at any time, and was only one careless act away.

The Sloan family had been nearly destroyed. William and little Katie were taken in by Rev. J.C. Taggart and his family. Everything that could be done was done to console the grief stricken father and husband. Fortunately, Katie was too young to fully comprehend the tragedy her life had become.

Brother James left early on Wednesday morning for Harrisville to inform the family of this tragedy. He had the awful duty to tell his sister Amanda that her husband Wilmer was dead. He also needed to see his own family and probably hold them in his arms in grateful thanksgiving.

Early on Thursday morning, a funeral service was held at the United Presbyterian Church. Rev. Taggart along with several other local pastors conducted the service. The church was filled to overflowing, and many people stood in the street outside the church. School had been suspended, and many of the children's classmates were present in the church.

William and Katie Sloan numbly sat in the front row as the bodies of their family were brought before the altar. The bodies had been placed in three caskets. Hannah and the youngest children had been placed in one, the older three children in a second, and Skeeles in the third.

Rev. Taggart spoke first, telling of God's mysterious ways and ending by urging the audience, *"to be also ready for in such an hour as you think not, the Son of Man cometh."* The Rev. T.V. Milligan spoke about *"seeing eggs in a bird's nest one day and then seeing only the broken shells the next. The birds had not died but had been released to soar above us singing melodiously. So it is with these precious little ones who perished in the flames. We see only the little broken shells now for their spirits are now soaring in Heaven."* He also said that little Katie, *"was the one little lamb snatched from the flames to be a comfort to her sadly bereft father."* Rev. G.G. Westfall gave the closing prayer while Rev. John Williams offered the benediction and dismissed the audience.

"In Heaven above-
Where all is love-
We shall meet all the little ones there"

A large crowd walked behind the procession which bore the caskets and the family to the train station. William and Katie boarded the 10:45 a.m. southbound train. They would escort the remains of their family first to Bridgeport, Ohio and then the twelve miles overland to Harrisville. The family is laid to rest in the Olive Branch Cemetery in Harrisville, Ohio. The citizens of East Liverpool donated money for all of the funeral expenses and the train fare, as well as some needed funds for William and Katie.

Unknown at the time, the furnace had overheated and caught the underside of the church floor on fire during the service. However, thanks to the quick action and cool thinking of a couple of men, the fire was extinguished by the use of several buckets of water. The service went on upstairs without any panic and only the slight smell of smoke.

At three o'clock that afternoon, a Coroner's Inquest was held with acting Coroner Squire Mills presiding. First, William Sloan's deposition was read.

Sloan had testified about the horse incident and how he saw the leaking oil. He said that the gas service in his section was never used, that his family used lanterns for light. Sloan said he had few combustible items in his store except for a small amount of turpentine and alcohol that was kept behind the counter in the drug store. He also explained his action up until the time when he was dragged from the burning staircase. He also thought the loud noise that awakened him may have been the oil barrel exploding. Sloan said he had forgotten to lock his cellar door, so maybe an intruder had set the fire.

George Kaufman was confined to bed due to injuries following the fire. He said he had secured his broken cellar door with a prop. He did not know his oil barrel was leaking. He also said his store was securely locked and all lights were out except for one gas light which he always kept burning. It was located over his desk in the rear storeroom of the grocery store. It was visible from the street. Kaufman said he knew nothing about how the fire had started.

Frank Stewart testified that in his portion of the basement, he had a boiler, an engine to lift his elevator and a milling machine for grinding grain. He usually used them about twice a week; however, they had been idle for several days. He denied that the third floor was filled with bales of hay, as had been reported. He said it was used mostly to dry clothes. He had closed up around 8 p.m., and had turned off all the gas lights. The fire in his stove was very nearly burned out at the time. He then went home to his residence that adjoined the feed store.

The last witness was Jack Bucher, who lived across from the building on 6th Street. Mr. Bucher said a noise woke him up. He got up and looked out the window, but saw nothing amiss. He said he could see the light in Kaufman's grocery store, but that it was always that way. He went back to bed. A few minutes later, at about 2 a.m., he heard another noise, but again saw nothing. A few minutes later a third noise aroused him. This time the building was on fire. He hurriedly got dressed and ran to awaken Mr. Stewart.

What was not said was that by this time the Sloan family was already fighting for their lives.

Squire Mills found that all the occupants had taken proper care to extinguish all open fires within the building. So Mills ruled that in his judgment that left only incendiarism as the probable cause of the fire. He ruled that an intruder had entered through the unlocked cellar door bent on robbery. The intruder had then either, by intent or by accident, started this horrific fire. *(* There is absolutely no evidence to support this ruling. The fact that the cellar door was unlocked is of interest, but certainly not conclusive.)*

Ruins of the Stewart Feed Mill

Life again returned to normal in East Liverpool. However, things were not the same for the fire department. Following the fire, the firefighters were praised and thanked for their heroic work. But behind the scenes rumors were spreading. *(* A careful study of the various city newspapers and fire department records revealed nothing except some interesting clues.)*

In early March, the Crockery City Fire Department paid for the following ad to run in all the city newspapers;

> *Whereas, Certain parties in our community have meddled with things not concerning them, and*
>
> *Whereas, They have circulated false reports as regards our sentiments toward our Chief, therefore be it,*
>
> *Resolved, That we denounce all such reports as unjust, unwarranted and uncalled for,*

Resolved, That we are satisfied with our Chief, so far as regards his capabilities as an officer, and his conduct as a gentleman.

*E.N. Croxall,
Secretary C.C.F.D.*

The company also voted to give Chief Hague a gold watch.

On April 9, 1881, the owner and editor of the *East Liverpool Tribune*, Jeremiah Simms, published an editorial about the use of too much water by firefighters. The story from Boston, Massachusetts, told of the proper use of fire hoses so as to prevent unwarranted water damage. Mr. Simms had been a critic of the use of fire hoses in the past.

Also, at the risk of sounding conspiratorial, the *Tribune* ran a joke during this period of time. The story goes, *"A housepainter had fallen three stories from his ladder. A crowd of people gathered around to see if they could help the poor man. As he was coming around someone gave him a drink of water. The painter exclaimed how many stories do I have to fall before someone gives me brandy?"*

There is no explanation for this joke and it appears to be completely out of context. Chief Hague was, however, a housepainter. Was this a subtle way of branding him as a drinking man? Again it may sound conspiratorial, but something was certainly going on. The end came on June 14th when Robert Hague offered his resignation from the Fire Department. Council accepted it with a vote of thanks for past efficient service.

City Council appointed Louis Love as the next Fire Chief on June 28th. *The East Liverpool Tribune* expressed how pleased they were with Love's appointment. They called him a man of "good judgment." They also said that there could be no better choice. Perhaps Mr. Simms had got his man?

Frank Stewart wasted no time in getting back into business. As soon as the weather broke, he began to rebuild on his lot. This time it would be a brick structure; again, three stories tall. This new building faced onto Washington Street and had two store fronts divided by a center stairway to the upper floors. There was also a third store front facing onto 6th Street toward the rear of the building.

The upper floors of this building for many years were occupied by a hotel. First it was the Hotel Grand, and by the 1920s the Hollenden Hotel. The building changed owners and occupants over time, but for ninety-three years it was a city landmark. That ended on a cold January night in 1974 when fire would once again claim this corner of 6th Street.

Louis Love lasted about a year as fire chief. The fire department had had a successful fair in May of 1882. They were raising money to pay for their operation. Chief Love was given $300 to pay some of the outstanding bills. Chief Love took the money and vanished. He was finally located in late August, living in Maryland and working in a Baltimore pottery. City Marshall John Wyman traveled by train to Baltimore and arrested him. Love was tossed into jail upon his arrival back in East Liverpool. At his hearing he claimed that he never had any intention of stealing the fire department's money. He said that he had returned to town voluntarily, and had not been extradited. He then paid for Marshall Wyman's expenses, and gave the fire department $100 in cash and a personal check for $200. He maintained his innocence and was allowed to return to Baltimore with his family. Louis Love was gone from East Liverpool for good, but he never did explain just what he was doing in Baltimore with the fire department's money.

Robert Hague returned to the fire department as a firefighter under the new Chief, Phil Morley, and served four more years. He continued to ply his trade as a painter. Mary, his wife, passed away on October 10, 1894, leaving Robert alone. In those days before pensions and Social Security, people worked until they could not do it any longer. At some point, Hague was unable to care for himself so he entered into the Columbiana County Home. Hague died from bronchial asthma on January 18, 1928 at age 74. He is buried in the County Home Cemetery.

Frank Stewart died on October 9, 1901 at the age of 51. The cause of his death was listed as typhoid fever. This was not an uncommon occurrence in those days, since the drinking water came directly from the Ohio River.

William and Katie Sloan moved away from East Liverpool, possibly to Belmont County, Ohio.

Postscript

On July 23, 1901 a serious fire broke out in the basement of J.J. Rose's tobacco and news store. The fire was first discovered when a passerby saw smoke pouring through the sidewalk grates.

The alarm was turned in and the fire department arrived quickly. The Central Fire Station was only two blocks away. Fire Chief Clint Morley quickly sized up the situation as the men entered the smoke filled basement hoping to quickly snuff out the flames. In those days, there was no protection from smoke except for a wet cloth tied over the firefighter's nose and mouth.

Once inside the basement, they found a large stock of tobacco products. Mr. Rose had just received a large supply. They also found a significant amount of fireworks. Some of the shells were quite large. The firefighters directed water onto these items and gave them a thorough soaking for fear they might explode in the cramped basement.

The smoke was intense and only grew worse as water was introduced. Unable to ventilate the basement, the firefighters suffered greatly from the lack of oxygen. Before the blaze was quelled, five firefighters were overcome by the smoke and had to be carried from the basement. They included Chief Morley, Assistant Chief James McCullough, and firefighters Bill Ruhe, George Betteridge, and Pat Wood. Several other men were sickened by the noxious smoke. The fire was finally extinguished after two hours of the hardest work the firefighters had ever done.

It was reported that the men returned to Central Station where Dr. Bailey came and attended them. All were suffering from smoke inhalation. Later, Mike O'Malley, a saloon keeper came to the station and gave them a good rubdown with towels and whiskey. The *News-Review* reported that it did them great good. The next day, although all the men were at their posts, not one of them was fit for duty. No one had eaten anything, and none had been able to sleep. They were totally exhausted.

The East Liverpool News-Review reported that the men had faced death in the same place were twenty years earlier the Sloan family was destroyed.

Chapter 3
"Siren's Song"
The Mysterious Murder of Joseph Martin
December 7, 1918

Pasquale Fiesule left his home in Italy in 1914. Leaving behind a wife and two small children, the 26-year-old man was off to seek his fortune in America. Like many others, he planned to send for his family once he was settled. After arriving in the United States, Fiesule made his way to Columbus, Ohio. Two years later he came to East Liverpool. By now he had stopped using his real name, and had adopted the American name of Joseph Martin. He found part time work on the streetcar line. Martin was a sober, good natured man without an enemy in the world; at least not that anyone knew of.

While waiting for the right time to send for his family, Martin found a girlfriend. His lady friend was never identified, but was described as being a very attractive, fun-loving Italian widow. It was said that she lived part time in East Liverpool and part time in Midland, Pennsylvania. It was also true that their relationship was at times somewhat stormy. Martin, however, was completely smitten by her and lavishly spent all his money trying to please her. She was insatiable.

Friday, December 6th was payday, and Martin drew $35 dollars from the streetcar company. That night at his boarding house located at 419 Market Street, Joseph Martin prepared himself for a big night on the town. He dressed in his finest attire. His suit was cleaned and pressed, a freshly laundered linen shirt with a starched white collar, a silk tie, and perfectly shined shoes. He was meeting his lady friend later that night, and all was well; or was it? At around 9:30 that night Martin asked his friend, one of the other boarders, if he could borrow a revolver and some cartridges. The friend did not have a gun, so Joe ventured out without one. He had a date to keep. His friend thought the request was odd because no one had ever known Martin to carry a gun, or even a knife. The friend began to wonder, did he feel he needed protection, or did he have something else in mind?

Dawn had not yet broken as the work train was making its way toward East Liverpool on the Cleveland & Pittsburgh Railroad. The train was coming from Wellsville, and had just passed Walkers when the crew saw something on the tracks. Upon stopping, the work crew was confronted with a ghastly sight. The torn and mangled body of a young well-dressed man was lying partly on the tracks. His feet had been severed by the 3:00 a.m. westbound passenger train. There were several deep cuts and bruises on the head of the victim. However, the train had not killed him. The victim had had his throat cut from ear to ear, just above his starched white collar, which was now crimson, as was his shirt.

When the police arrived, it was light enough to see so they began searching for clues. The place where the killing took place was quite evident from the blood soaked gravel between the tracks, several feet from where the body now lay. They soon determined that the victim was Joseph Martin, and that he had been robbed. All his money was gone except for 65 cents in his pocket. Gone, too, was the pocket watch and chain he always carried. A small piece of the chain was found in the gravel ballast of the railroad tracks. The police thought that the killers broke the chain when it was pulled free. One clue baffled the officers. Lying near the body was a large black overcoat; it was much too large for Martin to wear. The coat had been badly torn, and none of Martin's friends could identify the coat as belonging to the victim.

Police theorized that Martin had been lured to the remote area, possibly by his mysterious girlfriend. Once there, he had been attacked from behind and his throat cut, probably with a straight razor. After the deed was done, they thought the woman and her accomplice simply disappeared into the night. The East Liverpool police had very little to go on, and no real way to investigate. They could contact police departments around the area and ask if anyone saw the mysterious woman, but they did not even know her name. These were the days before the FBI or state police forces. Many times killers just moved on, apparently just like the killer of Joseph Martin, and his mysterious lady friend.

Chapter 4
Hurtling to Destruction!
Accidents on Streetcars

In the days before the automobile gave the common man a personal means of transportation, reliable public transient was a necessity. East Liverpool had been blessed (and sometimes cursed), since 1891 with an efficient streetcar system that linked the city neighborhoods as well as the surrounding communities. However, due to the hilly nature of the East Liverpool area there was always the danger of accidents, and some inevitably occurred. Here is a sampling of just a few;

"Walking the Trestle"
December 1, 1893

It was a good party and no one was ready to go home. The large crowd was enjoying the music and dancing at the home of John Robinson on Ohio Avenue. But it was getting late, already past midnight on December 1st 1893. Charles Karcher stopped a passing streetcar and asked Motorman Eckes if his was the last car of the night. Eckes said it was his last run. A little while later the party broke up and everyone headed home. Since the streetcars had stopped running everyone would have to walk. A group of thirteen men and women began the long three mile walk to downtown East Liverpool.

The weather was pleasant for December, so the walk would be leisurely with much talking and laughter. The group decided to take a short-cut across the trestle since there would be no streetcars running until morning.

The East End trestle ran downhill from near the end of Ohio Avenue across the marshy area known as Ralston's Crossing. This bridge allowed the streetcar line to cross over the East End Run where it joins the Ohio River. The track then followed along what is now the River Road.

The party of walkers had reached about the middle of the 294 foot long trestle when they were suddenly illuminated. Over the hill from Ohio Avenue, came Car # 16 operated by Motorman Benjamin Gregg.

Gregg later said that as the car straightened after the slight curve and dropped over the hill, he saw in his light that the track ahead was "*black with people.*" He could see their frightened faces as he jammed the brake on and reversed the power, but it was too late to stop. The car traveled the last 40 feet within a second and slammed into the crowd. People were scattered like bowling pins. Some jumped the fifteen to twenty feet from the trestle, and others were knocked off as the car plowed through the crowd. When it came to a stop, Gregg jumped off and grabbed the headlamp to see what he could do. He quickly saw he could do nothing without help. He then turned and ran up the track to the power house to get help. Soon a car was speeding from downtown carrying East Liverpool Street Railway Superintendent Robert Andrews and, oddly enough, Undertaker John Rinehart, among others.

Beneath the wheels of the car lay the mangled body of Estella Harsha; she had died instantly. The right side of her head was crushed and her right arm was nearly severed. As the first rescuers arrived, they saw her husband Miller Harsha, standing front of the car with their baby in his arms. Mr. Harsha had escaped death by jumping or falling between the ties; he did not know which. A nasty gash on the back of his head was his only injury, besides being in shock. He had been carrying the baby when the accident occurred, how he managed to hold on no one could tell.

The car was carefully moved, and Mrs. Harsha's body was pulled free. In all, nine other people suffered injuries from being hit by the car or jumping from the bridge. The Martin sisters, Laura and Dell were the most seriously injured. Both girls had been hit, and knocked off the trestle. The car hit Dell in the back and side. She fell nearly 40 feet over the hillside. Her sixteen-year-old sister Laura, suffered from head injuries.

In the coming days, some people blamed Motorman Gregg and wanted him to be arrested. Squire Manley held an inquest into the accident. It was testimony from the victims themselves that cleared Gregg of any wrongdoing. They said he had done all he could do. The accusations soon faded away. However, Gregg himself was pretty shaken by the death of Mrs. Harsha.

There were also those who wanted to lay the blame at the city's door step. City officials were able to prove the accident had occurred on private property. The partygoers also could have taken the longer wagon road to get back to town. The railway company braced for possible lawsuits, but they too were on solid ground since the victims were walking illegally on their trestle. All the other victims would recover. Maybe now, people would think twice before "walking the trestle."

Trouble on Franklin Street

There were many accidents on East Liverpool's hills. You could expect there to be problems negotiating Lisbon Street, and St. Clair Avenue, since they are so long and steep. However, even a short hill like Jefferson Street, then known as Franklin Street, had its share of excitement.

"The First Trip was His Last"
July 8, 1895

On a typical summer afternoon of July 8, 1895, Car #31 passed along 6th Street picking up passengers and freight, as was the custom of the day. The ultimate destination was Wellsville, and the car was pretty full with 20 or more passengers. Motorman James Hamilton, who had been on the job for only a week was working alone for the first time, as a motorman.

The car turned onto Franklin Avenue, (now Jefferson Street) and started down the hill heading toward West Eighth Street. As it passed Seventh Street it began to pick up speed. Hamilton began to apply the brakes trying to slow the car. Witnesses later said the car passed by them at a terrific rate of speed. A railroad spur known as the "Horn Switch" lay at the bottom of the grade, and the crossing was rough. Car #31 sped across it and went a few yards more before coming to a culvert. The tracks and the road had to pass over the meandering stream known as Carpenter's run.

(*Today the freeway interchange covers this stream as it flows underground to the river.)

As the car approached the narrow culvert, it jumped the tracks and slammed into the stream bed at full speed. Hamilton either jumped or was thrown from the car. A barrel filled with potatoes may have slammed against him shoving him out; we will never know. However, he landed head first into the stone abutment of the culvert, and was killed instantly from a fractured skull. Rescuers found his body lying next to the mangled car in the stream bed. The passengers were hurled forward, piling on top of each other. Rescuers, who rushed to the scene, were confronted with a mass of struggling bleeding bodies. Nearly all of the passengers suffered injury. However, three were more serious than the others. Frank Green, a young boy was badly crushed he was given up for dead several times over the next few days. He did however, recover. Miss F. A. Nessly was found near the bottom of the pile. She had suffered serious trauma to her head. East Liverpool had no hospital at the time, so she was taken by train to the West Penn Hospital in Pittsburgh, Pennsylvania. Mrs. Charles Manor had a severe laceration to her head, which took doctors nearly four hours to completely stop the bleeding. Several other passengers had jumped from the car before it had derailed.

(*This accident renewed the call for a hospital to be established. At this time neighborhood people would open their homes to the victims of nearby accidents.)

James Hamilton lived in the East End with his wife and six children. Mrs. Hamilton was inconsolable. It had been her idea for him to take the job. He had agreed only because of her insistence. The Hamilton's were well liked and it seemed as if all of the East End turned out to pay their respects.

East Liverpool Traction Company superintendent Robert Andrews, carefully inspected the wrecked car, and declared he could find no mechanical problems. Witnesses testified that it appeared Hamilton had done everything he could to control the car. Still they wondered if a more experienced man could have prevented the accident.

The culvert, over which the car crashed, had long been deemed as being insufficient for the traffic it carried. Ironically the city was awarding a contract to replace it that very night. However, no one felt that anything the city did to the culvert would have prevented this awful accident.

"Terror in the Afternoon"
October 18, 1902

Car #14, operated by Motorman William Kincaid was heading toward Wellsville, Ohio at about 2:00 p.m. The car was carrying nearly twenty passengers. The occupants had been in town that Saturday morning doing their shopping and socializing, and now it was time to go home.

Kincaid was a long time employee, and was known as one of the most careful men on the line. Kincaid guided the car onto the Franklin Street hill, and had just rounded the curve above Seventh Street, when he saw it. There was a freight train on the "Horn Switch" at the bottom of the hill.

The railroad spur known as the "Horn Switch" exited the main line near were the sewage treatment plant is now located, behind Westgate School. The spur allowed for rail cars to be moved through town to the potteries and other plants in the Bradshaw Street area. This section of track traveled along Webber Way toward Dresden Avenue.

When Kincaid saw the train blocking the right of way he applied the brakes, since he knew he would need to come to a full stop. The brakes however, failed to slow the car, and it began picking up speed. Evidently, the train engineer saw what was about to happen, since he applied power to the slow moving train. The train sprang forward but it was unable to clear the crossing.

Just before the collision, Motorman Kincaid and Conductor William Wade, jumped from the speeding car. This possibly saved their lives. Several of the passengers also managed to jump from car. However, most of the passengers were trapped in their seats, and simply rode it out.

The streetcar hit the last freight car broadside with such tremendous force that it caused it to overturn. The side of the railcar was caved in, and the truck wheels were broken away from from the body of the car. The front of the streetcar was crushed by the "T-Bone" accident.

Railroad Brakeman Frank Risher, was riding on top of the overturned railcar. He was trapped under it for a time. He suffered multiple injuries, including a broken arm and leg. Among the passengers, several suffered broken bones and lacerations. Nearly all of the twenty passengers suffered some type of injury. One man jumped out of a window of the wrecked car, only to be landed on by another jumper. The impact caused the first man's ankle to be severely injured. Incredibly, no one lost their life in the accident.

In the coming days the *Evening Review,* editorialized that the streetcar system was unsafe. They along with prominent citizens, called on city council to force the railway company, to fulfill the conditions of their franchise. They wanted the latest safety devises to be installed on the cars, and the rail lines. They complained of the runaways on the Calcutta line, and of the slipping backwards of cars climbing up the steep hill on Washington Street.

They pointed out that Pittsburgh has many hills, and they run many more cars, than East Liverpool with fewer accidents. Several people complained that the cars were running too fast on this line. They complained that the track was rough, and sometimes the motormen ate their lunch as the cars sped along. The streetcar company remained silent.

Franklin Street Again!
January 11, 1903

Less than three months later, there was another run away on the Franklin Street hill. Car # 1 was empty except for the crew, as it started down the hill on the way to Wellsville. Once again the car became unmanageable after the brakes failed again, to grip the icy rails. The crew jumped as the car began to pick up speed.

The car derailed as it crossed the "Horn Switch" rail spur. It crossed over the railroad and West Eighth Street, before smashing into the hillside. The front of the car was a severely damaged, and all the windows were shattered. The crew, Motorman William Kincaid and Conductor Heydenreich were unhurt. *(*Kincaid was probably ready for a different route.)*

"Calamity on the Grandview Line"

As the city grew, so did the need to extend the streetcar system. A new line was laid up the Calcutta Road (now St. Clair Avenue), opening on November 10th 1900. The route, which ran from the Diamond (the town square) to just above the Riverview Cemetery, was officially known as the Grandview Route. It included a steep, slightly winding hill, seven tenths of a mile long, with a hairpin turn, near the bottom. Just a month into its operation death came calling.

"Four Winter Days"
December 17, 1900

At only 31 years old, James Christie was one of the most respected men on the line. He had come from Scotland in 1887, and settled first in Cleveland. He worked at several different jobs over the next few years, and then he heard of the new streetcar line being constructed in East Liverpool. He came to help build the line, and stayed to become one of the company's first motormen. Christie was a single man who made his home in Wellsville, Ohio.

On December 17th 1900, Christie was assigned to the new Grandview route. He was reluctant to accept the assignment, because the men thought the cars were unsafe on the hill. After thinking it over, he decided to accept the assignment. He knew someone had to operate the car and he was one of the most experienced men. The streetcar's braking system was put to the test on this hill. The company had declared that the car would have the latest in safety devices. They claimed the car would be as safe on the hill as on level ground.

All went well until 3p.m. as car # 7 was due to make the return run down the hill to the "Diamond." The day was cold, and the tracks were icy due to the sleet that was beginning to fall. Mrs. Charles McKee asked Christie as she was boarding, *"Is it safe?"* Christie said *"If I did not think it was safe then I would not be here."* He then added, *"If anything happens don't jump off the car."* Christie started for town with three lady passengers, and Conductor Jim Morgan. He stopped the car just above Wall Street (now known as Morton Street), to take on more sand. He wanted it for the steepest part of the decent. Sand was dropped onto the tracks to give the steel wheels traction.

Upon starting out again the car began to pick up speed, and the brakes failed to slow it down. Christie dropped the "safety devise", a log designed to jam the wheels and stop the car. For a brief second it seemed to work as the car shuttered to a stop. However, the hold was lost in an instant, the car then continued to speed down the hill. Conductor Morgan set the rear brakes and rushed forward to help his friend gain control, but nothing they did could slow them down. Christie reversed the power, to no avail and began ringing the bell to warn those in his path.

William Crawford's wagon was just rounding the hairpin turn at Walnut Street when he saw the streetcar speeding toward him. Crawford applied his whip and the horses strained forward, clearing the track by not more than a few inches. As the car sped past, a small boy who had been seated on the rear of the wagon, jumped off and ran away as fast as he could, to where no one knew.

The car jumped the tracks at the sharp right turn, and crashed at full speed into the duplex home owned by Mrs. Sophia Wucherer. The William Stroud family lived on the north side of the home. Mrs. Stroud was washing curtains in her kitchen when the car stuck. She and her daughter Ethel were pinned against the wall with hardly enough room to stand as the runaway plowed to a stop in her kitchen. Her son was just then climbing up the steps to the rear porch when the concussion from the wreck threw him into the back yard. Incredibly, no one in the Stroud family was injured. However, Mrs. Stroud and Ethel had to be taken from the house through the kitchen win-

End of the Line

dow. Rescuers pulled them out nearly unconscious from shock. It was a miracle that they were not killed.

A section of the roof of the streetcar had to be removed to get to the passengers. The car was in shambles, but the three lady passengers were alive, and not too badly injured. Mrs. McKee had an ugly cut on her cheek that would require several stitches to close. Conductor Morgan was seriously injured with multiple cuts to his head and legs, and severe bruising over his body. Most tragic of all was the fact that Jim Christie was dead. He had been crushed in the wreckage. Once his body had been removed it was transported to the Burns & Quillen Funeral Home.

An estimated 3,000 people flocked to the tragic scene after the accident. By 5p.m., the East Liverpool Street Railway wreck crew had the car back on the tracks, and took it to the car barn. All the way down the hill one could see signs of the "safety devise" striking the brick pavement but never gaining hold.

Christie's remains were taken to Wellsville the following day. Local #52 of the Amalgamated Association of Street Railway Employees conducted his funeral. He was hailed for his character and dedication. East Liverpool firefighter, Elmer McMillan, said of his friend, *"He was a brave and true man, with nerve to spare."* Photographs of the casket, covered with flowers and a black draped streetcar were sent to his aged mother back in Scotland, as he had no living relatives in America.

January 19, 1901

Tragedy repeated itself a little over a year later. On the afternoon of January 19, 1901 the Grandview car headed toward the downtown at 1:30p.m. Motorman George Hales and Conductor Joe Davis, along with a young man, were all that were aboard.

After passing Wall Street, about halfway down the hill, the car began to speed up. Hales set the brakes, but the wheels could not grip the icy rails. He then dropped the "safety devise", and again it failed in its mission to stop the runaway. After doing everything he could,

Hales leaped from the speeding car. Hales had already decided that he would not follow Jim Christie to his death in the event of a runaway. The *Evening News-Review* commended Hales on his sound judgment. The young passenger decided to follow the motorman's lead and he too quickly jumped to safety. Conductor Davis made his mind up to ride it out, bracing himself for the worst as the car sped to its final destination.

Once again, the car left the tracks at the Walnut Street turn. It stuck a small frame building that had recently been completed on the Wucherer property, blasting it to pieces. The car then struck the northwest corner of the duplex ripping open a four foot section of the wall. The car was nearly destroyed, but there were no injuries this time, although Joe Davis was badly shaken by his death defying ride.

The Evening News-Review issued this call for safety on the day of the accident;

> *Our citizens should now demand that there be no more trifling with life. If a streetcar is liable to speed on a road that leads to death whenever it rains heavily, snows lightly, or freezes a sleet, it is high time to call a halt until it is demonstrated that proper precautionary measures have been taken and that the said car can be held under control in any emergency.*

George Wucherer demanded that the streetcar company do something to prevent these accidents. He feared, he would not be able to rent his property. The rival newspaper, *The Daily Crisis,* reported that an expert in track design said that the line had been built wrong. He said the outside rail on the turn should have been at least five inches higher than the inside rail.

The traction company suspended travel on the Calcutta Road route until April 6th, when service was resumed. They announced that new improved brakes had been installed on both ends of the car and further improvements were on order. They expected to have no more trouble. However, they did sink four steel rails into the ground at the hairpin turn, to act as a guardrail.

January 29, 1902

For the next year all went well until one winter night, when the cold slippery rails once again caused a streetcar to become uncontrollable. Car #17 had just passed Wall Street and was on the steepest section of the hill, when the motorman, T.L. Atkinson, realized they were out of control. He set the brakes and deployed the new safety devise, again without effect. Atkinson yelled that he was jumping and then leaped from the car. Conductor H. E. Neal and the only passenger, Police Officer Tom Stafford, quickly followed suit. All three were uninjured

The empty car sped on until once again it jumped the track at Walnut Street. It struck the rail barrier dead center, shearing off the center two rails as if they were matchsticks. The car passed neatly between the outer two rails and smashed full force into the north wall of the Wucherer property.

Sound asleep in his bed against the north wall was Ed Mercer. Jarred awake by the concussion, he found himself covered with debris. His bed had been shoved across the room. Except for the shock of what had just occurred he was uninjured, as were his parents. The Shaub family, who lived next door, also escaped injury although they were pretty shaken.

The car was completely destroyed; even the safety devise was bent and twisted. The wreck train soon pulled the car out of the house and back onto the tracks, leaving behind a huge gaping hole in the side of the house. People around town began to call the house, *"The Car Barn."*

January 24, 1903

Car #11 was one of the oldest and most dilapidated cars on the line. Motorman Charles Kontnier, and Conductor Lawrence Fisher, along with five male passengers, would soon find out how bad old # 11 was.

The car became unmanageable at the intersection with Avondale Street, and before anyone could react the speed had reached over forty miles an hour. The old car did not have an electrical braking system, and the hand brake was useless.

The five men all rushed to the rear of the car and began to jump for their lives. The conductor waited until all the passengers were gone, before he too leaped to safety. These men received cuts and bruises, but they were alive. Kontnier however, remained on the car doing all he could to stop the runaway.

The streetcar passed over the first derailing switch which failed to work. This was a new safety devise to help stop runaways. The second derailing switch worked, and the car derailed. It did not stop however it just went careening down the hill, running on the brick pavement.

Onlookers were horrified by the sight of Charles Kontnier, standing at the controls as the car sped toward destruction. Sometimes, the Good Lord intervenes, and maybe He did on this winter afternoon?

Something caused the car to veer to the right striking the curb, on the west side of the roadway. The car began to slow slightly as the wheels ground along the curb. It came to a sudden stop when it slammed a pole, carrying the electric wires, for the streetcar line. The trolley lines were torn down for several hundred feet. The runaway had covered over half a mile. It had traveled over 400 yards on the brick pavement. This time the Wucherer property was spared when the car wrecked just before the turn.

Kontnier stepped from the smashed car unhurt, except for a slight foot injury. The railway company blamed snowy conditions for the accident.

For the next few years the Grandview Route was relatively accident free. The same could not be said for other parts of the system.

(*The Wucherer property no longer exists. It is now the front lawn of the 1st Church of the Nazarene at 670 Walnut Street East Liverpool, Ohio.)

Lisbon Street Hill

East Liverpool is a city built on hills, so as the city grew, new neighborhoods were built on the mostly level hilltops. The streetcar system moved along with the growing city. The new line up the steep winding hill, to the Pleasant Heights neighborhood, began operation on March 14th, 1903. The single track ran from the "Diamond" out Dresden Avenue, turning onto West 9th Street, and then up the Lisbon Road. At the top of the hill it turned right proceeding up Northside Avenue, ending at Ceramic Street.

The *Evening News-Review,* reported that in the week since the opening of the new route, great numbers of people had been riding the car. People saw it as an opportunity to do some sightseeing. Many of them had never seen this part of the city, and it only cost a nickel.

"The Pleasant Heights Miracle"
March 22, 1903

It was a little before seven thirty, on Sunday evening March 22nd. Car #2 had made the journey up the steep hill and turned into the Pleasant Heights Addition. For some reason, Conductor Welsh decided to step off the car, and wait at the bottom, breaking company regulations by doing so. Motorman George Toland took the car on up Northside Avenue to its terminus at Ceramic Street. At the scheduled time, Toland released the front brake and removed the controlling handles, to walk back to the other end of the car. The rear of the car would now be the front on the downhill run. When the brake was released, the car began to roll down the hill. It gets a little confusing as to what happened next.

What we can be sure of is that the car began picking up speed, and within a short distance, witnesses said it was traveling nearly 40 miles per hour. The car negotiated the right turn at what is now Croft Street, but soon jumped the tracks and went airborne. Witnesses said it was thrown forward its own length and made a half revolution before crashing down onto its roof. The car slid to a stop about half way between the tracks and the St. Aloysius Cemetery fence.

The sound of splintering wood and breaking glass was deafening as the car was crushed to the tops of the seats. On board with Toland were fifteen passengers, and no one escaped injury. Miraculously, no one was killed. There were however, the usual broken bones and cuts and bruises that always occurred in these accidents.

Newspaper sketch

Waiting to get on the car at the turn, were a couple of men who nearly were hit by the runaway. They were the first to help the victims. Motorman Toland managed to crawl from the wreck, and began to help get people out. The congregation of the Pleasant Heights Chapel on Northside Avenue also rushed from Sunday evening services to help. As Toland was helping the injured passengers, he suffered what may have been a heart attack and fell nearly lifeless to the ground, bleeding from his mouth and nose.

Word was quickly sent to the power house, and company officials sent a relief car to the scene with as many doctors as could be found. Physicians were at the scene within forty-five minutes. Toland was revived by a doctor. The injured passengers were taken in by neighbors until other arrangements could be made. No more cars ran up the hill that day, but dozens of spectators made their way up the hill to see the wreck.

As soon as the passengers were freed from the wreckage, they began to blame the motorman for the accident. They told whoever would listen that Toland was walking with the control levers in his hands as the car began to run away. Toland, however, claimed this was untrue. He swore he was at his post doing all that was possible to slow the car. To prove this, he even crawled back into the wreckage with three witnesses. They found the brakes were set and the power off just as Toland claimed. This evidence however, did not stop the passengers from continuing their denouncement. There is, however, no doubt that the crew was not following regulations. Conductor Welsh was absent from his post. He was not holding the car with his brake while the controlling levers were being moved. It seems that even though Toland managed to get the controls into place, the speed was too great to stop the runaway.

The car was a total loss and the line was out of service while a new car was prepared. Toland told the *Evening News-Review*, that he had done all within his power to control the car. He said, *"The magnetic brake had refused to work. The speed was too great to be checked by the hand brake, I could do no more."*

The streetcar line began an investigation into the accident. Within a few days they announced that the investigation was completed, but they would withhold the results. Perhaps they wanted to give Toland and Welsh time to quit and silently fade away. Lawsuits however, were filed over the next few months. Twelve of the passengers filed suits of several thousands of dollars against the company. The company was able to settle out of court with all the plaintiffs with final settlements coming in June 1905.

"The Final Run was Nearly the End!"
March 26, 1903

Meanwhile, just after midnight, on March 26th the Pleasant Heights car was returning from its last run of the day. The car was empty except for the motorman John Hughes and the conductor Willis Green. The car had just started down the hill when Hughes applied the hand brake and the chain broke. The brake was now useless and the car began to gain speed. Hughes and Green did all they could to stop the run away, but could not.

The car continued to run down the steep hill until it hit the derailer switch which caused the car to jump the track. Fortunately, the car soon came to a stop. The two crewmen were shaken up, but not seriously hurt. The company wreck train soon had the car back on the track and it was taken to the car barn for repairs.

This was the second runaway in just four days. Clearly, safety on the new line was a work in progress.

Trestle over Jethro Run

A Few More Rides!
"Over the Bridge"
December 8, 1906

At around 10 o'clock in morning, car #103 was speeding toward East Liverpool from Wellsville. On board were Motorman Samuel Kerr and Conductor Albert Dietz. Eight passengers were on the ill-fated car as it approached the west end of the trestle across Jethro Run just inside the city limits. Sam Kerr was pouring on the speed trying to make up time. They had been delayed at least 15 minutes at Walkers, a small pottery community located between Wellsville and East Liverpool, due to the electrical power being off. They were behind schedule.

Kerr knew the track was straight and true all the way across the trestle so he gave the car all the power he could. As they began to cross the trestle, however the car struck something on the track, possibly a rock. The right wheel of the front truck was dislodged from the track, causing the car to derail. The car swerved left, crossed the west bound track, and smashed through the steel railing, plunging into the

Cleaning up the Wreck

ravine 30 feet below. It hit nose first and then settled upright against a small tree. It was a miracle that it did not roll over and continue all the way to the bottom, taking all on board to their deaths.

The passengers had been spread out within the car, each minding his or her own business never once worrying about the ride. The accident was over within seconds and there was nothing Kerr could do to stop it. Conductor Dietz was in the process of stepping onto the back platform when the car derailed, he was thrown the length of the car. When the car hit the embankment everyone was thrown headfirst into the front of the vehicle, piling on top of each other. The interior of the car was a mass of writhing bodies covered with broken glass and splintered wood.

A number of citizens of the west end had witnessed the tragic event and soon the city patrol wagon on the scene. An ambulance from Miller's Funeral Home was also sent, along with several local physicians. The victims were pulled from the wreckage, all of them suffering from head injuries, and numerous other cuts and bruises, and at least one broken bone.

Once the passengers were untangled, it was discovered that James Vale who had been sitting near the front, was dead. He had been crushed under the weight of all the others. His skull was also badly fractured. Vale was 65 years old and a widower. He left behind four grown sons. Motorman Kerr was also badly injured since he too was on the bottom of the pile. The victims were transported to the city hospital where doctors thought some might die from their injuries.

Shortly after the accident a representative from the East Liverpool Traction & Light Company arrived on the scene. He determined that no blame could be placed at the feet of the company or its employees. Although the car was speeding, the track was good. Besides, the car could not come off the rails unless an obstruction was on the rail. Although he deeply regretted the accident, the company could not be held responsible.

The next day it was reported that the victims were all doing well. Fourteen-year-old Ethel Golden, who had been unconscious since the accident, had finally woken up.

Within a couple of days the accident was no longer news. The city did make a request for additional railings to be installed on both the Jethro Trestle and the 6th Street Viaduct. The traction company also spoke of installing the rule of coming to a stop before crossing a bridge. The Pittsburgh traction company had installed that requirement, following a terrible accident in that city. The company now also said they did not think Kerr had *really* been speeding.

"The Grandview Line Again!"
March 19, 1915

Things had been fairly quiet on the "Grandview" line for the last few years, but that was about to change. March 19th 1915 started like any other day, and streetcar #127 was on its first run of the day. At 6:10a.m. the car was just passing the Northside Fire Station at McKinnon Avenue, starting down St. Clair Avenue toward town. On board were Motorman S.T. Galloway and Conductor J.C. Roseplier along with sixteen passengers. East Liverpool Police officer George Toland and Firefighter William Rider were among the passengers on their way to work.

Motorman Galloway began applying the brakes but something was wrong, the car just increased speed. Conductor Roseplier and Toland and Rider perceiving the danger, stepped to the rear of the car and shouted for the passengers to remain seated and to brace themselves. Toland had been through this before. He had been the motorman during the Pleasant Heights wreck back in 1903.

Galloway threw the car into reverse, to no avail, the runaway car continued to gain speed. Seeing there was nothing else he could do, he jumped from the car, sustaining painful bruises to his hip and arm. A streetcar is not like a ship at sea, and taking a cue from Galloway, both Toland and Rider decided not to go down with the ship. They leaped from the speeding car just before the tracks made the sharp right turn at St. Clair and Walnut Street. Both men escaped with bruises and torn uniforms and maybe some fractured pride.

The car had blown through three derailing switches before leaving the tracks at Walnut Street. It climbed over the sidewalk, and then smashed through a fence and a billboard before coming to a stop in the yard just short of the Wucherer property on Walnut Street.

The remaining passengers were all badly shaken, but sustained only a few injuries. Goldie Watkins age 19, the only female on board was knocked unconscious with cuts to her face and right leg. After she regained consciousness she was taken home by the fire department. Most of the injuries happened when passengers were thrown from their seats. Some passengers escaped injury, and Conductor Roseplier stayed at his post all the way to the end.

Once the streetcar company got the car back on the tracks, it made the trip to the car barn in the East End under its own power. It was reported that the brakes seemed to be in working order. So what caused the runaway? Traction Company officials decided that the most likely cause was as usual, wet slippery rails.

The call was raised again to divert the tracks at Young's Alley, over on to Avondale Street to get away from the sharp turn at Walnut Street.

"Autumn Leaves"
October 27, 1902

At 10:00 a.m. on that Monday morning car # 12 of the East Liverpool & Rock Springs line was making a run back to Chester, West Virginia. Leaving the business district of East Liverpool the car turned onto Washington Street and started down the steep hill. The motorman Seth Rauch applied the electric brakes but nothing happened. Rauch then pulled the hand brake with the same results. They were out of control.

Autumn had brought down the leaves from the many trees lining the route, and they were covering the rails. Rauch did his best to get the brakes to take hold but the steel wheels could not grip the leaf covered track. The car was supposed to come to a stop at Third Street so a switch could be thrown, that would allow them to divert onto the line leading across the bridge, and on to Chester. Rauch could not stop the car and it continued past Third Street on the route to East End.

Just a few feet beyond Third Street the tracks were clear and the motorman tried again to regain control. Unfortunately, the rough ride had caused the control wire to slip off the electric power line, which left the car without power. The eight passengers were in a panic as the Ohio River was only seconds away. Pottery worker John Wallace decided to take his chances and jump. He landed hard onto the brick pavement badly bruising his side and arms. The others mostly remained in their seats calling fervently for Devine intervention.

When the car reached the turn at Second Street, it jumped the track continuing down Washington Street heading for the river. The heavy car began to cut furrows into the brick pavement. This caused it to veer to the right where it smashed headlong into a tree, stopping only a few feet from the river's edge. Everyone was shaken up but the only injury was to John Wallace when he jumped from the car.

Large crowds gathered to watch as a team of horses pulled the wreck back to the Third Street switch were it was towed to Chester. All were amazed that there had been no serious injuries for after they had reached the dizzying speed of at least 20 miles an hour.

"Coming Home from the Dance"
October 15, 1910

One final episode is included because it is a little different from the other stories.

At 8p.m., on October 14, Harry Finley and Willis Cunningham went into J.S. Rayl's livery stable in East Liverpool to rent a surrey and two horses. They had dates with Bessie Naut and LuLu Reed for the dance that night over in Fairview, West Virginia (now known as New Manchester.) After the dance, the happy couples headed home, crossing back over the Newell Bridge at about 2:30a.m. They were having so much fun; they never wanted their "joy ride" to end, so they drove down to Wellsville.

By now the young lovers and the horses were probably getting sleepy, and a heavy fog had settled in the Ohio River valley, as is common for that time of year. The road between Wellsville and East Liverpool at that time was a rutted dirt trail that ran alongside the streetcar tracks. Did Harry Finley decide to drive on the right of way? Or did the horses wander onto the tracks as the couples slept or were otherwise occupied?

The time was 5:30a.m. October 15th, and the west bound interurban car was moving through the heavy fog. The motorman was Charles Kontnier an experienced man who was accustomed to excitement at work.

(*The interurban was a transit system that ran between Steubenville, Ohio and Beaver, Pennsylvania, connecting with each city along the way. A passenger could make connections and travel to Cleveland and Pittsburgh on the system.)

Just west of the East Liverpool city limits, the interurban hit the surrey head on. The impact was so violent, that one of the horses was instantly killed and the surrey was destroyed. The four occupants were ejected from the coach. LuLu Reed was thrown under the front of the interurban car. Fortunately, Kontnier and Conductor Charles Goodman managed to stop the car before the wheels ran over her. The four "joy riders" were taken to the hospital. Finley a 25-year-old carpenter from Chester, West Virginia was badly bruised and cut. He was suffering from shock, so he remained in the hospital overnight. Bessie Naut, from East Liverpool was also kept in the hospital. She sustained much the same injuries as Finley. LuLu Reed of Chester was treated for minor injuries and sent home. She was a very fortunate young woman.

Willis Cunningham was not badly hurt. He gave the name William Allison to the hospital officials. However, it did not take long to discover his true identity. It turns out that, Cunningham was a married mill worker from Chester, West Virginia. He must have had a whole lot of explaining to do once he got back home.

Postscript

The street railway system in the East Liverpool area lasted less than fifty years, and in that time, many such accidents occurred. Streetcars ran into other vehicles and into each other. They ran away with tragic results, they derailed and fell off bridges. People fell off of them and people got run over by them. They frightened horses causing them to become hazardous to the public welfare. In short one's idea of a slower more relaxed era of men with handlebar mustaches and ladies in hoop skirts with parasols, comfortably riding to a picnic, on a streetcar has been shattered. It appears to me that accepting a ride on the streetcar system in the East Liverpool area was a gamble and in bad weather an even bigger gamble. Surely the systems in other cities had their fair share of accidents. However, here, too often, East Liverpool's citizens went *Hurtling to Destruction!*

Chapter 5
Taken for a Ride
The Roy Marino Murder
September 10, 1937

The 1930s were a tumultuous time in America. The nation was gripped by the Great Depression, and East Liverpool was no different. Depression had hit the city hard by 1936, and people were becoming desperate. Although money was tight, many people were willing to take a gamble on getting rich. If one was lucky, a few pennies could bring prosperity, at least temporarily.

Prohibition had made bootleggers and big city gangsters rich and famous. However, the making and smuggling of illegal alcohol was a thing of the past. Prohibition had come to an end, but the gangsters liked the rich lifestyle, and they weren't about to go out of business. So they turned to another source of easy money- illegal gambling. Gambling came in many forms, from slot machines to dice games and poker. The biggest play however came from the numbers. The desire to get rich was not confined to the big cities. There were plenty of hoods available to fill the gambling needs of small town America.

East Liverpool of the 1930s was a smoky, hardworking, pottery town that had a thirst for bootleg whiskey during Prohibition, and now had a thirst for gambling. Gangsters were more than willing to quench that thirst. The town was controlled by the numbers operation run by the P.H. Brogan and James Cascelli syndicate from Steubenville, Ohio. They had numerous number writers covering the city, selling chances to win. At 5-1 odds, a one penny bet could result in a $5.00 win. Because wages were low in those days, the lure of extra cash was hard to resist. After all, it was just a couple of pennies. The number was determined from the results of the daily stock exchange. Soon Brogan's syndicate was entrenched, and thriving. However, they were about to have some competition.

William "Big Bill" Lias was a short, 300 pound Greek racketeer from Wheeling, West Virginia. He controlled crime in Wheeling and was looking to expand his territory. The Lias organization moved into East Liverpool and other towns along the Ohio River, bringing with him a new deal, 7-1 odds. The racketeers gathered their supporters and settled in for a fight. Both sides began working hard to woo the police and city government to their side. The police, undermanned due to layoffs, seemed willing to accept the numbers business as no big deal. Both of the numbers rackets were ready to pay for the right to operate in town.

On August 21, 1936, the *East Liverpool Review* reported that, "Big Bill" was upset over the deal he thought the Steubenville group had arranged with City Hall. He made a trip to town and met with City Solicitor G. Jay Clark in his office. Lias told Clark; "*I intend to stay until the last dog is hung. If I am forced to go, I'll do so, but I'll not take it lying down. If they stay, then I am going to stay.*"

This led Service and Safety Director E.B. Laughlin to declare that the city administration, "*was obligated to nobody, and if the racketeers want a fight they'll get it.*" City Council ordered the police to clear the city of number writers. Police Chief Hugh McDermott was ordered to arrest anyone caught in the act. The Chief said he did not think they would find many, but the beat cops would keep their eyes open just in case. The police did keep their eyes open. It seems however, a lot more of Lias's men got caught in the dragnet, than did Brogan's. Most of those pulled in received only a small fine and a suspended sentence. Regardless, the raids disrupted their business, and it was proving to be costly.

By November 1936, it appeared, "*the last dog was hung.*" "Big Bill" Lias had had enough. Granted, his mind and attention may have been elsewhere, for he was beginning to having trouble with his ex-partner, Mike Russell. He was also was recovering from a slight gunshot wound. Lias had been hit with a .45 caliber slug in the left elbow during a drive by shooting on November 11th, in Wheeling. Police quickly picked up Walter Sauvaguet, a member of Russell's gang. Unfortunately, there was not enough evidence to charge him for the shooting. Trouble was brewing back in Wheeling and the East Liverpool operation was being harassed by the police at every turn. Lias's "book" was also hit with some large pay outs, which caused the distracted racketeer to finally throw in the towel. He closed down his East Liverpool operation, paid off his debts, and complained loudly to anyone who would listen. When asked about the situation, Chief Hugh McDermott declared smugly, *"The numbers racket isn't what it used to be."* In regard to the closing of the Lias book, the chief commented *"Well, it's something like a boxing match- not always how hard you hit, but how often."* "Big Bill" had lost his first battle, but the war was not over. Over the next few years he would make a comeback, becoming the leader of the Upper Ohio Valley rackets, although for now he was looking a little vulnerable.

With the status quo returned, things ran quietly for the next few months. That is, until late summer of 1937, which brought on new concerns. At about 11:30 a.m.,on July 27th, three young boys were returning from picking berries just outside the village of Lisbon, Ohio. Suddenly they came across a grisly discovery. Under some bushes, they had found more than berries. There was the decomposing corpse of a middle-aged man. The victim was sprawled on his back with his arms outstretched. The boys ran to a nearby house and the police were called. Village police turned it over to the Sheriff's office since it was outside the village limits. County Sheriff Harry Gosney, sent Deputy Chris Pusey to the scene, and the investigation began.

The body was located on a wooded hillside, just outside the village limits, about 100 yards west of the U.S. Route 30 Bridge. The man appeared to have been shot in the right temple. The body was removed to the county morgue where Coroner Arnold Devon discovered two gunshot wounds. One bullet had entered his left breast just below the heart, while the other bullet had entered his right temple. Coroner Devon doubted suicide, since in all probability, he would have fallen face down if that were the case. Strangely, the bullet from the chest wound had penetrated his shirt and underwear but not his suit vest. Also, the victim's right hand had been mutilated by an animal. There was no identification on the body, but it was apparent that he had not been robbed. He was dressed in a light colored suit and was wearing black shoes. His wrist watch had stopped at 4:15, and $26.38 was found in his wallet and pockets.

Also found on his body was a pearl handled pocket knife, a pack of gum, two pencils, a box of matches and a pack of cigarettes. Authorities said he may have been an "educated man" since he had a current copy of the *"Readers Digest"* in his coat pocket. Also found in his pocket was the return portion of a bus ticket for passage from Youngstown to Lisbon and back. The Penn-Ohio Bus Company later determined that the ticket had been purchased at 2:00 p.m. on July 4th at the Youngstown terminal. There was no name on the ticket.

More ominously, tucked into the waistband of his trousers was a .25 caliber German made automatic pistol loaded with two bullets. Suicide was ruled out once and for all, since no one thought the victim could have slipped the pistol under his belt after shooting himself twice. The gun would be sent off to the FBI in Washington D.C.; however, they were unable to match it to any individual or crime.

Because the body was in such poor condition, it could not be identified through photography. However, the general height and weight of the victim were determined. A dental chart was made, and the personal effects were cataloged and kept. The description was sent to every police department within a 100 mile radius. Still no one came forward to identify the victim.

The county buried the victim in the County Home Cemetery on July 29th under the shade of a maple tree. A simple wooden cross, with the inscription "Buried July 29 - Name Unknown" marked the grave. Today the grave is unmarked and the exact location lost.

One of the first tips on the investigation came from an unidentified patron of a local Lisbon pool hall. He said that on July 2nd four suspicious, tough- looking men had come into the place. He said he thought they might be part of the "Jungle Inn" crowd. The Jungle Inn was a notorious gambling den and hangout for all sorts of gangsters and tough guys, located in Liberty Township, just north of Youngstown. He recalled seeing one of them back again on July 4th. Whoever the victim was, he must have been from out of town, since no one in Lisbon was missing.

On August 10th, a local woman came forth after reading about the body and seeing the police combing the area. She told investigators that she remembered hearing two gunshots around 3:30-4:00 p.m. on July 4th. She had not thought much of it at the time, since it was the Fourth of July. Inquiries came in from many places including the cities of Warren and Lorain, Ohio. Warren authorities were looking for a missing former boxer. However, nothing matched the missing men from those cities. The case was stalled.

Then, on August 23rd, Mrs. Donald McLean of Beaver Falls, Pennsylvania identified the victim as being her missing husband. Donald McLean was a 46-year-old ex-machinist at the Jones & Laughlin Co. in Beaver Falls, Pennsylvania. He had been missing since April 7th. Mrs. McLean traveled to Lisbon, and identified the watch and wallet, along with a piece of material from the victim's suit as well as his shoes, as belonging to her missing husband.

Mrs. McLean was the manager of a Beaver Falls restaurant, and she identified the watch as one she had taken in as collateral in lieu of payment. She said her husband began wearing it shortly before he disappeared. McLean was described by his wife as a frequent gambler who lost often, and sometimes heavily. She thought that it might have led to his death. There may also have been some marital problems. He had just been ordered by the court to pay $65 a month to his wife and child in support. He had made only one payment before disappearing. Donald's brother, John McLean, the publisher of the *Beaver Falls News-Tribune,* also viewed the victim's personal items, but could not be certain they belonged to his brother. He was of the opinion that his brother was still alive.

Mrs. McLean could give no legitimate explanation as to how her missing husband ended up dead in an Ohio berry patch. However, she did report two life threatening phone messages she had received since her identification of the body. The voice on one of the phone calls told her, *"If you don't keep your mouth shut, you'll get the same thing somebody else got."* Authorities did what they could to check on these calls, but found nothing. Mrs. McLean made no attempt to recover the body. County officials believed its condition was such that it should remain where it was. It still rests in the county cemetery today.

The case seemed to be on its way to being wrapped up. But it was not so. It turned out that Donald McLean was very much alive. He was found on August 28th, living at the Improvement of the Poor Farm in Warrendale, Pennsylvania. He had been living there since June 28th.

Investigators went to the farm immediately to question him. They wanted to know why his wife identified the dead man's wallet and watch as belonging to him. McLean said he did not know anything about that. He also told investigators his clothing had been stolen while he was sleeping in a transient hotel in Pittsburgh, and that he had reported it. He said perhaps that was how his valuables ended up in Lisbon. The police checked and found that the theft had indeed been reported. The investigators left for now, but they had a lot more questions to ask him in the coming days. They would not get a chance. McLean left the farm without explanation a few days later and once again, simply vanished.

The investigation was right back where it had started. Fortunately, on September 7th, another clue came to light. A curious local teenager was poking around the crime scene and found a spent bullet. The bullet was a couple of inches under the ground where the victim had been found lying. Investigators thought it was the bullet that had passed through the victim's head. A few feet away a spent shell casing was also found. Now, perhaps ballistics would be able to match the murder weapon, if one was ever found. No such luck. The FBI would report later in the month that they were unable to match the bullet or the casing to any weapon in their files.

While the county authorities were awaiting developments, events were developing elsewhere. Down the river in Wheeling, Mike Russell, the onetime cohort, and now arch rival of his cousin "Big Bill," had started his own numbers business. He and Lias had been at odds ever since Russell's wife Elsie had killed Lias' wife, Gladys, back in 1934.

At the time of his wife's death, Lias was serving an 18 month prison sentence on a bootlegging rap. While Bill was out of action in the Atlanta Federal Penitentiary, others would have to fight his battles. Gladys took on that role, and she was pretty upset. Elsie Russell was talking about "Big Bill" and his business, saying things that should not be said. Gladys went to the Russell home to complain about what Elsie Russell was saying about her family. She wanted satisfaction. The two exchanged harsh words, and then a gun was pulled. Both women struggled for it, and Gladys was shot three times. At the trial, the jury concluded it was an accident, so Elsie Russell was acquitted.

Now three years had passed since the shooting, and Bill had even remarried, but "Big Bill" was not the kind of man who forgot about things. He was the kind of man who patiently watched and waited for an opportunity to arise to strike back.

Mike Russell was not standing still either; in 1936 he went into the juke box business with John Anthoulis of Steubenville. They formed the C & J Music Company. Russell loaned Anthoulis the start-up money and forced him to take Charles Calaris as a third partner. Then, in 1937, Russell informed Anthoulis that he was putting 20 slot machines into operation with partner John O'Boyle. Anthoulis would not be a partner this time. He would just be a $35 a week employee.

John Anthoulis

No one could or would identify the short, stocky killer who pumped several slugs into Mike Russell. The Wheeling shooting took place in front of his own house in broad daylight. Russell's wife, Elsie, watched the August 25th killing from an upstairs window. She collapsed and was of no help to the police. John Anthoulis was so shook up by the killing that he suffered a nervous breakdown and went to bed for a couple of days. However, shortly after the funeral, Anthoulis was sufficiently recovered to accept Elsie Russell's offer to take over her husband's share of the slot machines on a 50-50 basis. Thus, Anthoulis became partners with O'Boyle. In late August, O'Boyle began building up the gang, bringing in Cleveland gangsters, Solly Hart and Herb Ross. Eddie Hegert was also hired as a slot machine mechanic and collector.

Meanwhile, in Youngstown, tavern operator James Tesone was shot and killed during a holdup of his Hazelton neighborhood saloon, on September 8th. The killers got away with over $9,000. Some witnesses thought this was the work of the notorious Al Brady gang, which was currently terrorizing the mid-west. Reports were that one of the holdup men was wounded in the getaway. For a short time police thought the unidentified corpse in Lisbon might be the wounded gang member. However, the evidence of the bus ticket and the condition of the corpse ruled against any connection. Local police were however, beginning to think all this violence was part of an ongoing gang war for control of the Youngstown-East Liverpool-Steubenville rackets. The question remained; who was the victim found under the berry bushes?

Youngstown, Ohio during the '30's was a hotbed for racketeers and shady characters, and one of them, Roy Marino, had big ideas. Roy "Happy" Marino was born on April 4, 1904 in Youngstown, Ohio one of six sons of Charles and Marie Marino. Roy had been married to Helen Foley Marino for 14 years. They had one child, a 12-year-old daughter, Mary. Marino was best described as a small time Youngstown racketeer with big

Roy "Happy" Marino

time aspirations. Over the last few years he had made headlines for his attempt "to muscle in on the bug," as the numbers racket was known in Youngstown. His biggest headlines came from his failed bank robbery in Louisville, Ohio on June 10, 1933. He was soon arrested and on November 21st, convicted and sentenced to 20 years to life. Somehow he received a parole after only 14 months. *(*This would become part of a scandal in the Ohio prison system within the next couple years.)* By September 1937, Marino was operating the Smoke Shop, a cigar store which was a front for his downtown Youngstown bookie joint.

Then there were the rumors, "Happy" was friends with "Big Bill." Or was it Mike Russell? Was he involved in the $20,000-$30,000 jewelry heist, from "Big Bill's" home? Was he the man that put Mike Russell "on the spot," or was he the shooter? Or maybe he had gone straight, as some people said. In any case, the police had their eye on him.

The police were not the only ones looking at Marino. The Steubenville boys were also getting fed up with him. One day, Eddie Hegert was in the gang's headquarters fixing a slot machine. He overheard Anthoulis say to gang members Solly Hart and Tom Galati, *"We have to get that _____. He's double-crossed once and he'll do it again. We've got to take care of him."* Later, Hegert heard O'Boyle talking with Herb Ross and Hart about a phone conversation. He heard O'Boyle make the remark, *"We have a date with Marino on Thursday."*

"Happy" was in the Smoke Shop on Thursday September 9th, when the phone rang just before six. Employees overheard Marino say *"If you want to see me you know where I live."* "Happy" soon left the shop. He first took one of his employees home, then drove to his parent's home on Pershing Avenue for supper. While enjoying the evening meal with his family, a car horn sounded. Outside was a new black sedan. Warily Roy sent his 12-year-old daughter Mary out to see what they wanted. His brother Andrew's six-year-old daughter went with her. No one knows what was said, but after a few minutes the girls came back in. Roy went out and talked for about five minutes. He came back inside, and the car drove away. Roy stayed a few minutes longer, then left, saying he had to meet some fellows.

Roy drove downtown, arriving about 7:30 p.m., at the Youngstown Hotel where Elizabeth "Betty" Jaynes, a former East Cleveland chorus girl, was living. Marino and Jaynes had been seeing each other for a couple of years. While in Betty's room, Roy received another phone call from a man who wanted him to go to New Castle, Pennsylvania. He told Roy to meet him at Chick's Café at Wilson & Forest Avenue on Youngstown's East Side. Roy and Betty drove to Chick's and parked across from the bar. Roy got out, telling Betty to wait in the car. *"I won't be gone long"*, he said. Marino entered the bar and ordered a whiskey, which he drank quickly, then left through the rear door. He was followed by a stranger. What happened next will never be known for certain, but Roy Marino had just a few hours to live.

Outside the tavern two high school boys were walking home. They noticed a new black sedan parked in the shadows near the home of one the boys. As the boys passed, the two men inside the car hid their faces, which aroused the suspicions of the teenagers. One of them wrote down the license number.

Meanwhile, Betty Jaynes sat patiently waiting in the car. At about 1:00 a.m., John Chick, the son of the bar owner, came over and asked her who she was waiting for. She described Marino, but Chick did not know him. Jaynes then went into the bar, and called for a taxi which took her back to the hotel. It had been quite an uneventful night for her.

Around 6:30 a.m., on September 10th, truck driver Albert Hess had just passed through the sleepy hamlet of Rogers, Ohio on State Route 7. He was heading south toward East Liverpool when he saw something which brought him to a halt. There, lying face up about ten feet off the west side of the highway, was a body. It was located about a mile south of Rogers, on the edge of a field on the J.C. Ashford farm. Middletown Township Constable John Bable was notified, and he called the sheriff's office. Three deputies were sent including Chris Pusey, who had been first on the scene of the Lisbon body a few weeks earlier. County Coroner Arnold Devon was called to the scene at 7 a.m. A large amount of blood was found at the scene, and also some vomit. A blood trail about 14 feet in length indicated that the victim had crawled or stumbled along the highway before dying. The body was transported to the Kelly Funeral Home in the East End of East Liverpool. There, Dr. Roy Costello, the pathologist at East Liverpool City Hospital, performed the autopsy. County officials contacted the Youngstown Police Department because labels in Marino's clothing came from stores in that city. Mahoning County Detective John Callan and Youngstown Detectives William Harrison and Thomas O'Hara came to the Kelly Funeral home and identified the victim as being Roy "Happy" Marino.

A strange phone call was received at the Columbiana County Jail at noon on the day Marino's body was found. Deputy Robert Case said the caller asked if the body had been identified. He told the caller that the deceased was Roy Marino. The caller said, *"Thank God"* and then hung up. The deputy tried, but was unable to trace the call.

Marino was wearing an expensive watch at the time of his death. Police thought it might be part of that big jewelry heist from the home of "Big Bill" Lias. They also knew that Marino had recently pawned a ring worth $1,200. At the time of the killing, "Big Bill" was in Federal Court in Clarksburg, West Virginia. He was there to answer charges of income tax evasion. A few days after the murder, police took the watch to him for identification. He denied ever seeing it before. Probably a wise decision, even if it was his. The last thing he needed was to be tied to Marino now.

It was also reported that Gomer Williams, a farmer who lived near the murder scene, had heard five shots early on the morning of the 10th. Williams later denied it when questioned by County Prosecutor Karl Stouffer. Sheriff deputies had not found any eye witnesses to this brutal murder. Now, perhaps no one had even heard the noise of "Happy Marino's" final seconds of life. At least no one was willing to talk.

Coroner Arnold Devon reported on September 11th that Marino had been shot at least six times at close range. According to Devon, the victim apparently stumbled ahead a few feet, his arms raised over his face or above his head, perhaps in a futile effort to defend himself from the hail of bullets. He then fell into the ditch on the edge of the farm field. Bullet wounds in his armpits showed his arms were raised. The autopsy results further showed that two guns may have been used in the killing. That meant two shooters in all probability.

Devon reported that four bullets from a .38 caliber police special had entered through the arms and chest, passing through his body and emerging through his back and side. One .38 slug was lodged near his backbone. A .32 caliber bullet had passed through his forehead lodging between his skull and the skin. His body was pierced with as many as 12 entry and exit wounds. In other words, he was shot to pieces. Dr. Costello reported that death would have resulted from at least of three of the wounds.

Devon signed the death certificate on the 11th, stating Marino had died *"of gunshot wounds inflicted by some unknown person or persons."* County authorities were beginning to wonder if rural Columbiana County was becoming a killing ground for the mob.

The day after the murder, Hegert went with Anthoulis to the village of Irondale, Ohio to pick up a broken slot machine. While they were there, Anthoulis spied a newspaper which had Marino's killing on the front page. Anthoulis picked it up and began to read. After a moment he turned to Hegert and said, *"There's another_____ full of slugs."*

Meanwhile, Mahoning County detectives began to put together "Happy" Marino's final hours. Andrew Marino, the victim's brother, revealed that they had dinner at their parent's home on Pershing Ave in Youngstown. While enjoying their meal, a large black Packard sedan drove up and blew the horn. Andrew said his brother seemed a little anxious, as if he was expecting them. Betty Jaynes told police that he seemed to be in good spirits the night he disappeared, not realizing he had been, *"put on the spot."* Jaynes said she did not know if he had any enemies or who might have been out to *"get"* him. Marino's car had been found where he and Jaynes had left it on Wilson Avenue, the keys still in the ignition. Police decided to hold

Jaynes, tagged by the press as the *"Chorine Friend,"* as a material witness. However, they must have held her pretty loosely, for as by the time the trial occurred several months later, she was nowhere to be found.

Marino's body was taken to the Schultz & Sons Funeral Home in Youngstown, where hundreds of friends and family paid their respects on Sunday. However, a couple of strange incidents occurred the night before. Shortly after midnight, three well-dressed middle-aged men arrived at the funeral home wanting to view the body. Even though they were told the home was closed, they insisted they were relatives from Cleveland and could not come in the daytime. They were allowed to view the body for a couple of minutes, and then left. Later, at around 2 a.m., an intoxicated man with two black eyes wanted to see the body, but was refused. This time the police were notified. Rocco Marino, one of the victim's brothers, was never able to identify any of the nocturnal visitors.

Funeral services were conducted by Rev. Oreste Salcini, pastor of St. Rocco's Episcopal Church where the Marino family were members. Roy "Happy" Marino was buried in Tod Cemetery on Monday, September 13, 1937. Now it was up to the police to figure out who the *"unknown person or persons"* were that had sent "Happy" *"to meet his Maker."*

Meanwhile, the numbers-slot machine rackets continued to flourish in the area. An investigation of the local rackets by the Columbiana County Grand Jury took place during late September. It resulted in the arrest of six minor gambling figures in East Liverpool. These people were all fined, but had their jail sentences suspended. They continued their activities, knowing that being arrested was part of doing business.

The Marino investigation was led by Mahoning County and Youngstown detectives. Columbiana County officials had stepped aside even though the body had been found in their jurisdiction. The Youngstown detectives were relentless in their pursuit. They began their investigation by questioning all of Marino's friends and associates. Little by little they began to gather evidence. They followed up on the theory that Marino was involved in the holdup and murder of Youngstown saloon keeper, James Tisone, on September 8th. They also looked into the rumor that he was trying to "muscle in" on a greyhound track in Fowler, Ohio.

Meanwhile, back in Steubenville, the Anthoulis – O'Boyle gang, was hard at work. While they certainly could not be called *"The gang that couldn't shoot straight,"* their attempts at a cover up, would prove them to be *"The gang that couldn't think straight."*

Eddie Hegert was a low level employee of the gang, but he soon had plenty to worry about. He was at work at around midnight a few days later, when Tom Galati and John O'Boyle drove Galati's Packard into Anthoulis's Novelty Amusement Co. garage. This was the gang's headquarters, and it was across the street from the police station. O'Boyle ordered Hegert to remove the car's upholstery. He saw that the back seat had dried blood on the upholstery, and a bullet hole through the roof. As he was doing so Anthoulis came in and excitedly ordered the car removed. He was scared because some Steubenville cops were hanging around on the corner.

Charlie Calaris said, *"I know where we can hide it."* Angelo Mantos owned a farm along U.S. Route 22 in Broadacre, near Cadiz, Ohio. Calaris contacted him, and the car was moved to the secluded farm. Once the car was hidden, Hegert and Calaris finished removing the bloody upholstery. They did not, however, destroy the telltale evidence.

| Herb Ross | Sol Hart | Thomas Galati |

The car was kept hidden at the Mantos farm for the next six days. Meanwhile, Solly Hart and Herb Ross traveled to Detroit, Michigan to find a match to the death car. They arrived in the "Motor City" on September 20th and checked into the Book-Cadillac Hotel. A couple of phone calls back to Steubenville resulted in two Western Union money transfers being sent to Ross. An identical Packard was purchased by a front man, and the two gangsters drove it back to Steubenville on September 24th.

After the upholstery was removed from the Michigan car and put into the death car, the Michigan car was hidden in the garage of gang employee Jack Sperry. It would remain there without seats until January 1938. The death car was then taken to the Standard Welding Co. to repair the bullet hole in the roof. O'Boyle had driven a wedge into the hole to disguise it. Later it was taken to be repainted at the auto body repair shop of Claude Wilson. Once it was finished, it was driven to Cleveland and sold, eventually ending up in Sacramento, California.

The organization of the gang began to change in October. On the 15th, O'Boyle called a meeting with Anthoulis at the Fort Steuben Hotel. O'Boyle was worried, telling his partner, *"I'm in bad shape; I'm hot. I've gotta get out of here, they're accusing me of taking $35,000 out of Russell's safe; I've got to leave!"* O'Boyle said he wanted $3,000 for his share of the business, but Anthoulis would not agree to that price. O'Boyle was desperate. He finally agreed to $600, with only $100 down. O'Boyle soon left town, and he never saw any of the remaining $500. Now John Anthoulis was the "Boss" of the gang.

On October 18th, Ross, Hart, and Galati called the employees together and informed them of the change. Ross laid the law down, telling Hegert they were cutting his pay. From now on he would be paid just $35 a week. Ross also said *"There will be no more pockets full of nickels going home after work each day."* Ross told him, *"If you don't like it you can quit."* But he left him with a warning, *"You won't get to any prosecutor's office, because we have ways of taking care of that."* Hegert knew he had to get away from the gang, and soon. By the end of October he saw his chance. First he went to work fixing machinery for his brother-in-law. After a while, he was able to leave town, getting away from the gang. He went home to Cleveland, and tried to disappear into the crowd.

Even though Hegert was away from Steubenville, he was afraid of the gang. About a month later, he decided to call John Anthoulis and ask if they had any work for him. Anthoulis said no. Hegert later said he did this to feel them out. If he thought they were after him he would flee the country.

The Anthoulis gang was continuing to run their illegal gambling operations, probably thinking they were safe. However, Youngstown Detectives John Callan, Robert Jeffrey, and W.J. Harrison had not given up. They were busy running down every clue they could find. Many of the leads were taking them to Steubenville. A few weeks after the murder, the Youngstown detectives arrested Robert "Toots" Calabrese, and George and Daniel Rackinac. The trio was quietly taken to Youngstown for questioning. They were released a couple of days later.

Meanwhile, the violence continued. On the night of December 22nd, Daniel Rackinac and Daniel Visnich were just leaving a bar on South 7th Street in Steubenville, when a car slowly drove past and a gunman opened fire with a shotgun. Visnich was killed, but Rackinac escaped uninjured. The two men were described as local underworld muscle. Police tried hard, but no link to the Marino murder could be found. One thing was sure, however; there was a war for control of the Upper Ohio Valley rackets going on. The *Steubenville Herald-Star* reported that as many as five different syndicates were vying for control.

Detectives knew they were on the right track when Tom Galati was picked up by the Cleveland police on January 10, 1938. They had been searching for him for several weeks. Witnesses had placed his Packard sedan at Chick's Café the night of the murder. Detectives John Callan and Bill Harrison rushed to Cleveland to question him. However, in the end they had to release him. They just did not have enough evidence yet. Galati could see *"the writing on the wall"*. He quickly and quietly left town.

About one month later, the detectives caught a break in the form of an anonymous tip. It would prove to be the deciding factor in breaking the case. It was said to involve the murder car, and the attempts to conceal it. Soon the detectives were running down the new leads. One lead led them to Eddie Hegert. At the request of Mahoning County authorities, the Cleveland police arrested Hegert on February 26th. He was brought to Youngstown and booked under the alias of Arthur Synder. Hegert was secretly placed in the Beaver County, Pennsylvania Jail under the alias. This was so he would remain hidden until the trial. Eddie was to be the State's star witness. Once the break came, the trail led to Cleveland, Detroit, to Steubenville, Ohio and even to Sacramento, California.

Detectives searched the Mantos farm, and Steubenville Policeman Lee Campbell found a piece of the bloody upholstery. Later the team found one of the license plates of the Michigan car in Bellaire, Ohio. It was under the floor mat of a truck owned by the Anthoulis gang. With Hegert now singing like a canary, the case was strong enough to go before the Grand Jury. Murder indictments were issued on April 6th against five members of the gang; John Anthoulis, Solly Hart, Herbert Ross, John O'Boyle, and Thomas Galati.

In the late afternoon of April 9th, Youngstown detectives and Steubenville police launched a series of raids on the Anthoulis gang. Herb Ross was arrested at the Novelty Amusement Co., the headquarters of the gang. He was carrying a .38 caliber police special pistol when taken into custody. Two other .38s were found on the premises. After questioning Ross for nearly an hour, he finally gave up his partners. Detectives Callan, Jeffrey and Harrison went to the law offices of John F. Nolan, Steubenville's political boss, and arrested Anthoulis and Hart. Nolan advised them to go quietly. Steubenville police raided several other places including the home of John Anthoulis, where they found Mrs. Mike Russell, wife of the slain Wheeling racketeer. By evening, Anthoulis, Hart and Ross were in custody but Galati and O'Boyle were nowhere to be found. The three suspects were booked at the Steubenville police station, and then they were taken to Youngstown in separate cars. Upon arrival at the Mahoning County Jail they were placed in separate cells on three different cell blocks.

The detectives and the county prosecutor questioned the men, but they all refused to talk.

Who were these men? Were they just some local boys trying to make a living? Or were they hardened criminals capable of murder?

John Anthoulis was described in the newspapers as the "Slot Machine Czar" of Jefferson County, Ohio. He was an ex-convict who had been convicted of bootlegging in 1929. He had done his time at the Federal Penitentiary in Atlanta, Georgia. After taking over the slot machine gang, he was convicted in January 1938 of illegal gambling and was fined. Police listed him as a onetime associate of "Big Bill" Lias.

Solly Hart was the biggest catch. The 32-year-old was from Cleveland, Ohio, and had a long police record, beginning in 1924 at age 18. He had arrests for driving a car without permission and for carrying concealed weapons. He was arrested for at least three robberies in the 1920s, but always managed to avoid jail. He was a suspect in several murders, including the famous murder of William E. Potter, in 1931. Potter was an ex-Cleveland city councilman, whose constituents thought would reveal corruption in city government. It was said that Hart had been with Potter less than an hour before the murder. (*The jury convicted his friend "Pittsburgh Hymie" Martin of the killing. Martin won a new trial and the conviction was overturned. The case was overturned due to some legal technicalities, and the alibi provided by a sometimes prostitute, Betty Grey, known to history as "Akron Mary.")

After the Potter trial, Hart was convicted of some old concealed weapons charges, and sent to the Ohio Penitentiary, in Columbus. He soon won a parole, and early in 1937 he was the suspect in a robbery and shooting at a disorderly house. Feeling the need to *"cool off,"* Hart came to the Ohio Valley to try his hand.

Herbert Ross age 35 also came from Cleveland and was described by police as Hart's bodyguard. Ross had done a year in the Ohio Penitentiary for carrying a concealed weapon. He was paroled in 1930. He was well known to the Cleveland Police Department.

The other two defendants, O'Boyle and Galati, were still on the run. Anthoulis, Hart, and Ross arranged for the services of Attorneys Hugo F. Chestosky and James S. Cooper, two high priced lawyers. An early trial was promised. Mahoning County claimed jurisdiction due to the crime originating in Youngstown. Columbiana County was okay with that.

First to go before Mahoning County Common Pleas Court Judge Erskine Maiden Jr. was John Anthoulis. The trial began on May 17th, and the state brought forth a parade of witnesses. Several were employees of the gang, such as Jack Sperry, who testified that his garage was used to hide the Michigan car. Ex-partner Charles Calaris also admitted to helping to change the upholstery in the death car, and hiding it on the Mantos farm. Western Union officials told the jury about the money orders sent to Detroit, and hotel clerks put Hart and Ross in that city at the same time. The high school boys placed Galati's Packard at Chick's Café. There were others, but the most telling testimony came from star witness Eddie Hegert. The defense tried hard to break him down, but in the end could not discredit his testimony. The trial lasted until May 27th. The jury of eight men and four women deliberated only a little over six hours before returning a verdict of guilty of first degree murder, with the recommendation of mercy. The verdict carried a sentence of life imprisonment, but no electric chair.

Herb Ross faced Judge Maiden next in a trial that lasted from June 8th until June 15th. The same evidence and witnesses were brought against him. A jury of nine women and three men took a little over 14 hours to bring in the same verdict, guilty, of first degree murder with the recommendation of mercy.

Solly Hart tried a different tactic when his trial came up on July 11th. He waived a jury trial and went before a panel of three judges. Once again the same evidence was brought forth, and once again the same result occurred. Hart was convicted on July 22nd. With the trials over, the three gangsters were quickly taken to the State Penitentiary at Columbus, Ohio.

The next day Tom Galati was captured at the home of his brother-in-law, Tommy Rizzo, on Oak St. in Marion, Ohio. A tip had brought police to the hideout, and the 29-year-old Galati came quietly. Galati had been arrested 12 times before, and his thirteenth would prove unlucky for him.

By now the high priced legal team had given up, and Galati had difficulty securing counsel. The trial which began in late September dragged on through October with delay upon delay, but on November 2nd, it was over. The results were the same.

All four of the killers had denied knowing anything about the Marino murder. So what really happened in the early hours of September 10, 1937? Although it will never be known, it could have happened like this. The gang in Steubenville was upset with Marino for any one of several reasons and decided to get rid of him. Three gunmen, probably Hart, Ross and Galati, went to Youngstown on September 9th to snatch him. They lured him to Chick's Café and kidnapped him. The next several hours are a mystery within a mystery. We can only guess what the conversation between Marino and his captors was like. Did he plead his innocence, or was he defiant? Where did they take him? Knowing he was in trouble, did he attempt to escape? Did he try to get a hold of the gun of one of his captors? In any case, shots were fired inside the moving vehicle. At least one wounded Marino, and one punctured the roof of the car. We can imagine the car sliding to a stop and Marino being pushed out onto the highway. His killers followed him, and as he held his arms up trying to shield himself, several more bullets tore into him as he stumbled or maybe crawled along the side of the highway. With the deed done, his killers got back into the car and sped on to Steubenville, leaving "Happy" lying dead in the ditch. Is that the way it happened? We do not know, but it seems likely from the evidence.

With four of the five killers doing life behind the bars of various Ohio penal institutions one might think the story was over. Wrong. As soon as they arrived at the prison, they began working to get out. Hart in particular began his transformation from Cleveland's Public Enemy No. 1 to a model prisoner. Shortly after arriving at the state penitentiary at Columbus, he was given the much sought after job of runner. The trio of Anthoulis, Hart, and Ross filed an appeal to the Ohio Supreme Court in the spring of 1939. Their contention was that two of the state's witnesses, Hegert and Calaris, had become co-conspirators, so their testimony was incompetent. They also claimed there was no evidence that Marino had been killed in Mahoning County, so the venue of the trial should have been Columbiana County. The Ohio Supreme Court ruled against these appeals in September, and the prisoners settled down to making life behind bars as easy as possible.

Solly Hart had a head start on the others. By April 26, 1941 he was a trustee in the prison which gave him more freedom of movement and privileges. By December, he was the warden's chauffeur. He would serve a succession of wardens as their personal driver.

Authorities finally tracked John O'Boyle down, arresting him in Chicago, Illinois in January 1945. He was picked up by the FBI in connection with a bond robbery in Los Angeles, California. Although not enough evidence could be found to connect him with the robbery, they did however, charge him with possessing stolen gasoline coupons. The Federal authorities then agreed to turn him over to Mahoning County on the murder charge. Unfortunately, he had the last laugh since the state's witnesses had all disappeared, and prosecutors could produce no one to testify. He was released back into federal custody on May 28, 1946, he was the only one to escape justice in Marino's murder.

For the next few years Solly Hart would be a model prisoner and thus reap all of the rewards available inside the walls. Making friends in high places certainly paid off. He was the chauffer for Warden Frank Henderson and then his replacement, Ralph Alvis. Prison officials began to express "grave doubts" about his guilt. Some began to think he had been "framed." Governor Thomas J. Herbert reduced his sentence to second degree murder on January 1, 1949, making him eligible for parole. However, the parole board denied him in February, much to the satisfaction of Judge Maiden and Mahoning County officials. Nevertheless, Governor Frank J. Lausche further reduced Hart's sentence to manslaughter on December 31, 1956, which carried a one to twenty year sentence. John Anthoulis did not fare as well, but one would assume he was not swinging a sledge hammer on a rock pile. He did, however, serve a life sentence, since he died as the result of a heart attack on October 9, 1956. Herb Ross had also impressed his captors. By now, he was a trustee at the London Prison Farm.

On January 29, 1958, Warden Alvis and Hart were driving in Columbus when they tried to pass a truck near an intersection. The truck made a legal left turn, striking Warden Alvis's convertible. Both Alvis and Hart were ejected from the car and severely injured. Warden Alvis lost an eye. The warden's vehicle was clearly at fault, but what is not so clear is why Warden Alvis was driving the car with Hart as *"his"* passenger.

It was announced a few months later that Solly Hart would receive his parole on July 21, 1958. He was interviewed a few days before his release. Reporters talked to him as he was sitting on Warden Alvis' front porch. He was dressed in dark blue trousers and wearing a summer-weight white sports shirt that concealed a brace he wore on his back. He said, *"I'm not sore at anybody. Seventeen newspapers said I wouldn't last three days as a trustee, but I'm still here."* When asked where he thought he would be if he had not spent the last twenty years in prison, he replied; *"That's a hard question to answer. You can't look twenty years ahead. I did a lot of things that weren't right, maybe. But I sure did twenty years for nothing this time. I was a foolish kid before I landed in prison. I never owned anything worthwhile. The older you get the more you learn."* Speaking about his sister whom he would be living with; *"She stuck with me all these twenty years. She never missed coming down to see me or worrying about me."*

Solly Hart gained his freedom at 12:05 p.m., July 21, 1958. He had served 19 years and 364 days, one day short of the 20 year maximum for manslaughter. Once again Mahoning County officials protested, but to no avail. Hart limped out of jail wearing neck and back braces. When asked about his plans he said, *"I'm going to Cleveland for medical treatments, and then maybe I'll come back to Columbus, and take one of the four jobs I've been offered."* He would be awarded $8,600 in injury compensation from the State of Ohio.

The "fully rehabilitated" Herb Ross was paroled on November 23, 1960 by Governor Michael DiSalle. Ross spent the remainder of his life in the Columbus area, working for an optical company. He died at age 79 in December of 1982. Tom Galati's sentence was reduced to second degree murder on January 14, 1963, and he was paroled in April. Galati lived in Cleveland until his death on June 15, 1968. He was 59 years old.

Solly Hart, however, would continue in his old ways. On June 2, 1967 he was convicted of book making in Miami, Florida. It seems he was working for his old bosses from Cleveland, who were in Miami for their "retirement" years. He was also working with another of his old acquaintances from the Potter murder more than thirty years earlier, "Pittsburgh Hymie" Martin, now known as "Fat Hymie." It goes to show you, true friends are a blessing. Solly's heath soon began to fail and he died in October 1976, at age 71.

The murder of Roy "Happy" Marino in 1937 and the discovery a few weeks earlier of the unknown corpse may or may not have been connected. We will probably never know; however, they do make for interesting reading about the days when the "mob" came to Columbiana County.

Chapter 6

Ninety Minutes of Terror!

The Dry Goods District Fire
March 3, 1892

The 1880s was a "boom time" for East Liverpool, Ohio. New buildings were springing up all over town. The population was booming too; by 1890 nearly 11,000 people had made their home here.

Fire protection was also growing from its humble beginnings. In 1885 the fire department acquired its first fire horses. In January two horses named "Sleepy George" and "Barney Golddust" joined the department. A new headquarters was built at City Hall on Third Street with a stable to house them. When the city bought these animals, they also had to hire someone to care for them.

H. Clinton Morley became the first full time paid firefighter in East Liverpool when he was hired to care for the horses. By May a third horse named "Grey Charlie" was added to the force. Firefighters converted the old hand drawn fire equipment to be pulled by the horses, much improving the department's response time to fires.

The Knowles, Taylor, & Knowles "China Works" Pottery on Bradshaw Avenue was destroyed on November 18, 1889. The fire was the result of a gas explosion. The loss was staggering; at least $250,000 dollars, millions in today's money. Poor water pressure played a part in the disaster and fed the movement to purchase a steam powered fire engine. The engine was purchased by the city from the Silsby Company in March of 1890, and that machine is currently in the Lou Holtz Upper Ohio Valley Hall of Fame Museum on E. 5th Street in East Liverpool.

East Liverpool Fire Department, circa 1890

By 1892, East Liverpool had developed somewhat haphazardly. There were no building regulations at that time. Retail stores stood beside private homes or stables. The main shopping area of town was located along 5th Street and into the "Diamond" on Market Street. This area was commonly called the "Dry Goods District." *(*The term "dry goods" was in common usage a hundred years ago. It refers to textiles goods like clothing and fabric.)* This area was occupied by two and three story buildings, many of which were built of wood frame. There were also smaller buildings and some private homes scattered amongst the business blocks.

The sun had not yet appeared above the surrounding hills on the cold morning of March 3, 1892. It was 5:30 a.m. The city was just shaking itself awake from a long night's slumber, when Sam Wallace noticed a problem. Wallace lived in an apartment on the third floor rear of the W. L. Thompson Building. He could see a fire burning fiercely in a narrow passage between the Thompson Building and the building owned by S.H. Porter.

These two buildings stood side by side along the east side of Market Street in the "Diamond." The dry goods store of Crosser &

Ogilvie occupied the first floor of the Porter building. The upper floors housed several other small businesses and apartments. On the first floor of the Thompson building was the huge dry goods firm known as the People's Store, operated by Henry E. Porter. This building was L-shaped with an entrance on Market Street and another on 5th Street. As with the other buildings in this area, the upper two floors housed a variety of businesses and apartments.

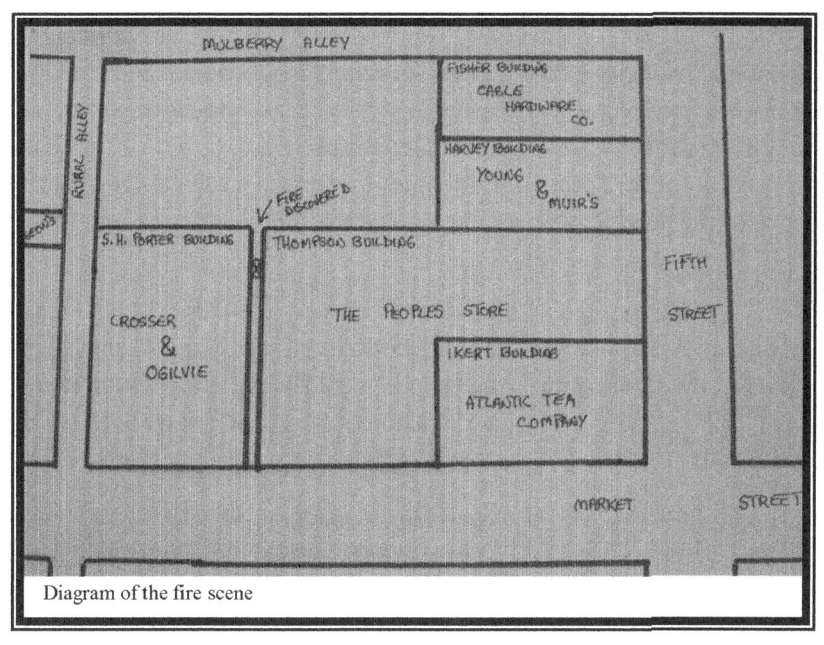

Diagram of the fire scene

Wallace said the fire was located within the eighteen inch wide passage between the two buildings when he first saw it. He could not tell which building the fire had started in but it was quickly eating its way up side of the Porter building. There was a chimney located in that section.

Almost before he could react, others tenants began to yell *"FIRE!"* Across the "Diamond" Jim Norris was just opening his butcher shop when he heard the commotion. Norris ran up Rural Alley, (later renamed Diamond Alley) to the rear of the Porter building, stopping in front of Geon's Saloon. It looked to him as if the fire had started from a pile of rubbish, but now perhaps a gas line had ruptured as the fire was burning with great intensity.

Norris continued to run up Rural Alley to Washington Street and pulled the fire alarm box at the Hotel Grand. The fire department soon arrived under the control of the fire chief, Melvin Bart Adam. The men quickly began to hook their hoses to a fire hydrant in the "Diamond." Unfortunately, an excited firefighter tried to turn it on the wrong way and broke the valve stem. This rendered the hydrant useless. Chief Adam ordered the hoses to be attached to another hydrant, but the delay was disastrous.

Chief Adam quickly called for the Silsby steam engine to be brought to the scene. The firefighters did not take the engine on every call because of its great weight. The department did not have enough horses to pull it along with the other apparatus, so it got left behind most of the time.

By now the fire had found its way into both the Crosser & Ogilvie's and the People's Store. Once inside, the flames found plenty of fuel and soon swept through the stock of clothing and other fabrics. On the floors above, the tenants were fleeing the burning buildings. All managed to escape unharmed although not without some close calls.

Within a very short time both buildings were fully engulfed in flames. Because the Thompson Building also faced onto 5th Street the fire was able to spread there as well. Located within the L of the Thompson Building was the Ikert Building. Located at the corner of 5th Street and Market, it was owned by Dr. George and J.J. Ikert. Flames now began to appear in it as well. The Atlantic Tea Company, a grocery store, occupied the first floor with the usual mix on the upper floors.

After it arrived, the Silsby steam engine was positioned on 5th Street near the intersection with Market Street. It took some time to get up steam and find some hose for it. All of the fire department's hoses were already being used, so several potteries loaned their private stock to help fight the blaze. Once the engine was in operation it would prove its worth. Called the "White Elephant" by its detractors, the steam engine nevertheless probably saved several buildings by pumping water onto the roofs.

By this time, the salvage operations were occurring all around the fire scene. Dozens of citizens organized into salvage gangs began carrying stock out of the endangered buildings. Soon large piles of merchandise was scattered all along 5th Street. One of the few injuries in this fire occurred during one of these operations. Harry Hughes lost his footing and fell down the steps in the Ikert building. He was bruised and shook up, but not severely injured.

Several smaller structures in the area were also burning, which helped communicate the fire to the larger buildings. John Harvey's building stood on 5th Street next to the Thompson Building. Young & Muir's Dry Goods store did business on the first floor. The rear and roof of the structure had begun to burn. However, thanks to the salvage crews, much of their stock was saved, although it suffered from smoke and water damage.

The Silsby steam engine was pumping thousands of gallons of water onto the roofs of the Harvey Building and the Fisher Building, which stood at the corner of 5th Street and Mulberry Alley. When the blaze was at its height a bolt blew out of the engine's boiler. It was pumping 800 gallons of water a minute at a pressure of 115 pounds per square inch. Scalding steam began shooting from the boiler causing all the people around it to run for their lives. Firefighters quickly drove a plug into the boiler, stopping the problem. Steam was restored and the fight was resumed.

The Thompson Building was by now a solid sheet of flame as the walls began to crumble. When they fell, a wave of intense heat drove back the crowd. The heat also blew out the plate glass windows of storefronts on the south side of 5th Street. For a time, many people feared that these stores would begin to burn as well.

The Fisher Building housed the Eagle Hardware Company, and for a while it appeared that it was doomed. Firefighters pulled the sheeting from the roof, allowing the steam engine to pump water throughout the building, which saved it.

However, when things still looked grim, a hero stepped forward. Frank Croxall was an insurance agent who had organized a salvage gang to save the merchandise from buildings his insurance covered.

He was trying to cut his losses. When he saw the Fisher Building catch fire, he remembered that the Eagle Hardware also stocked explosives.

He led his crew into the burning building to carry out eight kegs of gunpowder and two boxes of dynamite. The explosives were stacked in the intersection of Rural Alley and Mulberry Alley. Croxall was kept quite busy brushing away sparks and burning embers that landed on the pile. A large crowd had gathered in the intersection to get a good look at the blaze. They did not realize how much danger they were in. Croxall had sent for a wagon and after a tense wait, it finally arrived. The deadly cargo was quickly and quietly loaded. Croxall told the driver to *"Take this stuff as far out of town as you can!"* If this "stuff" would have exploded, who knows where the fire would have stopped?

At its height, the flames leapt hundreds of feet into the air. The surrounding area was so bright that people could see the glow from Rochester, Pennsylvania, nearly twenty miles away. Throughout the city, men were kept busy on rooftops putting out burning embers before they could take hold.

As the sun was beginning to rise over the West Virginia hills, it was evident that the fire was beginning to wane. The massive crowd took a deep breath and fervently thanked Almighty God for their deliverance. By 7:00 a.m. the fire was declared to be under control; however, it would continue to burn for several more hours.

The fire had destroyed the S.H. Porter, W.L. Thompson, and Ikert Buildings. The Harvey and Fisher Buildings had also been severely damaged. Nine large business firms had been burned out. In all, thirty-one different businesses and individuals suffered losses. Monetary loss was put at $150,000 dollars, several million in today's money.

East Liverpool's business community was made of stern stuff in those days. While the fire was still smoldering, store owners were already acquiring new locations. That day the building owners all vowed to rebuild at once, bigger and better than before.

Workmen began sifting through the ruins as soon as they were cool. They were searching the rubble to find the store safes. Most of the safes fared well through the blaze. Business owners were pleased to have the important papers and cash they contained. They would need it in the coming days. Dangerous walls that were left standing were quickly torn down, and debris hauled away.

East Liverpool had been lucky, and everyone knew it. If it had not been for the great many citizens that had joined in the fight, the whole of the business district could have been lost. The quality and the level of fire protection were inadequate for the fast growing community. The firefighters were dedicated and courageous, but they had neither the training nor the equipment that was necessary for a situation like this.

City Council and the business community met the following day to discuss the problem. Several proposals were made to buy more modern equipment and even to look into establishing a fully paid fire department. In the end, however, it came down to money and the city was unprepared to spend the amount that was required to accomplish these things.

Council did agree to purchase more hose and another hose reel for the rapidly developing Northside neighborhood. There had been 2,500 feet of hose used during the fire, a large portion of which belonged to private companies. They also called for Chief Adam to test the hydrants in the business district and look into the costs of paying the firefighters.

Things then went back to normal. New and better buildings sprang up in place of the ones that were destroyed. The business district soon showed little evidence of this near catastrophe. However, the problem still remained.

One year later, (on April 1, 1893), a major fire struck the Potters Co-Operative "Dresden Pottery." The blaze destroyed the plant, causing at least $80,000 dollars in damage. Once again the city was forced to look into the problem of fire protection.

In 1893, The Insurance Underwriters came to town to assess the quality of fire protection. This was so insurance companies could set the insurance rates. *(* This occurs periodically; in my time on the fire* *department, they evaluated the department at least twice.)* When their report came out in October, it contained many deficiencies.

The city knew the fire department needed to be improved, so in light of this evaluation the Council took action. In June they purchased a new hook & ladder wagon, and ordered another wagon to carry hose and equipment. Both were a vast improvement over the old hose reels and the old ladder wagon. The city also purchased Frank Dickey's livery stable on Broadway and what is now St. Clair Avenue. It became the Central Fire Station; the current fire station stands on the same spot. They also purchased another team of horses and more equipment.

The biggest improvement came in the way the department was staffed. Melvin Bart Adam remained the part time chief, but now there were full time men at the new station. H. Clinton Morley was named as Captain. He, along with James McCullough and Joshua Curfman, were the full time firefighters. In addition, four men spent their nights at the station. They were known as "sleepers."

In March of 1895, the East Liverpool Fire Department was organized as follows. Melvin Bart Adam was still the fire chief. He continued in the position part time. He and his brother owned and operated a harness and carriage shop. The three fulltime men were Captain H. Clinton Morley, Driver James McCullough, and Engineer Joshua Curfman.

The four "sleepers" were Tom Bryan, George Betteridge, Henry Diedrick, and Barney Peterson. All of these men, except for Chief Adam and Joshua Curfman, would be members of the full time fire department which would be organized in 1896. Chief Adam turned it down because of the work schedule and Curfman was deemed to be too old. Fourteen volunteer firefighters rounded out the force.

Six fire horses pulled the equipment, consisting of the Silsby steam engine, the new Babcock hook & ladder wagon and the new hose wagon. The city now owned 4,000 feet of fire hose and 100 fire hydrants were spread throughout the city. A fire alarm system was installed with 20 fire boxes and 50 police patrol boxes located on street corners or buildings. Private businesses installed 25 more alarm boxes in their buildings. In addition, there were volunteer hose reel companies in the East End and Northside sections of town.

The following year the department became full time with eight men under the direction of Chief H. Clinton Morley. Were they now prepared to handle another conflagration like what had occurred in 1892? In just thirteen years they would know the answer.

Chapter 7
Something Terrible has Happened!

The Tweed - Morris Murders
July 30, 1973

There is probably no greater mystery in East Liverpool, Ohio than the gruesome murder that snuffed out four innocent lives on July 30, 1973. Even forty years after the fact it still captures the imagination of this community. It has become an "Urban Legend" in East Liverpool. There are few adults who have never heard about it. For anyone interested in this story they can find it on the internet. Over the years the local newspaper the *East Liverpool Review* has written several stories about it. Recently an independent film maker who once lived in the area produced a documentary about the murders. The film is titled *759 Dresden,* which was the address of the crime scene. It first aired on November 20, 2010 on WQED Pittsburgh's Public Broadcasting Station.

The East Liverpool Police Department considers this to be an active murder investigation. They still receive tips from time to time which are always checked out. Evidence collected forty years ago has been sent to the FBI Laboratory for DNA and fingerprint checks. So far no match has been found.

It is hoped by authorities that with each retelling of the story maybe someone will remember some piece of the puzzle that will finally close this case. So what happened all those years ago?

Earl A. Tweed was the 75-year-old proprietor of the National Furniture and Upholstering and Repair Company located at 759 Dresden Avenue on the edge of the downtown district. Tweed was born in Steubenville, Ohio on August 18, 1897 and had lived in East Liverpool since 1912. He lived at 115 W. 3rd Street with his wife of many years, Marie. Earl and Marie were active members of the 1st United Methodist Church and many other clubs and service groups in town. They were well known and well liked members of the community. Their daughter Donna lived in Cambridge, Ohio with her husband James Ferguson and their family.

Along with the furniture business Tweed sold antiques and had some rental properties around town.

759 Dresden Avenue today

Arthur Lewis "Louie" Morris had just moved into town from eastern Pennsylvania. They had come to town to be closer to their family. His wife Linda was 22 years old and about four months pregnant. The couple also had a daughter Angela, a bright little girl of four. They were living at 684 Lincoln Avenue but with the baby on the way they were looking for a bigger apartment. Louie had just been hired in June by the city Street Department, under the Emergency Employment Act. While Louie was at work, Linda looked for apartments.

Charles Inman worked part time for Tweed and lived nearby on E. 8th Street. He went to the store in the late morning to talk with Mr. Tweed. Inman left about 11:30 a.m. Around 12:30 p.m. Tweed received a phone call from a relative and talked for a few minutes.

Shortly after 12:30 p.m. on that warm Monday afternoon, Linda and little Angela entered the National Furniture Store to talk to Mr. Tweed about renting an apartment.

Daniel and Frances Dugan of Chicago, Illinois were passing through town looking for antiques. They stopped in front of the store and Frances Dugan went in while Daniel waited in the car. The time was 12:55 p.m. Frances Dugan entered the dark cluttered shop and was shocked by the gruesome sight she found about thirty feet from the door. She turned and ran outside shouting to people across the street *"Call the Police, Something Terrible has happened."* Frances Dugan, a nurse, then stood guard outside the door until the police arrived.

Earl Tweed

The store was filled with furniture from Tweed's rental properties and antiques. Upon entering the building the police officers found the body of Linda Morris lying on a mattress that had partially fallen from a standing position. Just to her left was little Angela. Both had been badly beaten with a heavy object. Although it was too late for Linda, Angela was still breathing. A police officer scooped her up and rushed her to the City Hospital in hopes of saving her.

Police officers continued to warily move further into the dark room. Following a narrow aisleway they came into an open area near the top of the basement stairs. There they found the body of Earl Tweed.

Tweed had also been badly beaten and had been stabbed numerous times. Nearby, in a pool of blood lay a claw hammer, a knife and a wrench. On a chair were two slices of bread and some lunch meat. It looked as if Tweed had been fixing his lunch when his killer arrived.

By now the deafening roar of sirens had alerted the city. Word began to spread of the terrible killings.

Mrs. Lettie Morris, Louie's mother, was shopping uptown when she heard about the murder. She knew her daughter-in-law was going to see Tweed about an apartment. She hurried to the Dresden Avenue address where she told police about her daughter-in-law. The police described the clothing the victim was wearing. Mrs. Morris burst into tears upon hearing the details. She was taken to the hospital to be with her granddaughter.

Once the police had discovered the identity of Linda Morris they found out her husband was a fellow city employee. Mayor Norman Bucher was notified and he contacted Street Superintendent John Cornell *(*the author's father.)* Cornell drove the Mayor and Councilman Homer Mercer to the job site where Louie Morris was working. They then drove him to the hospital to be with his daughter. Sadly, doctors were unable to save little Angela; and she passed away at 1:56 p.m.

Linda Morris

Detective Bill Devon headed the investigation which swung into high gear as Chief Americo Radeschi mobilized the entire police department. Detectives found several potential murder weapons which were collected along with fingerprints and blood samples. Authorities conducted numerous interviews. A thorough search of the area revealed nothing.

An open rear window was determined to have been open for some time. A check of the rear door determined that it had not been opened, so it appears the killer left through the front door. He had walked out onto busy Dresden Avenue in the middle of the day and vanished.

Later that afternoon police received a phone call at headquarters. Patrolman William Buckley was dispatched to the freeway interchange at W. 8th and Webber Way. That location is about two blocks from the site of the murders. The city owns a set of steps that lead up to Ridgway Avenue. Scattered around the bottom of these steps were papers belonging to Earl Tweed. Buckley also found Tweed's wallet in the weeds. There was no money in it. The question is, did the killer go up the stairs or did he come down? Maybe he did not use them at all. From here several major highways can be accessed. The killer could have gone anywhere.

Later that night, Chief Deputy Coroner Dr. J. Keith Rugh, assisted by Dr. Oscar Budde of Salem, Ohio, conducted autopsies on the victims. Rugh reported that Tweed had been stabbed in the chest more than twenty times with what appeared to be an eight inch long serrated steak knife. All three of the victims had been badly beaten with a heavy object.

Freeway Stairs

Due to the fact that this is an open case, some details have been kept out of the newspapers and some seem to contradict themselves. Some reports state that Tweed had been stabbed with carpet shears instead of a knife. Both of these potential weapons had been sent to the crime lab for analysis.

Over the next few days a great many witnesses and potential suspects were interviewed. City police were assisted by members of the Ohio Bureau of Criminal Investigation, the Columbiana County Sheriff Department, and the County Prosecutor's staff. Police officers flew to a nearby city to interview a suspect who was picked up there. All of the physical evidence was sent to the Bureau of Criminal Investigation Laboratory in London, Ohio. The BCI never found a match linking anyone to this horrible crime.

Based on the investigation, police set a twenty five minute time frame for the murders to have been committed. They theorize that Tweed was killed during a robbery. He was known to have always carried a large sum of money. They also believe Linda and Angela Morris must have walked in on the murder and were killed to silence them. For the sake of a couple hundred dollars, four innocent lives were destroyed, Earl Tweed, Linda and Angela Morris and Linda's unborn child.

Over the next couple of days, stories began to appear in local newspapers like the one in the *Evening Review* of August 1st. It was reported that an unnamed boy said he was walking on Dresden Avenue at the time of the murders. The boy said a man ran from the store and bumped into him. The man grabbed the youth and demanded to know where he lived. The boy said something to the effect that he could not or would not tell his assailant. The man then said *"Tell me or I'll kill you!"* The boy broke free and began to run. When he looked back he saw the man run through the vacant lot between the National Furniture building and Allison's Meat Market, heading toward the freeway.

The Youngstown *Vindicator* ran this story also on August 1st. An unidentified driver was heading south on State Route 7 in the early afternoon of Monday, July 30th. He stopped and picked up a hitchhiker. In between State Route 213 and Port Homer, a report of the murders came over the car radio. The hitchhiker then pulled out a knife and ordered the man to stop the car. The hitchhiker got out and disappeared onto the heavily wooded hillside. The driver reported the incident to the authorities in Stratton, Ohio; however, a search of the area found nothing.

The *Evening Review* reported on August 8th, that police were searching for two dollar bills that Earl Tweed always carried in his wallet. The bills had been marked with the word DADDY and underneath the word was the letters XX OO standing for kisses and hugs. They had been given to him by his daughter.

From the various witnesses a general description was developed of a young man with red hair.

The Fraternal Order of Police Lodges of East Liverpool and Wellsville offered a $500 dollar reward for information leading to the arrest and conviction of the killer. By the end of August the reward had grown to $1650 dollars but still no break came. The case was stalled.

Funeral services were held on August 2nd with Earl Tweed being laid to rest in Riverview Cemetery and Linda and Angela Morris in Spring Grove Cemetery.

Within a few days the murder story had all but vanished from the newspapers, as nothing seemed to be happening. However, the investigation was continuing. The years have passed and everyone involved in the investigation is now retired; many have passed away. Like most cases, the detectives always have a prime suspect. However, there was not enough evidence to arrest him. We will probably never know.

Louie Morris moved away and eventually remarried and had a family. He would serve twenty-seven years on a police department in Michigan before retiring to St. Marys, West Virginia. He returned to East Liverpool to take part in the documentary *759 Dresden* in 2010. Louie passed away at age 63 on August 23, 2010. He is buried in Spring Grove Cemetery with his first wife, Linda and their daughter, Angela.

In a small city like East Liverpool it would be hard for a secret like this to remain after all these years. It is probable that whoever the killer is he or she no longer lives in town. Maybe they never did? Maybe they are dead? All we have are questions and an enduring mystery.

Chapter 8

Wrong Place at the Wrong Time

The Tragic Death of Herbert Sayre

October 8, 1925

In the early morning hours of October 8, 1925, the roof of the kiln shed of the T.A. McNicol Pottery caught fire. The plant occupied a three story brick and frame building, located on the eastern end of the River Road. Some bricks had come loose and fallen, allowing the intense heat to catch the surrounding wood on fire.

Herbert Sayre lived on Railroad Street across the tracks from the plant and worked there as a foreman. He was awakened by a neighbor and told about the fire. Sayre called the fire department, but they were already on their way. Dressing quickly, he rushed out to see if there was anything he could do.

The fire was eating its way up an airshaft in the wood frame warehouse when the firefighters arrived. Chief Tom Bryan and the crew from the Central Station arrived first, and were fighting the blaze when the East End truck arrived. Firefighter Bill Fowler was driving the East End

Bill Fowler

truck, and Chief Bryan ordered him to pull a hose line to the rear of the building. Fowler attached the hose to a nearby hydrant and started to drive the truck with the hose playing off the back of the truck. As Fowler made the turn around the burning building, he needed to pay close attention to the hose in case it caught on something. Looking away from where he was going for a second, he did not see the three men standing in the alley. One of the men yelled, *"LOOK OUT!"*, but it was too late.

Fowler struck Sayre, knocking him under the truck with both wheels passing over him. Unaware of what had happened; Fowler drove about fifty feet further, before another firefighter jumped onto the running board and told him to stop.

Firefighter Richard Stivason was the first one to reach Sayre. He saw at once that Sayre was in bad shape; his chest had been crushed. An ambulance was called for, but Sayre could not wait. Someone placed him in a private car and headed for the hospital. He would die on the way. Fowler later explained, *"I saw something fly up in front of the machine, but I could not tell what it was. There was no bump to the truck as it passed over his body. I knew nothing of the accident until I was told a little later."*

The fire was quickly extinguished after causing about $4,500 damage to the roof of the warehouse. After the fire was over, Chief Bryan conducted an investigation into the tragic accident. He cleared Bill Fowler of any wrongdoing saying he had been acting under orders. The chief declared the accident had been *"unavoidable."* Chief Bryan expressed the opinion that Sayre might have become confused and panicked, stepping into the path of the fire truck.

The next day Coroner J.M. Van Fossen handed down a verdict in the case. His ruling was a "probably unavoidable accident." The coroner arrived at the decision after interviewing Fowler, Chief Bryan, and the other members of the fire department.

Funeral services were held in the Sayre home on Railroad Street, with a burial in Riverview Cemetery. Sayre left behind his wife and seven children. Bill Fowler would continue to serve faithfully on the fire department until August 16, 1933, when he suffered a stroke and died.

Chapter 9
Death of a Firefighter
The Henry Avenue Tragedy
August 2, 1962

The city of East Liverpool has had a fulltime professional fire department since 1896, and in that time there have been four firefighters that have given their lives in the line of duty. The first was John Hamilton, who was electrocuted Christmas Eve of 1900, on Mulberry Street. The next two both occurred in 1907. George Betteridge was repairing the fire alarm system on Dresden Avenue when he fell from a telegraph pole on March 22nd. On September 3rd, Chief Henry "Clint" Morley was helping to fight a fire in the Wright Meat Market on Dresden Avenue when he suffered a heart attack and died a few minutes later. The fourth was Richard Plumley, who died in a rescue operation in 1962.

Firefighters the world over know that every call could be their last. Most never think about it; if they do worry, they usually move on to some other occupation. When I joined the department in 1975, many of the men that were involved in this terrible accident were still on the job. They rarely spoke of it, but when they did, it was with a sense of despair, anger, and unbelief. That night was still fresh in their minds, the night they *"fought the gas and lost."*

It was a cool Thursday evening, August 2, 1962. Mr. Robert Birbeck of 544 Henry Avenue was having trouble with his septic system. Richard's Sanitation Service was there pumping out the old bell shaped, brick cistern that had been converted into a septic tank.

Burton Richards was a World War II vet, who had been born in Spokane, Washington in 1917. He had lived in the East Liverpool area for the last twenty years. He was a district supervisor for the Darling & Co. of Cleveland, Ohio and had the sanitation business as a sideline. His helper this evening was young Lawrence Miller, only seventeen-years-old. Miller was born in Smithfield, West Virginia in 1945, and was from the Glenmoor neighborhood where he lived with his parents. Miller was working that evening because the regular helper had the day off.

The operation was progressing normally as the 13 foot deep cistern was beginning to empty. The liquid level had gone down five or six feet when some unknown trouble brought the pumping to a halt. Maybe tree roots had blocked the pumping hose, or maybe it had become plugged with the sludge. Richards and Miller decided to put a ladder into the tank to find the problem. Squeezing through the 22-inch opening, Miller descended into the cesspool. Because he was not wearing a protective mask, he was overcome by the noxious vapor within a few moments, collapsing into the murky water.

Richards, who had been watching from the top of the tank, saw that his partner was in trouble. He quickly climbed down the ladder to rescue him. Unfortunately, Richards was not wearing any protective gear either. As he descended into that foul pit, he too, was overcome by the deadly vapor and fell from the ladder. He managed only a weak cry of *"Help!"* before disappearing from view.

Scene of the tragedy

Robert Birbeck had been standing by, watching the operation. Now he rushed to his house to get a rope, something, anything to help. He yelled to his wife *"Call the fire department."* Mrs. Birbeck excitedly called the fire department at 9:11p.m. At the Central Station downtown, Firefighter Clarence Snediker answered the phone. During the frantic conversation, he thought the woman was saying that a boy had fallen into a well. What caused this confusion is unknown. That, however, is how the alarm went out. Snediker dispatched Engine Co. 3 at the Northside Station. Located at St. Clair and McKinnon Avenue, they were less than a mile from the scene. On duty that night were 25-year veteran Sheridan Pollock and Richard Plumley, a four year veteran of the department. Pollack was 65-years-old and had been appointed to the fire department in 1932; although the Great Depression had caused him to be laid off from 1936 until 1941. His fellow firefighters referred to him as *"Pappy."* Plumley was 28 and was born in East Liverpool; he had served honorably in the Army and worked at Crucible Steel before joining the department in 1958. His partner referred to him as *"Kid."*

James Sherwood, who lived a few doors away on St. Clair Avenue, had heard all the yelling. He and his eight-year-old son decided to go see what was going on. Sherwood was 51-years-old and had worked for the Ohio Power Company for the last 29 years. Details are a little murky but it is almost certain that Sherwood entered the septic tank before the arrival of the fire department in an attempt to rescue Richards and Miller. By this time many neighbors were responding, yet no one was quite sure when Mr. Sherwood had gone into the tank. Upon their arrival, the fire department discovered that now, there were *three* victims.

More neighbors arrived, and they began trying to do something, anything that would help. The ladder that Richards had been using had fallen into the pit. The neighborhood men tried to put in another ladder, but it was too short. Just then Engine Co. 3 arrived on the scene, and was confronted with utter chaos. Plumley quickly placed the fire department's aluminum ladder into the narrow hole. Pollock and Plumley came to the decision that the opening was too small to enter wearing a bulky self-contained breathing apparatus, an (SCBA.)

Looking into the tank, they could see at least one of the victims floating on the surface. Plumley knew then he had to try to get him out, with or without the SCBA.

(*Perhaps those who have never faced a chaotic life and death situation can understand the enormous pressure and urgency there is to do something. Firefighters are trained to act immediately. It is their job to save lives. Sometimes however, they must restrain themselves, for an unwise decision could cost them their own life.)

In those first frantic seconds Plumley decided to act. He fell back upon what he knew, and what he might have done before. He decided to go in after the victim he could see. He climbed down the ladder without any air mask, intent on tying a rope onto the floating victim. The gas, however, did not care how brave or determined Plumley was. Within in seconds, it claimed victim number four. True to his training, Plumley had hooked his leg through the rungs of the ladder, so that he could use both hands in the rescue attempt. The neighborhood men, including newspaper reporter Glen Waight and Water Department foreman Harold Peterson, could see his limp body hanging feet first from the ladder and began to pull the ladder from the tank. As the ladder reached the surface, Waight reached in and managed to grab hold of Plumley's belt as he and the others pulled the body out.

Richard Plumley

Acting Assistant Chief Gerald Goodballet was just arriving at the scene when he saw several men pulling Plumley's lifeless body away from the opening. He had come to the scene in the chief's car to check on what was going on, for he had heard Pollock's frantic cries over the radio, *"The kid is in the cesspool!"* Goodballet immediately began artificial respiration on Plumley assisted by police officers who had arrived by this time. At first there was no pulse and no breath, but after a couple of minutes a slight pulse was felt. Then Plumley took a deep, gasping breath; life was restored. However, his life hung by a thread. An oxygen mask was placed on him as the ambulances were arriving. Also more firefighters arrived from Central station as recovery of the other victims continued. Firefighter Snediker went into the tank tied to a rope and managed to tie another rope onto Sherwood's body before, he, too nearly passed out. His fellow firefighters pulled him out, dazed and groggy. No one else would enter the pit. It was now clear that this was no longer a rescue operation; it had become a recovery of bodies. Plumley and Sherwood were placed into the ambulance from Dawson's Funeral Home and sped to the hospital. Goodballet went along, still helping to keep his comrade alive. The time was 9:25 p.m.; a mere fourteen minutes had passed from the receiving of the call at Central Station.

Sheridan Pollock   Gerald Goodballet

It was during this time that further tragedy was averted when the brakes on the sanitation truck let go and the truck began to move. Quick action from a city police officer prevented further injuries. Officer Ken Mooney suffered a cut to his hand as he grabbed for the door of the moving truck and got snagged by a hook on the side of the bed. Mooney then climbed in and managed to stop the truck just as it was about to hit a couple of ambulance employees. Carmen Perorazio and Don Curran from Martin's Funeral Home were engaged in loading one of the victims. The truck came so close that they instinctively reached out trying to stop it. It came to a stop on the foot of Joe Wyand, one of Dawson Funeral Home's ambulance workers. The ground was soft and his foot was pressed into the muddy soil. The truck was slowly pulled away, leaving Wyand with a sore foot but no further injury.

Fire Chief Charles Bryan was now at the scene, directing the fire crew and police officers Bill Tice and Paul Burson to use grappling hooks to drag the foul sludge for the two remaining victims. The body of Burton Richards, the final victim, was pulled from the tank at 10:15 p.m., just over an hour from start to finish. It was a stark scene as the firefighters loaded the bodies into waiting ambulances and began gathering up their equipment. The large crowd began to drift away, slowly walking home in the darkness, their minds no doubt numbed as the events of this horrible night began to sink in.

The emergency room staff at the East Liverpool City Hospital sprang into action when Plumley arrived. Only a few minutes had passed since he was pulled out of the filth of that cesspool. Doctors performed a tracheotomy on him in an attempt to restore free breathing; it did not help. Plumley was then placed into an oxygen tent, and the vigil continued until 11:35 p.m., when he passed away, surrounded by his family. He had not regained consciousness. Doctor Keith Rue told his shaken family and fellow firefighters that there had been nothing they could do to save him.

Meanwhile, County Coroner Dr. William Kolozsi and his deputy, Dr. Roy Costello, had arrived and began to examine the victims. Dr. Costello announced the cause of death was exposure to hydrogen sulfide gas. Blood samples were taken from the four victims to be sent to a laboratory in Cleveland to determine toxic levels.

(*According to Ohio Safety and Health Administration, (OSHA) hydrogen sulfide is a colorless, flammable, extremely hazardous gas with the odor of rotten eggs. It is also heavier than air. (*Note, The vapor stayed in the tank and was unaffected by any wind that night.)

It results from a bacterial breakdown of organic matter, such as what takes place in a septic tank. The gas quickly overwhelms the sense of smell. The victims suffer a paralysis of the central nervous system and the lungs fill with fluid, stopping respiration. In concentrations of just 500 parts per million, death can occur from a single breath.) When the fire department arrived, the three victims were most likely already dead.

Chief Bryan and firefighters Russell Dray, Ralph Chapman, and Dolph Knott were checked at the Osteopathic Hospital, and Clarence Snediker was ordered home for bed rest. Sheridan Pollock was also sent home; it seems that he may have suffered a nervous breakdown at the scene. He was completely useless during the crisis, talking and acting hysterically. Upon his return to duty after the funeral, Pollock was transferred to Central Station for a while. After a time, he was sent back to Station 3. However, it appears he knew it was time for him to leave the job. As soon as he could, he retired. His last day was November 16, 1962, less than four months after the tragedy.

Burton Richards was buried in Columbiana Cemetery in Columbiana, Ohio on Sunday August 5th. He left a wife and four children. The other funerals took place the following day. James Sherwood is buried in Riverview Cemetery in East Liverpool; he left a wife and two children. Young Lawrence Miller was buried in Columbiana Memorial Cemetery in East Liverpool; he was survived by his parents and four sisters.

| Burton Richards | Richard Plumley | Lawrence Miller | James Sherwood |

Richard Plumley received a firefighter's funeral. The entire Fire Department marched to Martin's Funeral Home to attend calling hours on August 4th. At the funeral, which was on August 6th, he received the *"Last Alarm"* in front of Central Station on the way to Riverview Cemetery. Six of his fellow firefighter served as pall bearers and the rest of the department marched to the grave side. City police manned the fire station during the service. Richard Plumley was survived by his wife Sandra, two sons and a daughter. At the bottom of his grave stone is the Scripture; *John 15:13 Greater love has no one than this, that he lay down his life for his friends.*

The Ohio State Industrial Commission conducted an investigation recommending the City purchase an air mask attached to a long length of hose. That would have allowed Plumley to enter the tank and still breathe fresh air. Although the fire department is better trained today, they still do not have such a device.

It is never good history when writers try to put the standards of today upon an historical event. Were mistakes made nearly 50 years ago? Yes they were. That, however, does not take anything away from these brave men who gave their lives trying to save their fellow man. Miller should not have gone into the tank. Richards should not have sent him, or gone in after him. But in those first frantic seconds, he was driven only by his desire to rescue the youth. James Sherwood responded as any good neighbor should when someone is in distress. He became a victim through his moral integrity.

In 1962 the East Liverpool Fire Department was just like other small town departments. Most training was done in-house, and covered the situations the department had faced in the past. Their equipment was mostly designed for firefighting; not much attention or money was spent on rescue operations. The department had SCBA air masks; however, many of the "old timers" resisted using the heavy awkward gear. The SCBA had been in use nationwide since the end of World War II. During the chlorine gas fire at the city water filtration plant in 1958, East Liverpool had only three masks in service. As a result of that blaze the city purchased more, but the men still did not use them as they should have. Having said this, I am in no way implying that these men were either untrained or stupid. They were brave, highly motivated men who were just victims of inconsistent training and their own past practices.

The East Liverpool Fire Department of today is very different than it was in 1962. Today's firefighters are much better trained and equipped. However, more of both are needed. They now receive training in confined space entry, and have gas detecting meters. This does not, however, make them superior to their predecessors. In those first few seconds when life and death decisions must be made, we are blessed to have those courageous public servants who are willing to go where we dare not. It is in those times when instinct, common sense, and above all, training take over. Brave firefighters respond as they always have, seeking to save a life, even at the risk of their own. Let us hope and pray that another senseless tragedy like this one never happens again.

Chapter 10
Shootout in Little Italy
The Jim Kenney Murder
May 17, 1926

In the 1920's Wellsville, Ohio was a crowded town of over 8,000 people tucked neatly along a bend of the Ohio River with its back against the high hills that form the Ohio River Valley. It was a tough town, a blue collar town. Its railroad and mill workers lived hard, worked hard, and played hard.

Prohibition was in full swing in 1926, and the tri-state area had its share of illegal alcohol. The local newspaper, *The East Liverpool Review-Tribune*, was full of stories of raids and arrests in East Liverpool and Wellsville as the local police tried to stem the growing problem. However, just how hard they were trying sometimes came into question.

The newly elected mayor of Wellsville, Wallace I. Fogo, had run for office with the pledge of cleaning up the city. He had made no pretense of his dislike of Police Chief John H. Fultz. In fact, he had told many people that Fultz had to go. Mayor Fogo saw Chief Fultz as being corrupt and altogether too cozy with the bootleggers and gamblers. Then one day in March, a heated exchange took place between a bootlegger and Chief Fultz in Mayor Fogo's office. While conducting Mayor's court, Fogo held up a bottle of illegal booze and asked the accused if it belonged to him. The accused said he did not think it was his bottle; his bottle been a lot fuller when Chief Fultz had taken it from him. The chief jumped to his feet and began screaming insults at the defendant. He actually had to be restrained from attacking the man. This was just too much for the mayor.

Chief Fultz was suspended on March 20th, charged with twelve counts of misconduct, which involved a failure to crack down on the illegal liquor and gambling activities around town. Chief Fultz of course denied any wrongdoing and vowed to fight to clear his good name. Meanwhile, Arthur Newton was named as Acting Chief. However, the mayor also began taking part in police raids himself. The legal battle between the mayor and Fultz would go on for nearly a year.

Later, Mayor Fogo suspended Patrolman Harry Hurd on May 1st, for thirty days. He thought Hurd had been too friendly in helping Fultz fight for his job. Fogo also felt Hurd was tainted by the chief's illegal activities. Into this vacuum stepped James M. Kenney. Kenney had been employed with the City of Wellsville since July of 1919. He was officially a member of the fire department, but had filled in with the police when needed. Now with the suspension of Hurd, Jim Kenney was temporarily transferred to the police department.

Kenney was born across the river in New Cumberland, West Virginia on January 3, 1897. He and his wife Nancy lived on 10th Street. The couple had two very young children. A veteran of World War I,

Jim Kenney

he was a well-respected member of the community. Kenney aggressively joined Mayor Fogo's anti-bootlegging crusade. Maybe he was a little too aggressive?

Wellsville, like many other towns, had a thriving community of Italian citizens. Due to culture and language, these recent immigrants tended to live together in neighborhoods that became known as *Little Italy*. In Wellsville this area extended for several blocks, centered on Commerce Street between Tenth and Fifteenth Streets.

Unfortunately, the Italian community, which today proudly celebrates its ethnic heritage, was looked down on by many people at the time. Consequently, they tended to be clannish and wary of outsiders. The reputed leader of the neighborhood was Frank Fusco. Fusco was born in 1887, probably in Tricatica, Italy. In 1926 he lived at 500 Thirteenth Street with his family. There were also rumors that Fusco was the "Black Hand" boss of Wellsville. The Black Hand was the forerunner of what we know today as the "Mafia." It was mostly a "protection racket" that preyed on the Italian community. If you paid the "protection money" then you would be protected from violence. If you did not, well then, who knows? That was one of the reasons they were afraid to talk to outsiders.

The Italian neighborhood was dotted with small grocery stores that also served illegal alcohol in the back room. The 18th Amendment was not about to stop the Italian tradition of making and drinking wine. However, illegal alcohol was produced in homemade stills throughout the city, not just in "Little Italy."

The police, under the direction of Mayor Fogo, were causing a lot of anxiety with all their snooping and prying into the lives of the Italian citizens of Wellsville. Officer Kenney was an eager participant. He was going on raids with Mayor Fogo, and seeking information for future raids. Obviously, he was not appreciated or liked in the Italian neighborhood. There were also some who said that Kenney did not like Italians and was not bashful in letting them know it.

Kenney left his home at about midnight after taking a lunch break with his wife. He was on "beat patrol" and his "beat" stretched from 12th Street to the end of town, *"12th to Toronto"* the cops called it.

The city of Toronto is several miles downriver from Wellsville. Although the "beat" certainly did not extend to Toronto, the officer knew he was pretty much on his own.

Sunday night had turned into Monday morning May 17, 1926. At about 2:15 a.m., the neighborhood of Commerce Street between 12th and 13th Streets exploded in gunfire.

Neighbors rushed to their windows, having been shaken out of their slumber by at least eight to ten gunshots. What they saw was three or four men rush out of the front yard of the home of Frank and Dominica Maggio at 1224 Commerce Street. The men piled into the red Stutz automobile that was parked nearby. The engine fired, and the car sped away. The neighborhood went quiet as neighbors continued to watch the streets below from their darkened windows. Soon they saw a lone man emerge from the shadows between two houses and enter Brick Alley north of Commerce Street. The man was limping badly and nearly fell as he crossed 13th Street. He entered the yard of Frank Fusco. He began pounding on the door and yelling to be let into the house. This continued for about a minute; and then the neighbors heard a window break. For the next few minutes the night was once again quiet.

Mrs. Wilda McIntyre, a neighborhood woman, phoned the fire station and reported the location of the shooting. After reporting the shooting, Mrs. McIntyre went into the Maggio's yard to see what had happened. She saw the officer lying on the ground. He seemed to draw a breath or two and then became still. She was alone. Soon Officer James Barnes was on the scene. The residence of the Maggio family was typical of the neighborhood. It was a two story frame house crowded onto a postage stamp size city lot. The small front yard was enclosed by a wooden fence about four feet high. A small gate entered on the right side of the yard. A sidewalk led to the front door also on the right side of the house. The walk then led into the enclosed backyard. The house stands on the south or the river side of Commerce Street. *(* The house was destroyed by fire, March 20, 2014)*

As Barnes entered the dark yard he saw the outline of a body lying between the sidewalk and the fence line on the west side of the yard. Barnes knelt next to the body and lifted the head. A police cap fell to the ground, and Barnes realized it was the lifeless body of Officer Jim Kenney. Barnes began to shake Kenney's lifeless body, calling out his name, but he was gone.

Barnes quickly went to Mayor Fogo's home to inform him of the shooting. They called for a doctor and more help. Soon more police officers and the mayor were on the scene. By this time several neighbors had come out of their homes to see for themselves what had happened. Any thought of peace and tranquility had vanished for that night.

The scene showed signs of an intense confrontation, with blood on the ground. Kenney was found lying near the fence, as if he had been backed up against it with no avenue of escape. His revolver lay nearby with every bullet fired and blood streaking the barrel of the gun. One of the fence palings was broken or possibly shot away. A piece of lint from Kenney's overcoat was stuck to the fence.

Scene of shoot-out

Near the body was a guitar with what appeared to be stains on it. Whether the stains were blood is not known since the guitar quickly disappeared and was never seen again. Under Kenney's body a spent bullet was found. This was picked up by a civilian, which made it useless to the investigation, because the authorities could not be sure where it came from. Finally, the body was taken to the morgue at the John Hauge Funeral Home.

At the direction of Mayor Fogo and Acting Chief Newton, an intense search of the surrounding neighborhood was started. Wellsville authorities were soon joined by Columbiana County Sheriff George Wright and two Pennsylvania Railroad detectives. Rumors began to circulate about a loud party that Kenney may have interrupted.

Police could find little evidence of a party. The guitar had vanished and the Maggio family denied that they were having a party. Even though their living room was empty, all the furniture had been removed. A few straight backed chairs lined the walls of what could have been used as a dance floor. The Maggio's said they were asleep when the shooting had awakened them. They were puzzled by the apparent battle that had taken place in their front yard.

Police did, however, find two illegal liquor stills in the 1100 block of Commerce Street. Acting Chief Newton and Kenney had been working to gather evidence of these stills for several days before the murder.

Shortly after 8 a.m., the police received a "tip" that an Italian man had been shot and wounded last night. A full scale search soon led to 500 13th Street, the Fusco home. Police found blood stains and a broken window. After gaining entry to the home they entered an upstairs bedroom where they found Nicola "Nick" Scaccuto lying in bed. He had been shot and his three wounds had been crudely bandaged. He had bullet wounds in his groin, right leg and his right foot. He was immediately placed under arrest, taken to the East Liverpool City Hospital and placed under guard. At the hospital a bullet was removed from his right leg. The slug was lodged near his hip. Doctor J.S. McCullough took a scalpel and made a mark on the bullet. This was for later identification. After his wounds were treated, Wellsville authorities grilled him for over an hour. Scaccuto refused to talk, saying only that he did not understand.

Scaccuto was born in San Chiricco Nuovo, Italy near Naples. He was 28-years-old and had been in the United States since 1921. He could not read or write English or Italian; nor was he a U.S. citizen.

County Coroner J.M. Van Fossen conducted an autopsy later that afternoon. He found that Kenney had suffered five gunshot wounds. One bullet had entered the base of his skull and exited out the right side of his face. A second bullet entered his hip at the top of his hipbone and moved upward into his right lung. A third wound was to his left heel. A fourth bullet shattered the bone in his right arm. The fifth bullet entered his left side and was lodged three inches from his spine. The shoot-out must have been intense within the tiny fenced-in yard.

At 4:30 p.m. on May 18th, Mayor Fogo held court in Scaccuto's hospital room. Present were Sheriff Wright, Deputy Sheriff Lawrence Kinsvatter, Acting Chief Newton, and Special Officer Tom Madden. Attorney James E. O'Grady represented the accused. Scaccuto would only say he had been shot as he was walking along the street. He maintained that he had no idea who had shot him. His attorney waived a preliminary hearing and Scaccuto was held for trial. The inquest had been difficult due to the defendant's lack of understanding the English language. Within half an hour the hearing was over. Scaccuto was then placed in an ambulance and taken to the county jail in Lisbon, Ohio.

Wellsville City Council met, and with Mayor Fogo's agreement a reward of $1,000 was offered for information leading to the arrest of the guilty parties. Rumors were already being circulated that Scaccuto had not acted alone. Members of the fire department found a .38 caliber revolver lying on 17th Street, but authorities could not link it to the killing.

The funeral for James Kenney was held on May 19th at 2:30 p.m. at the First Christian Church on Main Street, and may have been the largest ever held in Wellsville. Hundreds of people crowded the church with many more standing outside in the street. Large numbers of ex-service men had marched en masse to the church at the request of the American Legion Post #70, and the Iris Lodge of the Odd Fellows also held a ceremony. Reverend L.E. Lee, assisted by Reverend R.R. Johnson of East Liverpool, conducted the service, which lasted well over two hours. Then the procession slowly made its way up 10th Street to the Spring Hill Cemetery. Local police from Wellsville, East Liverpool, Steubenville, and Bellaire led the way. The stone over Kenney's grave carries the inscription, *"Price of Loyalty"*. The Fraternal Oder of Police Lodge #11 placed a plaque at the foot of his grave with the inscription; *"Heroically gave his life in the line of duty."*

In the days after the funeral police arrested three men on suspicion. They were Joe Fusco (Frank's son), James Abbato, and Bennie Pepe. The police questioned them but had to release them for lack of evidence.

Patrolman Harry Hurd again met with Mayor Wallace Fogo's displeasure. He had been suspended for 30 days; on May 28th, just two days before the term was set to expire, the mayor fired him. Hurd vowed he would fight for his job. Patrolman James Barnes resigned in July. He sighted the mess that the Wellsville Police Department had become as his main reason. He said he lacked faith in the leadership.

Summer came and nothing new had come to light. It was as if a wall of silence had descended over the Italian community. Sheriff Wright and County Prosecutor Robert Brookes had become the lead investigators due to the turmoil with the local police department. Sheriff Wright appointed special investigators to assist. Due to their local experience, he appointed John Fultz and Harry Hurd. Mayor Fogo was not very happy. The sheriff assigned his deputies to walk the "beats" with orders to dig up any clue that would break the case.

Nancy Kenney received a check for $6,500 from the State Industrial Commission on July 23rd. Although no amount of money would replace her husband, it did represent several years pay.

Harry Hurd had his chance to clear himself on July 27th, but surprisingly, he resigned just as the hearing began. The hearing, however, was continued and several damaging things came to light. The mayor's decision to fire him was upheld.

There were no new developments in the case, but that did not mean the police were not actively pursuing the killer. All summer they kept up the pressure on the main suspects. Joe Fusco was arrested again in late August; this time on liquor charges. He was fined $600 and jailed until the fines were paid. He was soon on the street again.

He was hauled back to the police station on September 10th for questioning. After a two-and-a-half-hour grilling, police said Joe's answers failed to "dovetail." He was arrested and charged with the first degree murder of Officer Kenney. Joe Fusco operated the C&P Pool Hall in the 1300 block of Main Street. He ran the place for his father and he admitted that he owned a gun. Joe Fusco joined Nick Scaccuto in the County jail.

Joe's father, Frank, and his close associate, Rocco Carbicella, were not going to take this development lying down, so they "cooked up" a plan. Frank and Rocco went to visit the inmates at the jail a couple of days later. While they were there they spoke to Sheriff Wright, asking him to *"lay off"* on the investigation. *"It had all been a mistake,"* they said. They gave Wright a cigar and then stuffed a roll of money into his pants pocket. Wright quickly gave the money back saying *"Nothing doing."*

The following day, as the sheriff was driving east on U.S. Route 30 near West Point, two men flagged him down. One of the men was Rocco Carbicella. Rocco told the sheriff that he *"hoped (he) did not take offense to what had happened the night before."* The next day Sheriff Wright was in Wellsville and stopped by Carbicella's store. He talked to Rocco and made a date to meet with Frank and Rocco in the sheriff's office. The next day (Thursday, September 16$^{th)}$, Frank Fusco and Rocco Carbicella went to the jail to bring some candy and fruit to Joe and Nick. While they were there they went into Sheriff Wright's office. Once again they passed Wright some cigars and the roll of money. When they did, Wright said *"All right boys, that's fine."* Suddenly three members of the Burns Detective Agency of Pittsburgh stepped from their hiding places. The two men had been caught in a "sting" operation.

Fusco and Carbicella were arrested on the spot for attempted bribery. Thinking quickly, Carbicella said the money was not a bribe. He said it was instead a down payment on an illegal liquor fine he owed in Salem, Ohio. No one in the room believed that. Sheriff Wright unrolled the money and carefully counted it. It amounted to $390 in small denominations. He also recorded the serial numbers on each bill. Fusco and Carbicella were arraigned for trying to bribe the sheriff. They posted bail and were free to go.

The bribery trial began on October 19th and went to the jury two days later. The jury deliberated five hours and took eighteen ballets, before finally they found Frank and Rocco guilty of attempted bribery of a public official. The defense attorneys, W.A. O'Grady and Ben Bennett, immediately filed for a new trial and the defendants were released on $5,000 bonds.

While the bribery trial was going on, the police received a break in the murder investigation. On October 21st, John Fultz traveled to Cleveland with a young witness. The witness was a thirteen-year-old boy who was being kicked out of school and was in some other trouble. In the principal's office he made some comments that brought the police. He told the police he knew about the Kenney murder. Soon he was on his way to Cleveland with Fultz. The boy told authorities he had been at the "party" at the Maggio home the morning Kenney had been killed. He also knew who else was there.

Cleveland detectives accompanied by Fultz arrested two suspects at their residences. The two men, Michael Scoia and Michael Zionno, both denied being in Wellsville the day of the killing. The following day the group was joined by Sheriff Wright and Prosecutor Brookes. At the Cleveland Police Department the thirteen-year-old dictated a sworn statement of the events of May 17th.

He said there had been a party going on for several hours on Sunday, May 16th, stretching into the early morning hours of the 17th. He said there were several families at the party. They were singing and dancing with Joe Fusco playing the music on his guitar. He said Kenney came to the house early and told them to *"quit making so much noise."* He said they quieted down for a while; however soon the party was going again. Kenney returned, and something happened although the boy did not know what. This time guns were drawn. The young witness described several men firing at Kenney. They included Rocco Carbicella, Joe Fusco, Nick Scaccuto, Mike Scoia, and Bennie Carbicella. Later he said Bennie Carbicella did not do any shooting. The people at the party fled the scene. The shooters ran across the street and drove away in Rocco Carbicella's automobile. The boy and his father ran out the back door and went home. He said the party had been in the Maggio's front room. Police had found the room empty of furniture except for a few wooden chairs, possibly creating a dance floor. The young witness was given the statement which he read and signed in the presence of several witnesses.

The group returned to Wellsville that night with their prisoners. At 4:30 in the morning police swept in and arrested Rocco Carbicella and his brother Bennie at their homes. They were charged with first-degree murder. There were now a total of six suspects being held in the county jail. All six men pled not guilty.

Friday, October 21st had been a busy day, but there was still more as the attorney for Frank Fusco and Rocco Carbicella filed a motion for a new trial in the bribery case.

The police were now on a roll. A few days' later police in Detroit, Michigan arrested Antonia Scaccuto, (Nick's brother) as a material witness. However, by November 11th the tide had begun to turn. Three of the suspects, both Mike Scoia and Mike Zionno from Cleveland, and Antonia Scaccuto from Detroit made bail and were released. A preliminary hearing was held in Lisbon Common Pleas Court on November 12th. The court found there was not enough evidence to hold either Joe Fusco or Bennie Carbicella, and both were set free. Nick Scaccuto and Rocco Carbicella were held over on the murder charge. However, even Rocco was out the next day on a $20,000 bond.

The motion for a new trial on the bribery charges was granted on November 23rd. Both of the defendants were already out on bail with no new date set. Chief Fultz continued to struggle with Mayor Fogo. The court reinstated him; the mayor suspended him again.

The first-degree murder trial of Nicola Scaccuto began on December 20, 1926, with visiting Judge David Thomas of Marietta, Ohio presiding. County Prosecutor Robert Brookes and his assistant, Attorney John E. Bauknecht, handled the case for the people. The defense team consisted of Attorneys George T. Farrell, James E. O'Grady and W.B. Moore.

The state called a number of witnesses who testified to what they had seen and heard that spring night seven months ago. Much of this testimony laid the groundwork. Alleged Black Hand boss Frank Fusco provided testimony that he had been asleep, and had heard no gunshots. This is somewhat surprising since his home was no more than a couple hundred feet from the Maggio residence. Almost every other neighbor had heard the gunfire. Fusco testified that he first knew something was wrong when he heard Nick Scaccuto walking around in his house. He said Scaccuto asked to be allowed to sleep there, and he said he could. Fusco said he did not know Scaccuto had been wounded. Under cross examination Fusco said he let Scaccuto sleep there since he had lived with the Fusco family a few months earlier.

Railroad Patrolman Fred Herline testified that he was on Main Street with Officer Albert Oyster on the night of the shooting. He said after hearing the gunshots he and Officer Oyster started going west on Main Street. They saw Rocco Carbicella drive by in his red Stutz between 9th and 10th Streets.

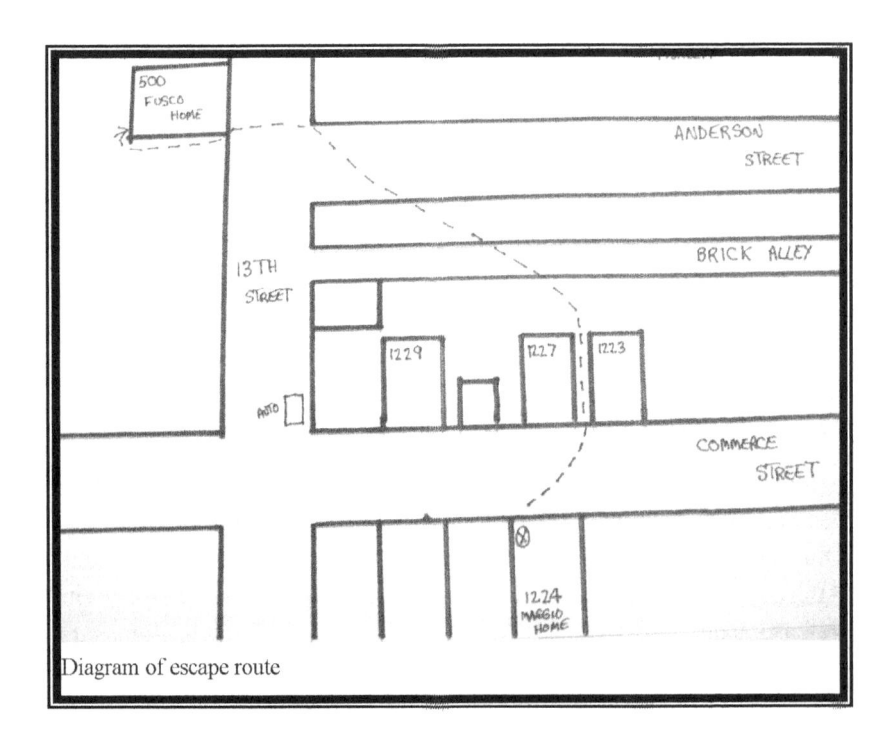

Diagram of escape route

Much of the day's testimony had to come through an interpreter since many of the Italian witnesses either could not, or pretended not, to understand the English language.

On the morning of day two of the trial the judge, the attorneys, and the jury were taken to the scene of the crime. The parade of automobiles caused a great stir in the congested neighborhood.

The afternoon session brought testimony from County Coroner Van Fossen, who described in detail the five bullet wounds that Officer Kenney suffered. Prosecutor Brookes asked which of the five wounds would have caused the officer's death. The coroner said the wounds to his head and his side would have caused death. He also identified a bullet then in evidence as being the one he removed from Kenney's right lung.

Former resident Richard Burns had lived across from the Fusco family on 13th Street at the time of the murder. He testified that he had been awakened by several gunshots. As he was watching from his darkened upstairs window he saw a man emerge from the shadows. The man started to cross the street then turned back. Burns lost sight of the man for about a minute. Then the man returned and crossed Brick Alley. He made his way onto 13th Street and quickly crossed the intersection under the glare of the street lights. The man was almost running but heavily favoring his left leg. He testified the man's leg *"nearly gave way on him."* He said the man entered through the front gate of the Fusco home and went around to the rear of the house. Burns heard pounding on the door and the man yelling to be let in. This lasted about a minute. Burns then said he heard glass breaking, and then it was quiet. Prosecutor Brookes asked Burns if the man he saw that night was in the courtroom. Burns said yes, and identified Nick Scaccuto.

Day three of the trial included Pittsburgh Police Captain William T. McCready, who testified as a ballistics expert. McCready testified that he had fired a test bullet from Kenney's revolver. The bullet was a match for the one removed from Nick Scaccuto by Dr. McCullough. There was no cross examination.

Frederick C. Buckminster, a chemist from Pittsburgh, followed McCready to the stand. He testified that there were powder burns on the trousers that Kenney wore that day. Called back to the stand Captain McCready testified that for powder burns to be present the shot had to be fired 10-18 inches from the victim.

The star witness for the prosecution was called to the stand during the afternoon session. It was the 13-year-old boy. However, it soon blew up in Prosecutor Brookes' face. When called to the stand, the young boy recanted his sworn statement. He claimed he knew nothing and had been forced to give the statement at the Cleveland Police Station.

This came as a quite a shock to Prosecutor Brookes. The prosecutor immediately asked to confer with Judge Thomas and the defense attorneys. He proved that the young witness had recanted only after being talked to by his mother and defense attorney William O'Grady.

Judge Thomas allowed the statement to be read in court. He also allowed the boy to be questioned as a hostile witness. After each question Brookes asked him, *"Did you say that?"* to which the boy would reply *"Yes, but it was a lie."* However, the testimony did get into the record.

The last state witness was John Fultz, who testified about various details of the murder scene and the investigation, after which the state rested.

The case for the defense was short. After a few character type witnesses, Nick Scaccuto took the stand in his own defense. He testified through an interpreter that he had been walking home from the home of Phillipo Rini. He said he had been there asking for permission to marry their daughter, Rose. He left at about 2 a.m. and as he was passing the Maggio home on Commerce Street, two unknown men began to shoot at him. He testified that he began to run for fear of his life. He went to the Fusco residence because he knew them and had lived there at one time. He said he knew nothing about Officer Kenney's murder. After Nick's testimony and the cross examination, the defense rested.

The case went to the jury at 12:25 p.m. on Christmas Eve. The jury of eight men and four women returned at 5:30 p.m. with a verdict of guilty. Nick Scaccuto was found guilty of first-degree murder in the second charge of the indictment. The jury determined there had been no premeditation. They recommended mercy, no death penalty. It had taken six ballets. Due to the Christmas holiday, sentencing was delayed until December 31st.

When asked by Judge Thomas if he had anything to say before passing sentence, Scaccuto said through his interpreter, *"Someone else killed the policeman and I got the blame."* Judge Thomas sentenced Nick Scaccuto to life imprisonment at the Ohio State Penitentiary in Columbus. Sheriff George Wright delivered Scaccuto on January 1, 1927.

The conviction of Nick Scaccuto did not end the story. Frank Fusco and Rocco Carbicella were re-indicted on the bribery charge on January 12th. The first conviction had been overturned back in November.

On February 14th, the Fultz-Fogo saga finally came to an end. Judge Thomas D. Price, in a 30-minute hearing, ruled that Mayor Fogo had been too severe in his punishment of Fultz. The judge gave Fultz a five day suspension without pay. Fultz returned to work the following day, and the city began looking for ways to repay the $1,605 they owed him in back pay.

Nick Scaccuto filed his appeal on February 23, 1927 with the Seventh District Court of Appeals. The court agreed to hear the case.

The second bribery case went to court in May. On the 12th the defendants, Fusco and Carbicella, both changed their plea from not guilty to guilty. Their attorney, William A. O'Grady denied having any part in the change of plea. He claimed that other people had talked them into it and he did not agree. Judge W.L. Lones handed down a sentence of between one and ten years in the state penitentiary. However, he suspended it and placed the men on probation for the term of the sentence.

The Seventh District Court meeting in St. Clairsville, Ohio upheld the conviction of Scaccuto on May 20th. *(*The Ohio Supreme*

Court would affirm the conviction on April 16, 1928.) Life in Wellsville began to return to normal.

In the years to come, the Italian community in Wellsville would grow and mature into a vital and respected part of the village. However, to this day they have been tight-lipped about the killing. Rumors have surfaced from time to time that the police had arrested the wrong man. Whether Scaccuto was the lone shooter or one of several is something we may never know. The $1,000 reward was never claimed. The reason for the murder also remains a mystery. Some say it was because of Kenney's dislike of Italians and his words and actions toward them. Others say he was just the victim of a mistake. There is also the rumor that the shooters were out to get another cop. Whatever the real cause, Kenney certainly paid the ultimate price.

Nick Scaccuto's sentence had been reduced to second-degree murder due to his good behavior, making him eligible for parole. In early December 1955, Governor Frank J. Lausche commuted his sentence, and on February 21, 1956, Nick Scaccuto was a free man.

The Fusco family continued to live in Wellsville for the rest of their lives. Frank passed away in 1945, and his son Joseph died in 1989.

In 1976, the Jim Kenney Center was built at the city marina as a memorial. To date, he is the only fulltime police officer in Columbiana County to give his life in the line of duty.

Chapter 11
Chlorine Gas!
The Water Filtration Plant Fire
April 3, 1958

East Liverpool put its first water lines in in 1879. The pump station was located on the River Road. It supplied water to the main part of town, feeding thirty-one fire hydrants. As the city grew so did the water system. Because of the danger of flood every year, the city decided to move the plant. In 1915 the city opened the current water filtration plant on several acres of high ground in the extreme east end of town.

The plant consists of a two story brick building with a tile roof along with holding tanks and other facilities. Built at a cost of $375,000, by 1958 the city still owed three annual $10,000 payments, the last one due in 1960.

At just past 1:00 pm, Clem Allison, water department supply man, was directing the unloading of a tractor trailer truck. The load consisted of powdered charcoal in heavy paper bags. Assisting in this were four part time employees, Eugene Beaver, Rex Kreefer, Hank Duncan, and Jim Reed.

The charcoal had to be taken up a freight elevator to the second floor. They had just unloaded the elevator when the electric power went off. Allison knew that the power usually kicked back on automatically, but not this time. He went to the switch box and tried to reset the power, but it kicked out again. A third try resulted in the same thing. Allison remarked to the others that there must be a major short circuit somewhere.

Just then Beaver saw sparks falling down the elevator shaft; he looked up the shaft and saw the flames. The men quickly exited the building and called for the fire department.

The weather was warm and dry that spring, and the department was battling a major brush fire along State Route 7 at Jethro Hollow when the call came in. With most of the department tied up in West End, the call went to the Engine Company 2 in the East End. Firefighter Don Hancock was the lone man on duty at Station 2. Engine Company 3 from the Northside was sent to assist on what was thought to be another grass fire.

By now the fire had melted the relief valves on the chlorine tanks, releasing the deadly vapor into the smoky building. When Hancock arrived he saw flames on the second floor of the building. He quickly set up a ladder, climbed up, and began spraying water onto the blaze. The chlorine filled smoke soon took its toll. Hancock found breathing to be hard, so he climbed back down the ladder before passing out. Soon after, Firefighter Merle McShane, who had arrived in Engine 3 was also felled by the thick yellow green vapor. There were now no firefighters left to fight the fire. Both men were rushed by ambulance to the Osteopathic Hospital on W. 6th Street.

Scene of the fire

About this time one of units fighting the brush fire in West End returned to Central Station to refill its water tank. Calls were coming into Central Station, reporting the serious situation at the water plant. Asst. Chief Dave Anderson ordered off duty firefighter Gail Mcfarland, who happened by to see what was going on, back to duty. He told McFarland to take two air packs and two extra air tanks to the fire and report back on how serious the fire was. Anderson did not know both his men were currently on their way to the hospital. At this time the department did not have two way radios in the trucks, so until a phone call could be made, the men were out of communication.

McFarland quickly assessed the situation and called for more men and equipment. The off-duty firefighters were called back to work. Soon all of East Liverpool's firefighting equipment and men, except for Engine Company 4, and the hook and ladder truck, were fighting the fire.

Because of the chlorine vapor, self-contained breathing apparatus masks were in desperate need. East Liverpool had three SCBA masks at the time of the fire, but could not refill the air bottles themselves. The call for mutual aid went out to the surrounding fire departments. Chief Robert Lewis of Wellsville responded with three SCBA masks and five extra air bottles. The Chester West Virginia Volunteer Fire Department supplied two masks and equipment. Both Liverpool Township Volunteer Companies (LaCroft and Dixonville) sent help. Due to the fact that East Liverpool could not refill the air bottles, a shuttle service had to set up. City police and the Highway Patrol ran empty bottles to the Wellsville Fire Station to be filled and then brought them back to the fire scene. All of this aid was greatly needed and appreciated.

Off-duty police officers were called back for crowd control as a large group of spectators had gathered. The crowd had to be kept out of the chlorine vapor or more victims would be claimed.

The blaze, though not very large, was extremely difficult to fight. The high pressure water hoses caused the charcoal bags to burst open. The fine powder then mixed with the already toxic smoke. Consequently, the water that poured from the building was as black as India ink.

The firefighters suffered greatly as the smoke turned them black as coal and as the vapor burned their skin and irritated their eyes, throats, and lungs. Even their wedding rings and watches were ruined. *(* When I joined the fire department in 1975 there were still a lot of guys working that had fought this fire. They talked about how hard the fire was on them. Their personnel records recorded their symptoms in case some health problems occurred later in life.)*

It was about 9:30 p.m. before firefighters were able to remove the eleven leaking chlorine tanks from the building. They were loaded onto a street department dump truck and then dumped into the Ohio River.

Confined to the filtration building, the fire caused about $20,000 in damages. Fire Chief Charles Bryan ruled that a short circuit in a light socket had caused the blaze. The water supply of the city was never in jeopardy since the reservoirs were pretty full and the water pumping building was not involved in the fire.

Firefighter Don Hancock remained in City Hospital for a few days while Merle McShane was kept overnight at the Osteopathic Hospital. Water department employee Eugene Beaver was also kept in the hospital. All three were treated in oxygen tents. Also suffering from the chlorine were police officer Orin Smith and two civilians, George Thayer of Michigan Avenue and ten-year-old Tom Leon of Ohio Avenue.

Immediately after this fire the city ordered an air compressor and more SCBA units. A new state law required two SCBA units on every fire truck and Chief Bryan had already requested them in his annual budget. The city had been slow to comply with this law and had nearly paid a very high price. In 1962, the East Liverpool Fire Department would face another toxic gas situation, with even more tragic consequences.

Chapter 12
"The Deadly Chain"
The Accidental Death of George Morley
June 5, 1898

In the early days of the East Liverpool Fire Department, there were only eight men on the full time force. These men were required to work six straight twenty-four hour shifts before receiving a day off. After that twenty-four hour break, the men returned to work for another six days. The only concession was that each man received one hour off for meals, three times per shift, although most of the men rarely took the full hour that was allotted. Because it was felt that the full force was needed each day, a system of substitutes was installed. These part-time men filled in when the regular men had their day off or were sick. Several different men filled this role, and George Morley was one of them.

Morley was twenty-one-years old. He had been working as a driver for the East Liverpool Ice Company, but had quit. For the past few months he had been subbing in the fire department, hoping one day to get a full time position. He was a well-liked, enthusiastic young man. He was also the nephew of Fire Chief H. Clinton Morley.

Saturday, June 4th was Tom Bryan's day off, and Morley was on duty. The day had been uneventful until early Sunday morning. At 1:00 a.m., Firefighter Pat Wood sent in a call for the patrol wagon to come to East Market Street (Dresden Avenue) to pick up a prisoner. In those days the firefighters were also required to perform police duty. The Patrol wagon or paddy wagon was also operated by the fire department. Asst. Chief Jim McCullough and Firefighter William Terrence took the wagon and headed for East Market Street.

When the call had come in, George Morley had come downstairs to the switchboard, which was located on the Broadway Avenue side of the fire station. At 1:15 a.m. a call from the police alarm box # 16 was sent in from 6th Street and Broadway by one of the police officers walking his beat. Morley was trying to read the alarm tape when firefighters William Mickey and Charlie Rose slid down the fire pole. Rose had counted the alarm bells when it rang, and told young Morley where the call was coming from. Excitedly, Morley yelled out, *"You call City Hall and I'll run to the "Diamond" and try to catch the wagon before they start down."* His intention was to stop the Patrol wagon and divert them to box #16, before they went all the way to City Hall at Third Street and Market.

After yelling his intentions to Rose, Morley started to run through the dimly lit station. Dodging the fire wagons, he decided to cut straight through the stall where the patrol horse was kept. The horse was gone, so the stall was empty. There was a door which opened onto West Market Street (St. Clair Avenue) next to the stall. There was no wall on this side of the stall, only a heavy chain suspended to keep the horse in and to prevent people from walking through. As Morley was taking his short cut, he either did not see the chain or tried to duck under it. Morley struck the chain and was thrown onto the brick floor.

Rose saw the youth fall and ran to his assistance. Morley was getting up when Rose reached him. He had a bad cut above his right ear, either from the chain or the floor. Rose and Mickey helped him to a wash stand to run water over the wound. Morley began to vomit. His fellow firefighters sat him down, and for the next half an hour they thought he was just shaken up. By now the Patrol wagon had returned, but Morley was feeling much worse. The men helped him upstairs and put him to bed. They then called for Doctor William Taylor to come to the station. Doctor Taylor had a contract with the city to provide medical treatment to the fire and police departments.

Doctor Taylor arrived quickly and began to treat the young man. Morley was conscious for about ten minutes after Doctor Taylor began treating him, and then he lapsed into a comatose state. When that happened, someone sent in a call for his father, Samuel Morley, to come to the station. George lingered for about half an hour more and then died at 2:30 a.m. His father arrived not more than two minutes later.

His body was removed to his home on Third Street, just after daylight. Doctor Taylor thought that a severe concussion and the possible rupture of the carotid artery were the probable cause of his death. George Morley was buried in Riverview Cemetery on Tuesday June 7th; his fellow firefighters served as his pallbearers.

*(*Sometimes while doing research for one story, another story is found; that was the case here. It also cleared up a minor mystery. In the photographic archives of the East Liverpool Fire Museum there is a photograph of, I believe, George Morley. No explanation accompanies the photo. Although it was apparent that he was probably related somehow to Chief Morley, I did not know anything about him, or why there is a picture of him. The records of the department are lost previous to 1899, so there was nothing there that could help. Now the mystery has been solved.*

In the long history of the department, four regular firefighters have lost their lives in the line of duty. They were John Hamilton who was electrocuted in 1900. Then, there was George Betteridge who fell from a telephone pole in 1907. He was working on the fire alarm system. Chief H. Clinton Morley suffered a heart attack and died while fighting a fire in 1907. Lastly, there was Richard Plumley, who died during a rescue attempt in 1962. However, before all of them, there was substitute firefighter George Morley.)

Chapter 13
Tragedies on the Mainline!
Four Railroad Accidents 1893-1948

The railroad came to this area before the Civil War, and for many years the city of Wellsville played a significant role. A steam locomotive required a massive amount of maintenance, with many moving parts that needed to be greased and oiled. This forced the railroads to provide maintenance yards at regular intervals along their routes, and Wellsville was chosen as one of those places.

Beginning in the 1850s, a large rail yard grew along the riverfront between 12th Street and 25th Street. There were repair shops and a roundhouse along with a marshaling yard with several sidings. At its height, over 100 men worked in the rail yard. The downfall came with the introduction of the diesel electric locomotive. The new locomotives required much less maintenance, so by 1954 the Wellsville yard was determined to be unnecessary and was closed.

The railroad brought jobs and prosperity. It also brought tragedy.

Out of the Fog!
The Wellsville Yard Wreck of 1893

A heavy fog blanketed the Ohio Valley as morning came on October 17, 1893. Fog is a common thing during autumn along the Ohio River. At 6:00 a.m., that Tuesday morning, it was thick as pea soup.

Even at that early hour the Cleveland & Pittsburgh rail yard in Wellsville was busy. Near 18th Street, Engineer Dan Cochenour and Fireman H. Phillips were proceeding to move freight train #626 from a siding on the north side of the mainline onto the westbound track. The warning switches had been thrown at the "block signal tower," and they were given right of way. As their west bound engine began to cross over the track, through the fog they saw an east bound passenger train coming fast.

The passenger train, the Fort Wayne Limited #2, was a special, due into Pittsburgh at 8:00 a.m. It was under the control of Conductor George Carothers. The engineer was Robert Jackson of Allegheny, Pennsylvania. The fireman was Jackson's son, Elmer. Express messenger Robert Ferry, baggage handler Alex Frazier, and electrician William Fowler rounded out the crew.

This was not their regular route. The Pittsburgh–Fort Wayne–Chicago line was blocked due to an accident at Beaver Falls, Pennsylvania. At Alliance, Ohio they were diverted onto the Cleveland & Pittsburgh line to bypass the accident. Railroad policy was that whenever a diversion was necessary, a "pilot" was taken aboard who knew that line and the signal locations. Carothers was acting as a pilot since he was familiar with this line.

With only seconds to react, Cochenhour and Phillips leaped from the engine. The crew of the Fort Wayne express did not. The two steam engines slammed together nearly head on. Within seconds the two powerful machines came to a grinding halt. The high pressure steam boilers ruptured sending scalding jets of steam into the crew compartment of the express engine.

Both engines were blasted into nearly unrecognizable piles of twisted iron and steel. The force of the collision caused the huge express engine to spin nearly around, facing the direction it had come from. It came to a stop upside down. The baggage car and the smoking car telescoped into one another, totally destroying both cars. Miraculously, the remaining cars did not derail, which saved many lives. Although, the sleeping passengers were thrown from their beds and tossed around none were seriously hurt.

Slowly the dazed victims climbed out of the wreckage into a surreal world of noise and fog. They had no idea of what had just happened, or where they were. Most just sat down along the track and probably thanked God to still be alive. The row of passengers stretched along the track for nearly half a mile.

Within minutes, the area was filled with spectators and rescue workers, as the citizens of the town began to respond to the terrible accident. Nearly every physician in town was quickly at the scene of the wreck. However, for some, there was nothing a doctor could do to help.

George Carothers had been killed instantly. His mangled body was found under the twisted wreckage of the express engine. Robert and Elmer Jackson were horribly burned and crushed. They were taken to nearby homes were doctors treated them. Both men lingered for hours, probably in excruciating pain. Both father and son died around ten o'clock that morning. Robert Ferry and Alex Frazier were also seriously injured. They were transported by train to the West Penn Hospital in Pittsburgh. Both men would succumb to their injuries that evening, bringing the death toll to five. The last victim, William Fowler, had suffered a crushed leg and serious steam burns, but he would recover.

As the fog slowly burned away, it revealed the scope of the disaster. Both trains were a wreck. The freight train engine laid on its side, a steaming twisted pile of metal. Two cars of the passenger train had partially telescoped, a railroad term meaning they jammed into each other like the folding of a telescope. Oddly enough, most of the cars of both trains did not derail. Yard engines pulled the undamaged cars out of the way so work could begin to clear the track.

An engine was attached to the rear of the passenger train and the dazed passengers climbed aboard. The train was taken to Steubenville, Ohio, and there crossed over the Ohio River, where they connected with the Panhandle line to go to Pittsburgh.

The work train began clearing the tracks with its heavy derrick, and after several hours, the mainline was reopened. Throughout the day and long into the night, crowds of curious people lingered around, watching the clearing of the accident.

If the crowd was hoping to be shocked, they were not disappointed. Shoes had been torn from the dead crewmen by the terrific impact. There were heaps of steam-soaked clothing with blood spots on them. However, the most gruesome sight was found after the fog burned away. Near the site of the impact was what appeared to be a glove hanging on a bush. Upon inspection, it was found to be the skin of a hand scalded and ripped away by the high pressure steam. On each finger the finger nail was still in place. It was later learned that this ghastly object had belonged to the dead conductor, George Carothers.

After a frightening delay, the passengers were safely on their way. They were no doubt glad to be leaving Wellsville. Now if only they could leave behind the memory of that horrible foggy morning along the Ohio River.

A Close Call in East Liverpool
The Derailment of 1902

Extra freight train #99 left the yard in Conway, Pennsylvania on July 6, 1902, bound for Mingo Junction, Ohio. The train consisted of eighty-five cars, nearly all loaded with coke to feed the furnaces of the National Steel Company. Conductor Willis Jordan, a native of Wellsville, Ohio, was in charge of the fast moving freight.

At 7 a.m., as the train was passing by the passenger depot at the foot of Washington Street, in East Liverpool, a spectator noticed a broken axle on one of the coke cars. In an instant, the cars began to leave the tracks. Sixteen railcars piled on top of each other in a twisted and shapeless mass of steel.

The wreck occurred between Union Street and Market Street. This area was a narrow passage, with houses and factories crowding the right of way. The Potters Supply Company fortunately had three rail cars standing on their siding at the time of the accident. These cars protected the factory from major damage, as eight cars piled into them. One of the derailed cars did strike the south end of the plant, tearing out the corner of the building.

Five other cars upset near the old Rinehart Livery Stable. They were totally destroyed; their trucks were ripped from the gondola cars. Several other cars remained upright although the tracks had spread from beneath them. Railroad workers were able to get them back on the tracks after repairs were made.

The home of Thomas Abrams, located at the foot of Market Street, was struck by one of the careening railcars. Mr. Abrams was sound asleep when the house was hit. He jumped from his bed, and fled unharmed.

Engineer Thomas Croft and Fireman W. H. Marshall, said they were just passing Union Street, when they felt the big mogul engine shudder. Croft immediately whistled for the brakes. The front brakeman J.F. Roof was riding on the third car behind the engine. He jumped and escaped injury. The rest of the crew was in the caboose, and except for being shaken up, they suffered no injuries.

Croft took the undamaged section to Wellsville, and by 8 a.m., the wreck train was on the scene. A dispatcher set a portable telegraph up at the scene of the accident, and he directed the movements of trains from there.

The fifty or so undamaged cars were sidetracked onto the spur at the C.C. Thompson Pottery, allowing the wreck train from Conway to work the north end of the accident. Wreck Master Aten, of Wellsville, took command; he also called for the wreck train from the Alliance, Ohio yard. The Conway and Alliance crews using big steam cranes moved the wreckage to the side, clearing the tracks. Crews then went to work repairing the tracks, and removing the large amount of spilled coke. The coke was ten or twelve feet deep in places, and removing it was a massive job. The crews worked through the night before the wreck was completely cleaned up.

While the cleanup was in progress the two passenger trains arrived, one going east, the other west. Passengers from two trains had to be unloaded and walk (carrying their luggage?) to the opposite side of the accident. There they boarded trains from Wellsville on the west, and Conway on the east. At those two locations, new trains were waiting to take them to their destinations.

The monetary loss was put at $15,000 to the train, and another $500 to property along the right of way. Fortunately, no injuries or deaths occurred. Even a drunken hobo sleeping in one of the boxcars on the Potters Supply Company siding escaped without injury. Without the three shielding railcars, the damage to the Potters Supply Company could have been severe.

By six p.m., the tracks were repaired and the trains rolled on.

The Bridge has Gone Down!
The 1904 Railroad Disaster on Yellow Creek

Heavy rain and the spring thaw of 1904 had been causing havoc with the schedule of the Cleveland & Pittsburgh Railroad for the last several days. High water in the Ohio River and its tributaries had covered the tracks, bringing traffic to a standstill. Another bout of heavy rain came on March 3rd.

At about 3:00 p.m. that Thursday afternoon, Engine #7176 was entering the roundhouse at the Wellsville yard. A roundhouse was a circular structure which contained a turntable on which the engine could be turned. The engine could come in and be serviced or turned onto another track, so that the engine would be moving forward on the line.

As the heavy engine entered the building, the track gave way. Undermined due to the heavy rains, the tracks spread apartderailing the engine. The tender behind the engine stuck one of the building's support posts, knocking it loose. This caused a section of the roof and walls to collapse.

Twenty-six-year-old Bert McCord, of Wellsville, Ohio, was working on top of Engine #7127 when the falling roof came crashing down on top of him. He was killed instantly, his skull crushed. His partner, twenty-eight-year-old William Armstrong of Petersburg, Pennsylvania, was luckier. Armstrong was working a little lower on the engine so he was not hit by as much debris. He was, however, buried and had to be dug out of the wreckage.

Armstrong suffered a broken arm and leg, along with some internal injuries. He was removed and taken to his boarding house on Nevada Street by the City Patrol Wagon. There, doctors looked after him. His condition was said to be precarious. He would, however, recover.

Bert McCord left a wife and baby girl, and was much esteemed by all who knew him.

Railroad workers immediately began repairs to the roundhouse which had suffered at least $2,500 in damages. Soon they would have more work.

The flood water began to recede on March 4th, and the Cleveland & Pittsburgh Railroad was anxious to get back on schedule. The flooding had struck the towns along Yellow Creek very hard. The towns of Irondale and Hammondsville in Jefferson County and Salineville in Columbiana County had been severely damaged. The rail line through the area was also badly damaged. Several bridges between Salineville and Hammondsville, over winding Yellow Creek, had already been closed to traffic until repairs could be made. The company had a work train in the Irondale area busy cleaning up debris and repairing washouts along the track.

Very early on Saturday March 5th, the men received orders to return to the Wellsville yard. The work train consisted of two engines, #1676 and #7617 along with two cabooses. Ten men made up the work crew. Engine #7617 was out of service and being towed back to Wellsville for repairs, so no crew was necessary. Engine #7676 held the normal crew with most of the other men riding in the first caboose.

Also working in the area was Master Carpenter F.R. Martin, and his crew of ten men. They were nearly finished with their repairs, and Martin asked Engineer Maas to wait for them. Maas refused, saying his boiler was nearly out of water, and he would need to leave right now if he were to make it to Wellsville. Martin had just been very lucky, although he did not think so at the time.

George Close lived near bridge #55 about half a mile east of the Hammondsville station. He was out walking when he noticed that the bridge's eastern abutment had been undermined by the flood waters. He saw the bridge beginning to sag. Close hurried a little farther down the track to the home of John Lucas. Lucas told him, *"I don't think the trains are running yet."* Lucas was on his way to work at a nearby mine and when he got there he told his foreman, a man named Bowden, about what Close had told him. Bowden told him, *"Go as fast as you can down to the Yellow Creek station, and tell them about it."* Lucas began to run. Once he got to the Yellow Creek station he told Operator Crowles, *"Bridge #55 is going to fall down."* Crowles immediately telegraphed the warning to Trainmaster A.J. Dawson at the Wellsville yard. Dawson received word of the weakened bridge at about 6:00 a.m. He boarded a shifter engine and started for the site to see for himself what the problem was.

The east bound work train had not received any warnings, and they had no idea of the danger. At 7:05 a.m., as the heavy train began to cross the swollen steam, the eastern bridge abutment just crumbled. The train plunged headlong into the muddy water. Steam and the roar of grinding metal filled the air, drowning out screams of surprise

Site of Bridge 55 collapse

from the doomed men. Both engines and the first caboose were submerged in about ten feet of water. The rear caboose overturned, but remained on the western end of the bridge. What remained of the bridge was twisted and wrecked beyond repair.

Dawson arrived just after the accident, and immediately called for help. Soon rescue crews were on the way. The wreck train out of Wellsville arrived with a full work crew. Several doctors also came on the wreck train. The scene they found was terrible to behold. The bodies of dead men could be seen pinned by wreckage beneath the fast flowing stream. It would be hours before the victims could be brought to the surface. Rescuers formed a human chain to pass the broken bodies up the steep bank. Once on top they were placed in a baggage car and covered with white sheets.

Doctors at the scene thought death was instantaneous, since Engineer Jacob F. Maas was found with his hand still holding the throttle. He had been impaled by a piece of the bridge framing. Six men were dead and another four were injured. Fireman Tom Graft was only slightly hurt, and he had walked to the Lucas home. He then pulled out a cigarette, and asked *"Got a match?"* Rescuers found him there upon their arrival. Graft stayed at the scene and joined in the recovery efforts.

Engineer Emmett Ralston, Conductor E. Dudy, and Flagman George McDermott survived the crash along with Graft.

Among the dead were, J.F. Maas, George Phillips, John Henderson, Thomas Keer, J.J. Kountz, and I.B. King. All of the dead except for Kerr were from the city of Wellsville. News of the disaster had quickly spread thoughout the town. The train carrying the bodies arrived that afternoon. It was met by grieving families and many curious onlookers. Family members received the broken bodies of their loved ones to prepare them for burial. Three were taken to the Haugh Funeral Home, while the others went to the McLane Funeral Parlor.

Before long it was discovered that Thomas Keer was in reality Thomas Powell. Powell was a longtime employee of the East Liverpool Street Railway Company. He was using the false name to hide the fact he was quitting the streetcar company. He wanted to be sure he had steady employment with the railroad before turning in his notice.

The C&P Railroad did not take much time to investigate this accident. On March 7th, it was announced in the *East Liverpool News Review,* that a crew of 300 men were working around the clock to rebuild bridge #55. The repairs continued through the night with the use of artificial lights, bonfires, and torches. Ironically, the company also announced that work on a new right-of-way would be completed within sixty days, if the weather cooperated. The new track would eliminate the need for bridges #55 and #56. Much of the new line was already in place. However, until then, #55 had to be rebuilt and rail service resumed.

The Riverside Jumble
The Big Derailment of 1948

August 12, 1948 was just like any other day in the city of Wellsville. It was about 10:20 in the morning and two freight trains were approaching each other along Riverside Avenue. The west bound diesel locomotive was pulling seventy cars, mostly empties. The east bound steam engine was out of Detroit, carrying auto parts from the Ford plants.

As they rounded a curve in the 9th Street area they sideswiped each other. The roar of grinding metal on metal was heard throughout the city. Soon hundreds of people were running toward the railroad tracks.

What they found were dozens of rail cars piled on top of each other in a jumble of twisted metal. Thirty to forty cars had derailed, with two cars lying on Riverside Avenue. The wreckage was strewn from 6th Street to 9th Street. Residents of the area said their homes literally shook during the wreck.

Only one minor injury was reported. Each of the trains carried a five man crew; only the conductor, H.B. Wilt was thrown against the bulkhead where he received a bump on his head and bruised knuckles. He was treated at the hospital and released.

Aerial view of wreck

Within hours a crew of 200 men and three work trains were busy cleaning up the debris. By 1:00 a.m. the next morning both tracks were reopened. Within a few days the wreckage was gone, and life along the rails resumed.

*(*As I write this story, I have good friends that live on Riverside Avenue within the wreck area. I have spent many quiet evenings sitting on their porch watching the river and the trains roll by. But you never know!)*

Chapter 14
Conflagration!
The Great "Diamond" Fire
February 28, 1905

William Jennings Bryan arrived unexpectedly in East Liverpool on Sunday morning February 26, 1905. Bryan was one of the most famous men in the country, a two time Democratic candidate for President of the United States. *(*He would run for President a third time in 1908.)* He was also a much sought after speaker, and was famous for his Christian faith. Bryan had not come to East Liverpool by accident; he had friends here.

Although he came as a surprise, he was certainly welcome. He arrived at the fine home of Doctor George P. Ikert, at 6th and Jackson Streets, and was warmly greeted. The two men had first met and become friends while both were in Congress back in the early 1890's. After leaving Congress, George Ikert had resumed his life as a wealthy physician and surgeon. He also was heavily involved in business, real estate, and the newspaper business.

Bryan spoke briefly at three different church services on Sunday evening, and lectured on the Christian faith at the Ceramic Theatre on Monday evening. Monday had been a very busy day, and he was worn out from his hectic schedule. That night he went to bed hoping for a good night's rest. Unlike previous nights, he did not sleep well. A vivid and disturbing dream ruined his slumber. As he came to breakfast on Tuesday morning, he was troubled. However, he was hesitant to reveal the dream to his hosts. After much soul searching, he finally decided to tell them. He had dreamed that the Ikert family had been the unfortunate victims of a huge fire. They had suffered massive losses, and it seemed to Bryan that they were the only ones affected. He said he could clearly see each member of the Ikert family in his dream. Neither Bryan nor Dr. Ikert were superstitious, so after some discussion they dismissed it. Later that morning Bryan made his goodbyes and left town. *(*It was reported that the Ikert family had suffered from 15 previous fires.)*

Thirteen years had passed since the terrible fire of 1892. Known as the Dry Goods District fire, it had destroyed three buildings, including one that was owned by Dr. Ikert. The area had been quickly rebuilt, and now a stately four story brick building stood on the property owned by the Ikert family.

Tuesday, February 28, 1905, was like many late winter days in Ohio, cold and windy. But even on that blustery evening there were people on the streets. It was 6:30 p.m. when Charles Grafton noticed a small boy watching as smoke began to rise from the basement of the Gass Shoe Store. The Gass Shoe Store was located on the Market Street side of the W.L. Thompson Building, in the Diamond. *(*The Diamond is the center of the business district.)* The smoke was coming from a sidewalk grate in front of the store. Grafton quickly ran to

The Diamond along Market Street before the fire

a nearby fire alarm box and notified the fire department. The long desperate night had begun.

In 1905, the East Liverpool Fire Department was a horse drawn full time company of ten men. H. Clinton Morley was the Chief. He had served with the department since 1885, and had been chief since 1896. The Central Fire Station was located just two blocks away. The fire department arrived quickly, and began to pull up the sidewalk grate. By now a crowd was forming, and a few of the men began to assist the regular firemen, as was the custom of the day. Once the grate was removed, dense smoke began to pour from the basement area of the building. Firefighters attempted to enter the basement, but without any type of breathing equipment it was impossible. Morley ordered two large hose lines attached to nearby fire hydrants, and the firefighters began to pour water into the basement of the Gass Shoe Store.

The chief then ordered another hose to be laid into the rear of the building. That hose was attached to a fire hydrant on E. 6th 6th Street and laid down Mulberry Alley, then up Diamond Alley to reach the back door of the Gass Shoe Store. Chief Morley, along with firefighters Tom Bryan and George Betteridge, broke down the door and entered the basement. They had gone only a few feet into the basement before the smoke and heat proved too much for them, forcing them to retreat. Morley returned to the Diamond and continued to direct the fight from there. By now, the East End Company had arrived. This unit was commanded by Captain William Terrence. Terrence and regular firefighter John Spence would take over half an hour to make the long run with their wagon, pulled by two horses. A number of residents from the East End also came along.

The Thompson Building was a backward L-shaped three story brick building. One side of the structure faced onto Market Street in the Diamond, and the other side faced 5th Street. The first floor housed the Boston Dry Goods Store, operated by A.S. Young. The Boston Store had entrances on both streets. The Gass Shoe Store shared the first floor, but only faced Market Street. The upper floors were occupied by the Eagles Lodge, the Trades and Labor Council, and a union meeting room known as Brotherhood Hall. A common

[Diagram: Market Street side of fire — showing T. Burke Residence (4), G. Bendheim Shoe Store (2), Bon Ton Store (Dry Goods), W. H. Gass Shoes, Boston Store (Dry Goods) (1), Store (3), Kirt Block Offices + Apartments (7), Cellar Extension]

Market Street side of fire

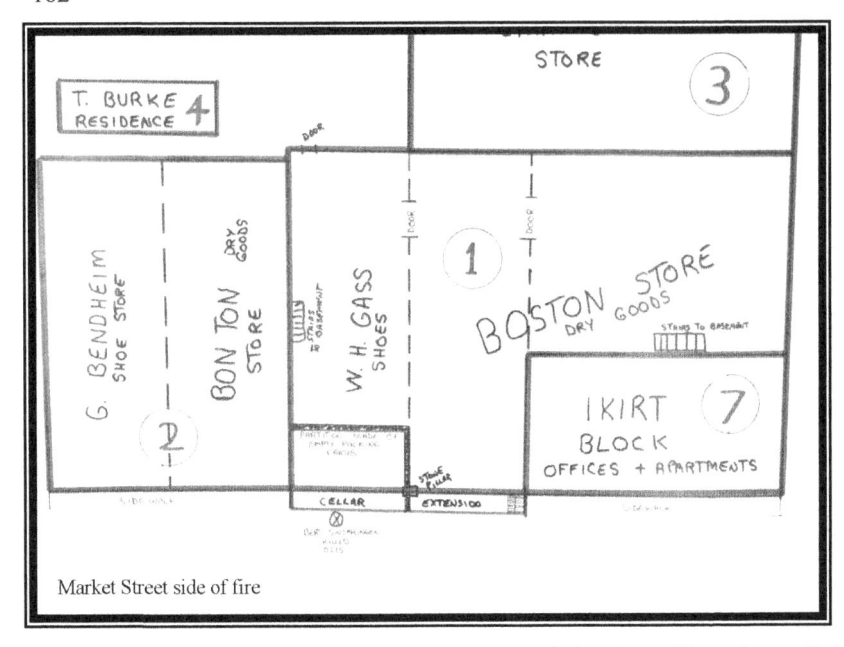

basement was shared by the Boston Store and the Gass Shoe Store. It was divided by a makeshift wall of stacked wooden packing crates. Mr. Young had signed a ten year lease, and had been given permission to remodel the building to suit his business, so he had cut more stairways into the basement.

Although there is no way to know for sure, the fire had almost certainly spread throughout the entire basement after eating its way through the packing crate wall. The efforts of the firefighters were not having any success, and they may have actually pushed the flames into other areas of the basement. Before long, the flames came roaring up the stairways onto the first floor, consuming in an instant the large stock of clothing and other fabric. With the stairways acting as chimneys, the fire spread quickly to the second floor. This all took place as dense smoke prevented the firefighters from entering the first floor of the building. The doors on the 5th Street entrance were kept shut in hopes of cutting off oxygen to the fire, so no firefighting had yet occurred from that side of the building.

On the north side of the Thompson Building stood the S. H. Porter Building. It was a three story brick structure, located at the south corner of Market Street and Diamond Alley. The first floor was occupied by the Bon Ton Dry Goods Store on the south side, and the Bendheim Shoe Store on the north side of the structure. The Columbiana Telephone Office was on the second floor. The other tenants were the Ohio Valley Business College, the Students Business College, Mary Donley's Millinery Shop and Dr. Laughlin's office.

While the fire was being fought next door, people entered the basement of the Porter Building, and found it filled with smoke. The porous sandstone wall was allowing the smoke to enter the building. As smoke continued to fill the Porter Building, it soon reached the upper floors. At the Columbiana Telephone Office, the young lady telephone operators held on as long as they could before abandoning their posts. Much of the telephone system was now out of service.

Firefighters were still having a problem getting water onto the fire because of the basement partition. They tried to push the box wall over with a ladder, but without success. At 7:00 p.m., Mayor William Weaver was standing beside Chief Morley when they saw flames in the second floor windows of the Thompson Building. They had lost the struggle to hold the fire in the basement. The Mayor had earlier asked Morley why he had not brought the steam fire engine to the fire. The Chief had said he thought it would hurt the water pressure, which was too low already.

However, after seeing the flames on the second floor, Chief Morley sent for the Silsby steam engine, and also requested more help. Although a number of civilians were already assisting the regular firefighters, it was not enough. Calls went out to nearby Wellsville, Ohio and Chester, West Virginia for assistance. Both would respond quickly.

The brisk wind was not helping either. The flames that were pouring from the upper windows of the Thompson Building were pushed by the strong wind into the adjoining Porter Building. The fire may also have spread through the basement wall; there was no way to tell. In any case, the Porter Building was soon ablaze.

The smoke in the Diamond was thick, and the firefighters and spectators were being showered with sparks and flying glass as the windows blew out from the intense heat. It was difficult for the men to remain at their posts, and though several were cut by the flying glass, they refused to flee. Fortunately, help was on the way. The Wellsville Volunteer Fire Department arrived by train and was soon on the fire scene. They left Wellsville at 7:30 p.m., making the trip in only fifteen minutes. Captain Ed Phillips had brought 35 volunteers along with much needed hose and other equipment. It was estimated that at least 200 citizens of that city had come along to watch. The Wellsville firefighters were placed along the eastern edge of the endangered zone. The volunteers from Chester had also arrived and were placed atop buildings in Diamond Alley, guarding the northern side of the fire zone.

Silsby Steam Engine

When the Silsby steam fire engine arrived, it was positioned in the Diamond to cut off the flames as they were being pushed northward by the gusting wind. The water in its boiler was cold, so it would take firefighters Charles Rose and Pat Wood about twenty minutes to get up steam and to attach the hose lines. Bystanders were shocked by how long it took before water could be pumped onto the blaze. A slab of bacon was thrown into the firebox, hoping the grease would increase the heat in the boiler and produce steam quicker. Then several men volunteered to pull a street department wagon by hand, back and forth, hauling coal from a coal yard several blocks away to keep the engine operating.

The flames were now leaping high above the Thompson and Porter Buildings, and sparks were falling like rain. Now the fire began to spread east, along the north side of 5th Street. The first structure to go was the two story brick building owned by Mendel Wasbutzky. Standing next to the Thompson Building, it was the home of the Star Bargain Store operated by Sol Whit. Firefighters had by now taken up the fight on 5th Street. Asst. Chief James McCullough commanded this side of the blaze. However, within minutes, the Wasbutzky Building was burning fiercely, with flames leaping from the roof. All along 5th Street, anxious store owners were organizing volunteers to remove the stock from their stores, which seemed to be doomed.

Mayor Weaver could stand it no longer. He was frightened and knew he had to do something. He contacted train dispatcher Joseph Moore at the Wellsville yard, and asked him to organize help from the neighboring communities. Moore quickly got the okay from his

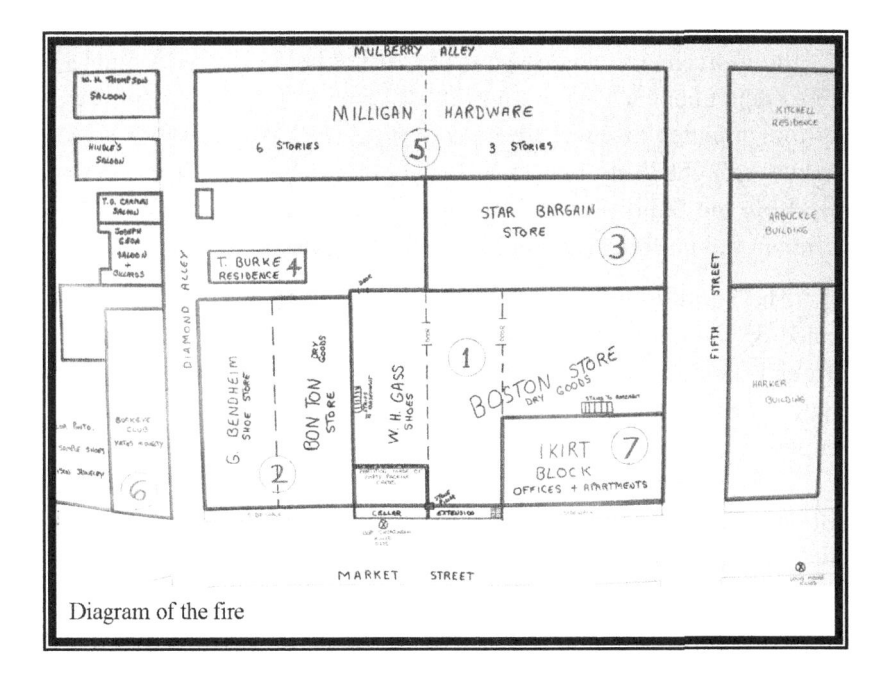

Diagram of the fire

superiors and contacted the Steubenville, Ohio Fire Department, and the Rochester, Pennsylvania Fire Department. Both departments said they would come, and began to organize their forces. Moore began clearing the tracks for the emergency trains that would bring those reinforcements.

Theodore Burke lived in a frame house on Diamond Alley in the rear of the Wasbutzky Building. His home would burn to the ground. He had some time however, and with several people helping him, he managed to save all his possessions, even the carpets off the floor.

Next to the Wasbutzky Building was the Milligan Hardware Company. It was located at the corner of 5th Street and Mulberry Alley. The building was constructed like a stair step, three stories on 5th Street and six stories in the rear, running all the way to Diamond Alley. The six story section was fairly new, and was full of all sorts of combustible material. With the Wasbutzky Building ablaze, the flames soon extended into the third floor of the Milligan Building. Rumors began to spread about the large quantity of dynamite that was in the building. These rumors were untrue, but large stock of ammunition, gasoline, and oil provided more than enough explosions, to keep the spectators at bay.

Reinforcements now began to arrive. The Rochester Volunteer Fire Department arrived in town at 9:12 p.m. It had taken them twenty-four minutes to cover the twenty miles to East Liverpool. Chief White brought thirty-two men and more equipment. They went to work on the Smith Fowler Building, which was now burning. They came in full uniforms, and put on quite a "parade ground" display.

The Smith Fowler Building was a three story brick structure, located on the north corner of Market Street and Diamond Alley. The ground floor was occupied by the R.W. Sample Shoe Store, the Yates Novelty Store, and Pattison Jewelry Store. The upper floors were occupied by Naylor Photography, The Buckeye Club, and the Senate Bar. It had begun to burn when the walls of the Porter and Thompson Buildings fell. The intense heat and burning debris had allowed the fire to leap across Diamond Alley. Along the north side of Diamond Alley were several taverns, and throughout the night they had been doing good business. However, several telephone poles had caught fire, and after burning through, they came crashing down onto the roofs of these taverns. The establishments of A.E. Hinkle, T.O Carmen and William Thompson suffered great damage. Fortunately, the crowd had evacuated these saloons before they were crushed.

Newspaper illustration of fire

Around 9:30 p.m. the Milligan Building was in its final moments. The walls began to buckle, and with a loud crash they came tumbling down. The Milligan Building towered over the surrounding structures. Now, tons of bricks came raining down onto the roof of the two story Exchange Building on the east side of Mulberry Alley. The bricks and burning debris broke through into the Lewis Brothers Furniture Store, causing considerable damage. Fortunately however, the stock had been mostly removed. Wellsville firefighters stationed on the roof of the Exchange Building quickly extinguished the fire. Most of the resulting damage came from water. The falling walls also crushed the front of Frank Marks' Saloon, in Diamond Alley. A large crowd had gathered there to watch the excitement. Everyone decided to move along after the front windows were shattered by falling bricks.

Firefighters Tom Bryan, William Ruhe, and George Betteridge had been fighting the blaze along Diamond Alley all night. The Chester volunteers and many civilians had been working there as well. When the Milligan Building collapsed, leaving nothing but a burning pile of rubble, the regular firefighters moved to the Smith Fowler Building. They climbed through a rear window and began to fight the fire. Before long they had the fire there under control. In the Diamond the Rochester men were still regaling the crowd with their firefighting *"skills."* Many would give them credit for saving the building. However, the East Liverpool firefighters would later testify that the fire was under control when the Rochester department started to work

At the height of the fire, there were fourteen fire hoses in use. Each one required at least three men to hold it, and more men were needed if it had to be moved very far. Water pressure, however, was not good. The water lines were too small, and clogged with silt. The river water that fed them was not yet being properly filtered. Chief Morley would later complain about so many fire hoses being in operation. Too many hose lines reduced the water pressure. He did not authorize many of them and had ordered some to be disconnected; however, he could not be everywhere, although it was his responsibility to be in control of the fire scene.

All evening the brisk wind had been blowing toward the northeast, pushing the fire in that direction. Left standing on the corner of 5th Street and Market Street was the four story Ikert Building. Thus far it had not caught fire, but it was filled with smoke and heat. This building was the home to several small businesses. The ground floor was occupied by M.E. Miskall's Real Estate, Enoch Elden's Hat Shop, The People's Building & Loan, and F.M. Leasure's Millinery Shop. The upper floors held offices and a few apartments. The building had long been evacuated. Throughout the night, Dr. George Ikert pleaded with every fire official he could find, trying to get them to deploy hoses into his building. They all ignored him, and continued to fight the fire in other buildings.

Ikert Building during the fire

The Steubenville Fire Department finally arrived at 10:30 p.m. Their trip had taken nearly an hour and a half. The only engine that was available was an old yard engine that had experienced problems, which delayed their arrival. Chief W.H. Martin had brought four regular firefighters and thirty-five volunteers along with several city officials. They also brought an old steam engine and a hose reel. They were sent to the Diamond. They went to work assisting Rochester in the front of the Fowler Building, and along Diamond Alley.

The Ikert Building had been spared until now, but it was so hot in the building, that no one was able to get above the second floor. Several men had tried to check out the situation, including Police Chief John Wyman. They were all driven out. Even Dr. Ikert tried, but was restrained by his son. The building was an inferno waiting to happen. About 10:30 the wind began to shift, and the flames turned toward the Ikert Building. The building, which had been super-heated, exploded in flames, and within half an hour it was destroyed. Very little effort was made to save it. Water pressure was low, and the water would not reach the fourth floor. Chief Morley refused to pull men and equipment away from the perimeter. He was concerned that the fire would continue to spread. Unfortunately, Dr. Ikert's building had to be sacrificed.

Chief Morley declared the fire under control around midnight; however, the fire would continue burning for several more hours. Within the fire zone flames still leaped high into the sky. The firefighters were exhausted, but they finally had the fire in check. It is remarkable that with the magnitude of the blaze there were few injuries, and only one fatality. The most tragic loss came at about 2:30 a.m. when a portion of Thompson Building collapsed. Twenty one-year-old Bert Swearingen was killed when he was struck by falling bricks and knocked into the basement. He died from a crushed skull. East Liverpool was served by two newspapers at the time, and sometimes they did not agree on things. Swearingen was praised by the *Evening Review,* as a brave and courageous volunteer. They reported that he had worked all night alongside of Will Terrence, the son of Fire Captain William Terrence. The paper ran an illustration of his likeness, a rare occurrence in the days before newspapers used photographs. The other daily paper, the *East Liverpool Tribune,* saw the tragic accident in a different light. In their story, Swearingen was where he should not have been. They related that the police had chased him off several times, but he kept sneaking back inside the fire lines. They saw him as just a curiosity seeker, who was in the wrong place at the wrong time, and tragically paid for it with his life. There were also many cuts and bruises, but one of the worst injuries happened to Asst. Chief Jim McCullough. During the fire one of the hoses got away from the men, and began to whip around wildly, striking McCullough, who received a severely bruised ankle. *(* In my years on the job, this happened only a couple of times, and it was always*

Bert Swearingen

Market & Diamond Alley

scary. In one incident a fellow firefighter received a broken ankle and another required stitches in his head.)

As the sun rose over the surrounding hills, the battle had been won, but at a terrible price. The once proud Thompson Building was reduced to a heap of smoldering rubble, as were the Porter and Wasbutzky Buildings. The huge Milligan Building had collapsed, with only broken portions of the walls still standing. The Ikert Building still stood at its full height, although nothing was left except the walls. On the north side of Diamond Alley, the Smith Fowler Building was gutted, and the several saloons that stood side by side were all crushed by fallen telephone poles and debris. Across Mulberry Alley, the western half of the Exchange Building had a steaming, gaping hole in its roof. Other buildings on the opposite side of 5th Street and Market Street had broken windows and burnt awnings. Fully, one quarter block had been totally destroyed. The insurance companies would cover losses of at least $700,000, but the true loss would be nearer to one million dollars, worth many times that amount in today's money.

With the fire out, the neighboring departments packed up their equipment, and with the grateful thanks of the citizens of East Liverpool, boarded the trains and headed back home. Over the coming days, the newspapers and people on the street heaped praise on the visitors at the expense of the hometown boys. Local papers praised the Rochester Fire Department, saying that they had performed like *"New Yorkers."* Sadly, Chief White, of the Rochester Fire Department took the opportunity to criticize the hometown firefighters for what he thought was a poor job. He related that he was shocked to hear that East Liverpool had a full time fire department. Apparently, the fancy uniforms, and precision maneuvers had impressed the citizens far more than their actual contribution. *(* The Rochester Volunteer Fire Department would send a bill to the City Council for their services, threatening a lawsuit if not paid. City Council, however, was not interested.)*

The next day, stories were told of how the play, *"The Sign of the Cross"* was delivered by candle light at the Ceramic Theatre, due to the electric power being shut off in the business district. Another was how a local teamster named Myler was helping firefighters lay the lines of fire hose in the Diamond. A streetcar employee cut the trolley power lines down for safety purposes. The line fell, hitting Mr. Myler in the head, knocking him unconscious for several minutes. He was dragged into a nearby store where he regained consciousness, and found that he was not badly hurt. Then there was the self-appointed policeman who enforced his rules with a wooden slat, striking those who disobeyed. After several offenders complained

5th Street Ruins

to a real police officer, the man was relieved of his weapon. That is when the victims of the zealot tried to take revenge. The police officer quickly restored order, and sent both parties on their way.

Many business owners had enlisted help in carrying their stock to safety; unfortunately, some of the stock made its way to a place of safety unknown to its former owner. However, even these few looters could not overshadow the large number of concerned citizens that stepped forward to help in the time of crisis. Men with no firefighting experience rushed forward to assist the beleaguered firefighters and in doing so, put themselves in harm's way. Restaurants and nearby residents provided food and hot coffee. Men and women helping wherever they could demonstrated the true spirit of East Liverpool.

Ruins of Ikert building

Long after the fire was out, firefighters continued to pour water onto the rubble to cool it down. Once the debris was cool enough, businessmen could search for their fireproof safes. Most were found to have worked well, saving the important papers and cash inside. Once the salvage operation was over, the most pressing need was to knock down the hazardous walls. Harvey McHenry was awarded the contract to raze the ruins of the Milligan Building. He accomplished the task without incident on March 4th.

The Ikert Building would be a much tougher job. The stately four-story structure was completely gutted. However, the walls remained intact, standing like an empty cardboard box. Contractor John White was awarded the contract. He decided that dynamite was the only solution. On the same day, he set his first charge in a hole he dug under the 5th Street wall. The explosion went off, failing to accomplish anything. As every red-blooded American man knows, more dynamite was needed. White doubled the second charge, and it went off with a great crash as the wall came tumbling down. The whole area was enveloped in a great cloud of dust, which lasted for several minutes. Unfortunately, the blast had also blown out all the remaining windows in the Harker Building, on the opposite side of 5th Street.

After the dust had cleared, White prepared the charge for his third shot, which would topple the Market Street wall. Police had stretched a safety rope at Market Street and Drury Alley, to protect the crowd of onlookers. There was a problem with this. From behind the rope the people could not see the walls fall. A number of people crossed over the rope, and were standing in front of the Brookes Building at the southwest corner of 5th and Market Street. One of these men was Louis Moore, a nineteen-year-old potter from Newell, West Virginia. When the third charge went off, pieces of broken bricks shot into the crowd of spectators, as if they had been fired from cannon. A piece of brick stuck Moore in the forehead, carrying the top of his head away and killing him instantly. The force of the brick then pierced a three quarter inch plank protecting the front of the Brookes Building. The wound was as neat as if had been cut with a knife; the top of Moore's head remained in his hat. Standing beside him was J.M. Willison, who was hit on the side of his face by a shard of brick. He was knocked off his feet. Bystanders carried him to a nearby doctor who treated his wound. Also injured was Walter Sweet, who was slightly hurt from a flying fragment.

Fire Chief H. Clinton Morley

The wall, however, remained intact for the most part, so a fourth charge would be needed. The dynamite was placed under a stone pillar at the corner of 5th and Market Streets. When it went off, the remaining wall fell, breaking several windows along the west side of Market Street. However, this time no one was hurt since the crowd had decided they could see just fine from behind the rope.

Smith Fowler hired a number of workmen, and they began tearing down the south wall of his building along Diamond Alley. He said the work would be done to the satisfaction of the fire chief, and he would raze the entire building if need be. *(*The entire building was razed and rebuilt.)* Others also set about repairing their damaged properties.

East Liverpool had never experienced such a destructive fire and everyone was in shock. Businessmen had suffered massive losses, and their insurance did not cover it all. Every day that they were out of business cost even more money, and they wanted answers. Mayor Weaver felt the same way; someone needed to answer for the catastrophe. He called for an inquiry into the conduct of the fire department. The Safety Board of City Council would sit in judgment and conduct the questioning. On March 3rd Mayor Weaver gave a statement to the city papers saying; *"The city must face the fact that East Liverpool is no longer a village, and the water system is woefully inadequate.* He went on to say, *"The fire department is poorly equipped, and there was misuse of the equipment they do have."*

The inquiry began on Monday evening, March 6th, in the council chambers at City Hall. A number of people had been subpoenaed to give their testimony. The vocal opposition was led by Dr. George Ikert, and consisted of others who had lost heavily. The defendant was Fire Chief H. Clinton Morley, who was charged *"with incompetency,*

Dr. George Ikert

gross negligence and being *devoid of the natural instincts of a leader.*" The Fire Department was charged as well and was represented by Firefighter William Ruhe.

The first witness called was W.S. Gass; he, however, said he had no criticism to make about the fire department, testifying; *"They were trying. If a mistake was made it was not knowingly."*

Dr. W.R. Clarke testified that he thought, *"The firemen should have flooded the floor of the Boston Store, to keep the fire from eating its way through."* Chief Morley replied, *"That would not work because the water would run down the stairways."* A few more witnesses were called with no new information being revealed.

Then Dr. Ikert was called. He took the stand and asked that he be excused for a week, so matters of insurance could be taken care of. He also said, people needed time to *"cool off"*, and think things over. *"You will reap riper judgment if you wait a week."*

A member of the Safety Board asked him, *"If he would like to wait a week with a cloud of criticism hanging over him, and if he thought it was unjust to the firemen to prolong the date of the hearing."*

Dr. Ikert replied, *"No sir, I do not. ....He (Morley) should have no more rights than anyone else. If this is to be a whitewash it is one thing. If it is to be for the benefit of the city it is quite another."*

Safety Board President James H. Grafton angrily interposed, *"It is an insult to the Board to even intimate a whitewash."*

Dr. Ikert replied, *"The people do not know. The people have confidence in the Board, but I know they cannot reach the right decision so soon."* He went on; *"In my opinion it would be better to wait a week. Now do as you please. I will be here at your command any time you want me."* Mayor Weaver excused Dr. Ikert for a week, saying the hearing would last several days anyway.

A few more witnesses were called with some (like a reporter for the *Evening Review)*, criticizing the firefighters' tactics, while others gave them credit for doing everything they could. The meeting was then adjourned.

The inquest resumed on Wednesday evening, March 8th, and again there was a parade of inconclusive testimony. On one side were the businessmen who had suffered loss, and bystanders who were sure they could have done a better job than the fire chief. On the other side were the firefighters and those civilians who had actually fought the fire. Chief Morley and Firefighter Ruhe tried to answer each charge with what they felt were the correct responses. Then Dr. George Ikert was recalled. This time he had come prepared. Among other statements, he related how he had given Asst. Chief McCullough advice on what he should do, but he had been ignored. Ikert said, *"The firemen worked hard, but simply lacked intelligence."* He then went on to explain how the fire should have been fought, saying first, *"They should have moved from the Gass Store to the 5th Street entrance of the Boston Store.* Secondly, *"They should have left the burning buildings and saved the buildings that were still standing."* (*His building)

The Board asked, *"Have you got any other criticisms to make?"*

Ikert went on, *"I could not be everywhere at once."* I asked two firemen to go up into my building and they refused. I do not know who they were. They were throwing water on the embers that were strewn on the streets. There was no danger in my opinion. But the firemen thought there was. I told him to follow me that I would not ask him to go where I would not go myself. I could not find the chief. (* Other testimony told of Ikert's son restraining him from entering his building.)

The Board asked, *"Have you any criticism to make concerning the Chief, for the water not being turned on your building?"*

Ikert responded, *"The criticism is due somebody. I asked for a hose. However, it is not my duty to lay blame."* He then continued, *"When the Rochester Department arrived they asked me what to do, and I told them to go over and fight the fire in its face. It was then in the Fowler Building, and it was not under control. The Rochester men got the fire checked in 20 minutes after they got at it. My argument is to the effect that a company should fight a fire in such a manner that it will be driven from a building instead of into it, is accepted by all fire departments. I learned it from Chief Murphy of Pittsburgh many years ago. It is the proper thing to try to put a fire out wherever it may be, and if it cannot be accomplished it is then the duty of firemen to get between it and other property." With that "Chief" Ikert ended his firefighting lesson for the day.

A summary of the testimony came down to the question, were proper tactics used? Did the firefighters attack the fire from the rear of the Gass Shoe Store, and if so, when? Why was the Ikert Building allowed to burn? Why was the water pressure so poor?

The inquest took a different turn on Monday March 13th. Until now Dr. Ikert had been a witness. During the recess he had written a letter to Mayor Weaver, requesting an attorney be appointed to prosecute the case on behalf of the people. Mayor Weaver offered the job to him, and Dr. Ikert readily accepted.

Chief Morley was called to the stand, and was closely grilled by Prosecutor Ikert. The questions centered on why the water pressure was low, why the chief did not use the steam engine sooner, and why the aerial ladder was not used. Chief Morley turned all questions on the water pressure over to the water department. He said he did not know why the pressure was low; maybe the lines are corroded. He said he feared the steam engine would draw water away from other hoses. *(*Probably a mistake.)* He said the steam was up in 20 minutes and no one could have done it any quicker. He did not think the aerial ladder was necessary. *(*The East Liverpool Fire Department used their aerial ladder as a rescue tool. The wagon had a 50 foot hand cranked extension ladder that was not suited to be used free standing, but was normally rested against a building.)*

Morley said his men were quite experienced, most of them having served for several years. He said they had fought enough fires that they did not need to drill. *(*Also, probably a mistake.)* He also stated that he did not know of a general set of firefighting rules that could be relied on, since each fire is different. *(*Questionable)*

Morley continued with his statement, *"I attacked the fire in the front, because that is where I found it. It had spread under the Young Store. (Boston Store) It had destroyed the box partition. We put two* lines into the Gass basement and within seven minutes had a line in the rear. I went to the rear and tore down the gate with an ax. I got into the cellar about ten feet. The smoke was intense, and the partition was warm. I left men there working and returned to Market Street. We tried to push the boxes out of the way with a ladder, but could not." He then told of going to the 5th Street side and saw heavy smoke. He had hoped to hold the fire in the basement."*At about 7:00 p.m. the fire was visible on the second floor and the Mayor asked about the steam engine. I did not think it was needed. With the town's ordinary water pressure it takes three men to hold a hose. Two men were needed to operate the steamer I did not have the manpower."* (* testimony was paraphrased)

The area that worried the Chief most was north of Diamond Alley. He said he ordered two hose lines into the rear to cut off the fire. When asked why the Ikert Building was sacrificed. Chief Morley responded; *"With the water pressure low we needed it for the Fowler Building. We could not safely take a stream from it. I believe the whole square including the Opera House and the Thompson Building would have been destroyed had we done so."*

(* He is speaking of the Grand Opera House on 6th Street and the new Thompson Building at 6th Street and Market on the northeast corner of the Diamond.)

Several other witnesses testified that they saw East Liverpool men fighting the fire in the Fowler Building, which they thought was under control, before the Rochester firefighters got there.

The inquest resumed on Wednesday, March 15th with Dr. Ikert serving as Prosecutor once more. This time he tried to confine the answers to his very leading questions, to either yes or no. Failing in that, he went on in a very confrontational manner. He grilled Water Department Clerk J.W. Gipner on the poor water pressure, and refused to accept his answer that the pipes may be corroded. He argued with witnesses on the question of why the fire department did not try earlier to fight the fire from 5th Street, not accepting the answer that the smoke was too dense.

Finally, Dr. Ikert sarcastically posed a hypothetical question to no one in particular, *"With an aerial ladder, and a force of firemen as good as any in the cities, and so good that they do not need to drill, under the command of a chief who has years of experience, who never loses his head; with a steamer known to work perfectly when properly manned, and with a high pressure (water) system that cost the city thousands of dollars, do you believe all this destruction was either necessary or unavoidable?*

Finally, Mayor Weaver had heard enough, and declared the hearings closed. After a parade of witnesses, the testimony was split equally, for and against. It was useless to continue. Not yet prepared to give up, Dr. Ikert interjected, *"Mayor Weaver, do you intend to ignore the other witnesses who have not yet testified?"* Weaver replied, *"I don't want to impose on the commission any longer."*

Dr. Ikert was not pleased. He was angry, and he wanted heads to roll, namely Chief Morley's. Mayor Weaver announced that no decision could be made until all the testimony was in typewritten form. He stated that it may comprise 500 pages, so it would take considerable time. In fact, history is still waiting on the document. The stenographer, who had taken the notes in shorthand, wanted to be paid before turning them over. The problem was no one wanted to pay her. City Council flatly refused to foot the bill. Even Dr. Ikert declined. Maybe he felt the decision would not bring the results he sought, or maybe he had just needed to get this frustration off his chest. At any rate, the inquest ended not in a bang, but in a laughable whimper.

However, several positive actions did result from the inquest. On March 16th the Safety Board issued their recommendations to improve the fire protection of the city.

- To organize a volunteer force of 25 men, under the direction of the Safety Board and the chief. Pay them 50 cents an hour when called out by the chief. Provide them with rubber coats and helmets.
- Add two more fulltime firefighters at the Central Station.
- Buy two more horses and harness so the steamer could respond to every fire.

- Install a "dry chemical" battery system for the alarm system.
- Buy a combination chemical hose wagon for Central Station.
- Open the Northside Fire Station.
- Pass a Fire Limits ordinance.

Although not all of these recommendations were carried out, several were. Two more firefighters were hired in 1906, bringing the force to twelve. A chemical hose wagon was purchased for Central Station in 1906 and another one for the East End Station in 1907. *(* These units carried twin 45 gallon soda acid fire extinguishers that were hooked to a small hose to be used on small fires in a much faster time.)* The Northside Fire Station opened in 1906, and plans were put in motion for the West End Station, which would open in 1908. The horses were bought, and the improvements to the alarm system would come in a few years. The volunteer force was never organized. Council also ordered the regular firefighters to buy their own helmets, and gave them until April to do so.

A new 16-inch water main was completed into the business district in 1906. In that busy year, Council also passed the Fire Limits Ordinance, which mandated that all construction within the zone would be of fire resistant materials. No new wood frame buildings could be built within the fire limits zone. *(* The entire business district.)*

The buildings that had been destroyed were all replaced with even better ones. By June 1905, all the buildings were under construction, with the Ikert Building being the last to get started. Today several of them are gone, only the Thompson Building (still L-Shaped) and the Porter Building remain. The Milligan and Wasbutzky Buildings, rebuilt in 1905, were again destroyed by a fire in 1925. The Smith Fowler Building likewise was lost in a 1968 blaze. As for the Ikert Building, it was razed in the 1950s, and replaced with a two story building which still stands today.

Several of the firefighters who fought the great "Diamond Fire" did not live to see all of these improvements. The year of 1907 was a tragic one for the East Liverpool Fire Department. Charles Rose developed pneumonia while fighting a fire on Sophia Street, near the downtown, and passed away on February 14, 1907. Just over one month later, on March 22nd, George Betteridge was killed when he fell from the top of a telephone pole on Dresden Avenue, near Webber Way. He had been repairing the fire alarm lines. Lastly, Chief H. Clinton Morley suffered a heart attack on September 3, 1907, and died at the scene of the Wright Building fire, on W. Market Street (now Dresden Avenue). His longtime assistant, James McCullough, was named to replace him.

Dr. George P. Ikert continued with his medical practice and his business career until his death on February 12, 1927.

The "Great Diamond Fire of 1905" was the biggest blaze ever to occur in East Liverpool. To be sure, many more would come, including another Diamond Fire in 1968. But so far none has surpassed it. William Jennings Bryan's dream was truly a "Nightmare."

Chapter 15
In - Flu - Enza
The Spanish Influenza Pandemic of 1918

Every year as autumn rolls around, we begin to see signs on local businesses advertising flu shots. Many people get one every year, and the elderly are encouraged to do so by their doctors. In 1918, you did not see anything about flu shots because they did not exist. However, if you were to listen to the children singing as they skipped rope you may well have heard this rhyme;

I had a little bird
Its name was Enza
I opened the window
and in- flu- enza

The worldwide influenza pandemic, known to history as the Spanish Influenza, occurred between January 1918 and December 1920. It was the first of two massive outbreaks involving the H1N1 virus. An outbreak in 2009 was much less severe due to new medications. The 1918 outbreak occurred during the last year of World War I and was devastating on battlefields across Europe. Thousands of soldiers on both sides died, and many more were seriously ill. The civilian population of war torn Europe was also devastated.

It was called the Spanish Influenza not because it started in Spain, but because Spain did not fight in the war. Because of this, their press was uncensored and the sickness was heavily reported on. Even King Alfonso XIII was gravely ill. Spain however, was not hit any harder than other countries. The warring nations had tried to ignore the growing threat, for fear it would demoralize their war weary populations.

By the time it had run its course, nearly every corner of the Earth had been affected. China and Japan, along with the Pacific Islands, were ravaged. Whole Eskimo villages were wiped out. Worldwide, between 20 and 50 million people would die, perhaps five percent of the world's population. Some medical scientists have described it as *"the greatest medical holocaust in history."*

This disease acted differently from the normal strains of flu. It was the most devastating to the young healthy population. It has been estimated that as much as 99% of the deaths occurred to people under 65 years old. More than half were in the 20 to 40 age group. The mortality rate was nearly one in five. This strain affected the immune system, causing it to overreact in what is known as a "cytokine storm." The stronger your system, the stronger the infection.

No one is completely sure of just where the flu started. One theory is the crowded army camps in Kansas were the breeding grounds of the flu. Others say war-ravaged France. We may never truly know. What we do know is influenza came to East Liverpool in October of 1918.

World War I was in its final days, and the people of East Liverpool were riveted by the reports coming from France. The pages of the local papers told how the once mighty German Army was now being pushed back by the hard charging American "Doughboys." Hundreds of young men from East Liverpool were in the thick of the fighting, and the folks back here on the front could not get enough information. There was little other news on the front pages of the newspaper. However, soon stories began to appear reporting the new sickness that was sweeping across the nation.

The northern part of Columbiana County was affected first. In early October, reports were appearing in the newspapers about the city of East Palestine. This small city of about 5,000 people had 1,000 cases of the influenza. By October 10th, cases were being reported in Lisbon and Leetonia, Ohio, and Chester, West Virginia. So far, East Liverpool and Wellsville had been spared. That was about to change.

Doctor J. Wallace Chetwynd was thirty-seven-years-old. For the past year he had been the head of the East Liverpool Health Department. Dr. Chetwynd was an ear, nose, and throat specialist. Originally from Wheeling, West Virginia, he had come to East Liverpool and set up his practice in 1915. His actions over the next few months would be critical to the health and well-being of the community.

Based on the reports coming from the surrounding towns, Dr. Chetwynd knew he must take action. In an attempt to get ahead of disease he exercised his authority by cancelling the Liberty Day celebrations. On Saturday, October 12th, there was to be a huge parade in downtown East Liverpool. This was for the fourth war bond drive, and an estimated 5,000 people would take part in the parade and rally.

The following day he saw the first cases of the flu in East Liverpool. Immediately, Chetwynd took further action by ordering a ban on all public gatherings. He shut down all churches, public and parochial schools, dance halls, pool and billiard halls, theatres, and worst of all, the saloons. The many saloons obeyed the order, but the wholesale liquor distributors opened as usual, and for a while did a brisk business. By 3:00 p.m. Police Chief Hugh McDermott had closed that loophole. Liquor could not be bought, sold or moved from building to building. East Liverpool was officially "dry."

Also, restrictions were placed on soda fountains and ice cream parlors. They could sell soft drinks by the bottle but not by the glass. Ice cream could be bought for home consumption by the pint or quart. However, nothing could be eaten in the store. All retail stores were ordered closed at 5:30 p.m. each day. Grocery stores and meat markets were allowed to remain open until 9:00 p.m.

Despite such precautions, the virus continued to ravage the area. On Monday, October 13th, the Columbiana County Health Board reported that 48 people had died so far. East Palestine had suffered forty-one of those deaths, and the other seven were from Salem, Ohio. East Liverpool had twenty-seven confirmed cases. Wellsville authorities followed East Liverpool's suit and banned all public meetings. Within a few days East Palestine had 2,400 cases, nearly half of the town's population. Not all these people were sick at the same time as some people either recovered or died. It does show, however, the number of people affected.

On Saturday, October 19th, it was announced that at 11:00 a.m. Sunday, all the church bells in town would be rung. This would call the people to a time of city-wide prayer and Bible study in their homes.

The call was also put out for volunteer nurses to staff the emergency quarantine hospital. City Council had appropriated $1,500 dollars to turn the unused West End Fire Station into a temporary hospital. Health officials did not want to mix influenza patients with other patients in the hospital.

The Evening Review reported on Monday that the first death had occurred in East Liverpool, over the weekend. There were also 185 confirmed cases in town. For the next several weeks deaths would be reported every day.

The war news continued to fill the front page of the city newspapers, but the inside pages were filled with the "cures" for the flu. Advertisements like these gave their customers hope with these claims;

Tanic – The Master Medicine It will aid a rundown system to combat the disease

Another was;

Father John's Medicine gives resistance to the disease through its laxative effect which drives the poisons from your system. Remember Father John's is a pure wholesome food guaranteed to be absolutely free of opium, morphine, heroin, codeine, or any other dangerous drug or alcohol. Get it in the large size, it contains more than twice as much as the small size.

The Vicks Vapor Rub Company ran an advertisement each day, giving ideas for preventing the disease and testimonials of how their product was being applied. The liberal use of their product was, of course, part of the cure. They must have been successful, because by November, doctors were being warned about a possible nationwide shortage of Vicks Vapor Rub.

In spite of these remedies, people continued to die. On October 28th East Liverpool city councilman Joseph Judge died. He was only thirty-three-years-old. *(*The flu would claim his brother James, on December 23rd. He was just twenty four.)*

Early November brought stories from other towns, who believing that the worst was over, relaxed a bit, only to be hit hard again within a couple of days. The Health Board in East Liverpool fell victim to this optimism as well. They made this announcement on November 4th. Just four days later there were 92 new cases. However, health officials ruled that most of these new cases were "mild reactions" and, bowing to immense public pressure, they partially lifted the ban on public gatherings.

World War I came to an end on November 11th, and the killing stopped, but the flu continued, and its death toll continued to grow. The ban was lifted on November 15th; however, all schools remained closed. That same day the *Evening Review* called for a strict in home quarantine for infected residences. Up until now, no quarantine was in effect.

The emergency quarantine hospital had not been as successful as had been hoped for. One of the problems was providing adequate nursing staff. Few people were interested in working among the sick and dying. However, one group was praised by the *Evening Review* for the wonderful job they were doing. The nuns from the Sisters of Mary Convent at St. Aloysius Catholic Church had been serving at the emergency hospital from the start. The newspaper said they had served with distinction.

As the epidemic raged on, fear was on everyone's mind, for one never knew if tomorrow they would be stricken. Over the weekend of November 20th to 23rd, for example the health department reported 15 deaths and 161 new cases.

On November 23rd the *Evening Review* reported that Mrs. Gertrude Coles, age 43, of W. 4th Street, had died from the flu after being sick only a couple of hours. Her son, a high school senior, had come down with the disease. His mother labored around the clock for several days, nursing her son through the worst of the disease. At about 3:00 p.m. on November 22nd, the boy began to improve, and would eventually recover. Two hours later, Mrs. Coles suddenly collapsed and died. She had sacrificed her health and her life to save her son.

Probably the most tragic event in this crisis was the destruction of the Hancock family of Bank Street. All of the family members would contract the flu. Mrs. Jennie Hancock was the first to come down with the disease. In an attempt to prevent the children from becoming sick, they were sent to their grandmother's home on Union Street. Meanwhile, Mrs. Hancock was removed to the emergency quarantine hospital. The children became sick anyway. On November 18th, the first death occurred when three-year-old Mary Jane passed away. On the 22nd Jennie died, and later that day so did little Ethel, who was under two-years-old. The next day, six-month-old John joined his mother and sisters in death. Four deaths in just one family. Ethel was already buried when the other family members died. Mrs. Hancock was buried along with the other two children in a single grave, at Riverview Cemetery in East Liverpool. Mr. Samuel Hancock would recover from the influenza, but not from his loss.

A few days later, the Health Board imposed the ban once more. However, the quarantine hospital was closed on November 25th. The remaining patients were transferred to the third floor of City Hospital. Between November 23rd and the 26th, nine more deaths occurred. The flu claimed Oliver I. Jones on November 30th. Jones was the editor of the *Evening Review*. He was originally from Cleveland, and his body was taken there for burial.

The city was able to help solve one pressing problem involved with this crisis. Due to the number of deaths and people who were sick, a shortage had appeared. There were not enough grave diggers. Mayor Joe Wilson and Police Chief Hugh McDermott solved that problem by ordering that prisoners being held at the city jail be put to use in this role.

By December 9th Dr. Chetwynd reported that the disease was beginning to lose its strength. People, however, were continuing to die. Miss Ida Walters, a student nurse, passed away on December 10th. Miss Walters was only nineteen-years-old. Her family had moved to East Liverpool from New Brighton, Pennsylvania when she was about nine-years-old. After high school she entered the nursing school at the City Hospital, and when the epidemic occurred she was assigned to the quarantine section of the hospital. Miss Walters worked untiringly, until she also fell victim to the flu early in December.

Just before Christmas, Dr. Chetwynd lifted the ban on public gatherings, and the stores and saloons reopened. Church services were held the next day for the first time in weeks. The schools remained closed until January 6, 1919. The children had not been in school since October 14th.

The Spanish Flu had moved on and the area began its slow recovery. A few more people would get sick, and a couple of people would die; however, most people recovered. On December 28th the Health Department reported that since October there had been 1,443 confirmed flu cases in East Liverpool, resulting in 135 deaths. It could be said that a few of these people had come from outside of the city limits, but is that important? Neighboring towns also had suffered during this epidemic, like Wellsville, who reported 36 flu related deaths.

America had helped to win the Great War. World War I was called, "*The war to end all wars.*" It failed to achieve that, but we had been victorious on the battlefield. Could we make the same claim over that even greater enemy, the Spanish Influenza? Or did it just run its course and leave on its own? Medical authorities say nearly 28% of the American population had contracted the disease. Between 500,000 and 675,000 Americans died from the flu or its complications during the outbreak. The war on the influenza virus continues every year and so far medical science is holding its own, but the enemy remains undefeated. The "flu" returns each year and usually in a little different form. It is an unrelenting foe and we must remain vigilant.

Chapter 16
Morning of Mayhem!
Samuel Mann's Insane Rampage
November 16, 1902

Samuel Mann lived with his wife and child in a humble home near the Golding Flint Mill. This area between the Newell Bridge and what is now Westgate School, was an inhospitable place. It was a place of railroad tracks, factories, and shanty boats. For many years there were a number of families who lived in houseboats (shanty boats) tied to the shore line of the Ohio River. This area became known as the Shanty Boat District. All in all, it was a bleak and depressing place. Sam Mann lived here with his family. Depressed, and filled with a smoldering rage, he had been drinking heavily for a couple of weeks.

Mrs. Mann and her three-year-old had just finished breakfast, and while clearing away the dishes, Sam suddenly attacked her. Laughing like a madman, Sam began to violently throw his wife and child around the kitchen. During the scuffle, a piece of carpet caught fire from the stove Mann picked it up and threw it onto the bed. Still laughing maniacally, Mann stood and watched as the flames took hold and the bed clothing began to blaze. Seemingly pleased, Mann ran from the house as smoke began to pour from the windows. He stopped only long enough to pick up a hatchet he saw lying nearby. With the deadly weapon in hand he ran onto the nearby houseboat of the Call family. Upon seeing this madman burst through the door brandishing the hatchet, the occupants fled in all directions. Mann managed to capture two young men, Moses Call and Ralph Wooley. Swinging the hatchet wildly, he ordered his two captives to, *"Get down on your knees and pray to God."* The two frightened men dropped to their knees and began to call upon the Lord for their deliverance. For fully ten minutes the men prayed, more fervently than either had ever done before. All the while Sam Mann hovered over them, hatchet in hand. Finally he told them to get up. Seizing their opportunity, the two men bolted from the boat, escaping with their very lives.

Mann, realizing he was alone, also left the Call houseboat. Shoeless and without a coat, he climbed up the embankment and onto the railroad tracks. Walking a short distance, he came to the bridge over Carpenter's Run. It was undergoing some repairs, and several of the workmen restrained him from jumping off, possibly to his death. As they tried to calm him he became violent again and broke away. Mann raced back to the shanty boats and climbed onto the boat belonging to the John Brighouse family.

Fortunately, these folks had witnessed the rampage and had barricaded themselves in. Mann, in a demented rage, began to smash at the door with the hatchet and his fists, all the while ranting violently. The fact that he was unable to break in only increased his anger.

At this point the police arrived. Officers Mike Mahoney and C.E. Morris approached the howling maniac warily, ready for anything. When Mann saw them, he became instantly calm. The officers disarmed him without the least bit of resistance and took him to jail. A large crowd of excited citizens followed behind. Once at the jail in the City Hall, Mann was locked up in one of the women's cells. Exhausted by his wild rampage he virtually collapsed onto the bunk. He remained quiet for several hours.

Suddenly, Mann was seized by another fit of madness. He began to hallucinate, and nothing Police Chief Tom Thompson or Officer Cliff Dawson could do would calm him down. He told the chief, *"When I am ready to leave, the Angel will unlock the cell."* Spying an empty jug near his cell, he became frightened and begged that it would be removed. He told the officers it was full of nitroglycerin. In an attempt to calm him down they removed the jug. Later his parents came up from Wellsville and his wife and child visited him. Although they all tried to reach him, his delusions continued. For some unknown reason his wife gave him four handkerchiefs, which he accepted without comment. During one particularly violent episode Mann smashed the window of his cell. Officers began to think about taking him into one of the men's cells. Mann again told them, *"You need not think of taking me out of here, when I want to go this little Angel will unlock the door."* He then showed them a picture of a girl, his Angel. Some of the officers thought he should be committed to the insane asylum in Massillon, Ohio. Chief Thompson, however, thought it best to wait and see if once he sobered up, he would come to his senses. Mann slept all night, but in the morning he was no better. Sometime during the night, Mann tied the four handkerchiefs to the bars of his cell, saying they were possessed with demons. Once again there was a crowd gathered outside his cell. Mann called out, *"Say, I guess you people had better get out of here. The Lord told me you were all devils and I want you to get out!"* Then without warning, he dropped to his knees and began to pray. After a few minutes he jumped up and told one of the men, *"You can stay, I talked it over with the Lord, and he says you're alright. You got the Lord to save me didn't you?"* Mann refused to eat or drink anything, saying it was poison. He said on his drunken spree he had, *"Drunk a thousand devils, and they will never get out of me until my Angel commands them to leave."* Frequently he raved about a pretty girl he had met last week. He said she was in the hallway and that they were married. A doctor did manage to get him to take some medicine, but it did not calm him down. Seeing no improvement, it was decided to send him to Lisbon, so an Inquest of Lunacy could be held. The problem was how they would manage to get him there.

East Liverpool Mayor William Davidson came up with an idea. He pretended to be Mann's good friend, Charles Moore. Mann accepted this pretense and warmly greeted the mayor. Then when Columbiana County Sheriff Charles Leonard was introduced as Charlie Moore's father, Mann went over and kissed Sheriff Leonard on the cheek. With the greetings out of the way, Mayor Davidson told Mann, *"Some other fellow has been trying to get us to put these cuffs on him. We want you to wear them, so you better get them on before that other fellow comes."* Mann smiled and held out his wrists. Sheriff Leonard slapped the handcuffs on him saying, *"We are going to take you for a nice ride."*

On November 20th, an Inquest of Lunacy was held before Judge J.C. Boone, and Sam Mann was found to be insane. The presiding doctors hoped that this unnatural behavior was brought on by the abuse of alcohol, and thus might be temporary. He was committed to the asylum in Massillon, along with his angels and demons, for an undetermined term.

Chapter 17
I'm not Drunk; I'm Crazy!
The Murder of Letha Barrett
May 23, 1946

It was warm that Thursday afternoon, and Lawrence Abraham Wheatley was ready to let off some steam. When quitting time at the Edwin M. Knowles Pottery came at 3:30, he was ready. Best of all, it was payday. Abe Wheatley was a ruggedly built 26-year-old pottery worker who lived in Newell, West Virginia with his wife and two young children. With his paycheck in hand, Abe headed for East Liverpool.

Downtown East Liverpool was a bustling place in the late spring of 1946. The wartime shortages were beginning to ease, and people were ready for their lives to return to normal. One group that was looking to make up for lost time was the drivers of the city bus line. They were on strike for better wages and benefits. If you did not have your own car this made things a little inconvenient, but you could always share a ride with someone, and there were always the taxi cabs.

Lawrence "Abe" Wheatley

Abe's first stop was a tavern, where he cashed his paycheck. Then he went into a nearby hardware store and looked over some fishing tackle. Before leaving, he bought a box of .22 caliber cartridges. His next stop was the State Liquor Store at E. 6th and Walnut Street, where he bought a "fifth" of brandy.

Abe then began bar hopping. He walked into a bar and began drinking "doubleheaders." At his third bar he ran into a co-worker, Emmett Howell, and the two men had a beer. Abe wanted to open the brandy, but he could not get the top off. They decided to go to Howell's apartment. Howell wanted to get cleaned up for a night on the town. While there, Abe managed to open his brandy, and by the time Howell was ready, Wheatley had drunk most of the liquor. Before too long, Howell decided that Abe was not the best partner, so the two men went their separate ways. Abe finished his brandy and then bought another bottle.

Letha Barrett

Finding himself in the Diamond, Abe climbed into a taxi that was parked in front of the Diamond Cab Company Office. He was ready to go home to Newell. There was already a male passenger waiting in the cab. Due to the strike, this was a common occurrence. The cab was about to pull away from the curb, when Wheatley saw her.

Letha Barrett was a middle aged grandmother who lived on Price Street in the East End of town with her husband and unmarried daughter. Earlier in the day, Mrs. Barrett had caught a ride to town with a neighbor, Louise Bratt. She did light housekeeping for Mrs. Bratt, who paid her the six dollars she had coming, and then the two went their separate ways. She was walking along the sidewalk when Wheatley saw her, and told the cab driver to *"Stop! There comes Letha Barrett. I'd like to throw her in the river."* Jumping from the cab, Wheatley stopped her, and began talking to her. *"Com'on get in the cab,"* Wheatley said.

"No. said Barrett; *I'm going to East End to visit a friend."*

Showing her the bottle of brandy Wheatley said, *"We can drink this and then go visit your friend."* Finally, Barrett agreed, and climbed into the cab. It was 6:25 p.m. Cab driver Roy Frondorf drove out Dresden Avenue, letting the third passenger off at a local grocery store. Turning to his remaining passengers, Frondorf asked, *"Where to?"*

Wheatley spoke up and said, *"Drive us down the Wellsville Road."*

Mrs. Barrett protested, *"I don't want to go to Wellsville. I want to go to East End."*

Wheatley leaned over and gave the driver a wink and two dollars, saying, *"Take us down the Wellsville Road."*

Mrs. Barrett continued to say she did not want to go to Wellsville, but not too forcefully. Just outside the East Liverpool city limits on the way to Wellsville is an area that was then known as Brady's Cut. *(*Ohio State Route 7 is now a four lane highway through this area and many of the landmarks are lost to history.)* Wheatley told the cab driver to turn onto the old dirt road that led down to the river, and the abandoned sewer pipes works. The old sewer pipe pottery of N.U. Walker had been closed for a long time. Not much remained except for ruins and a couple of old kiln stacks. The cab had gone about 200 feet down the dirt track that led to Walkers, when Wheatley told the driver to stop. Wheatley got out and Mrs. Barrett followed. She looked around and said, *"I want to go to East End."*

Wheatley pulled out the bottle of brandy and said, *"We'll drink this bottle and then we'll go to East End."* Then he winked at the cab driver. Frondorf turned the cab around and left. He decided that they were both drunk. He thought the woman was more intoxicated than the man. Arriving back at the cab office, Frondorf filed his report, telling the dispatcher were he had taken the fares, and about his $2.00 tip.

Later that evening, Wheatley was walking across the Newell Bridge, on his way home. About halfway across the bridge he met Lawrence Drumm and Robert Vaughn, who were walking toward East Liverpool. Wheatley was very drunk, and he offered the men a drink from his bottle. Drumm said Wheatley suddenly blurted out, *"I killed somebody."*

The two startled men asked, *"Who and Where?"*

Wheatley replied, *"You'll find out tomorrow."*

Wheatley walked into Clarence Nease's service station at 5th and Washington Street in Newell, at 8:15 that evening. There were several men in the station sitting around talking. Wheatley went straight into the men's room. When he came out he turned to Nease and said, *"Nease, I want to tell you something, and you won't like it. I killed a woman this afternoon."* He began to cry. *"I know I killed that woman. I tramped her head right down into the ground. She's down on East Liverpool-Wellsville road near the two stacks."*

Nease said *"Abe you're drunk."*

Wheatley replied, *"I'm not drunk, I'm crazy. I stomped her to death."* Holding out his left hand the men saw it was swollen and encrusted with dried blood. Wheatley then took out his wallet and handed it to Nease. He said *"Give this to Mary and tell her to get the kids out of the house- there's going to be trouble."* There was $167 dollars in his wallet. He turned and left the station. Everyone looked at each other and then dismissed it since he was so drunk.

A short time later the men heard a gunshot and the bullet hit the window of the service station. Nease looked across the street, and saw Wheatley standing at the second floor window of his apartment. He raised his revolver and again shot through the window of the service station. The men scattered and made their way out the rear door to safety. Finding a telephone, Nease called Squire John Talbott. Talbott quickly arrived and found Wheatley on the sidewalk. With the help of a passerby, the two men overpowered Wheatley and disarmed him. Wheatley was loaded into a car, driven to New Cumberland, West Virginia, and locked in the Hancock County Jail. He was charged with malicious assault with intent to kill.

Meanwhile, Mr. Barrett had come home from work, and found his wife missing. He called friends, but they were of no help. He then went to town to look for her. He did not find her.

Once Wheatley was locked up he continued to rant about what he had done. Because of this, West Virginia authorities contacted the East Liverpool police, and gave them the details. By now it was dark. The police made a brief search of the area, but found nothing. Because Wheatley was so intoxicated, police were skeptical of what he was telling them. During the first few hours in jail, Wheatley had said the woman he had killed was his sister-in-law. Police checked on all his family members, but everyone was all right. This led the police to further discount his story.

Meanwhile, the Barrett family spent all of Friday searching and waiting for Letha to return. Finally, at noon on Saturday Mr. Barrett reported his wife missing to East Liverpool police officer, John Graham.

Leo Payne had gone down to the river to do a little fishing on Sunday afternoon. About 4:00 p.m., he was pushing through some brush when he was met with a shocking spectacle. Lying in a shallow gully was the nearly nude body of a woman. Payne immediately hailed a nearby fisherman, Jim Merriman, and the two men hurried to a phone to call the police.

The police arrived quickly and began to collect evidence. The body was lying face up and was nude except for shoes and stockings. Nearby was the rest of her clothing, which appeared to have been ripped from her body. She had been badly beaten around her face and head. *(* The coroner would later report that her nose, septum, upper jaw, maxillary processes and hard palate were fractured. The left hyoid bone (at the base of her tongue) was dislocated and there were lacerations and heavy bruising. The injuries resulted in internal hemorrhaging.)*

The area also showed signs of a struggle. The contents of her purse were scattered near her outstretched right arm. The coroner found $36 dollars on the body, six dollars in the foot of one stocking and $30 dollars in the other. The murder scene was about 75 feet south of Ohio Route 7. Photographs were taken of the body and the crime scene. Then the body was removed. Police determined that they had been within 10-12 feet of the victim during their search Thursday night.

While still trying to put two and two together, the police received a break. Cab driver Roy Frondorf was returning from a trip to Wellsville when he saw all the police cars along the highway. Word of the murder was just then circulating on the street. Remembering the couple he had taken to the area on Thursday, he notified the authorities. Frondorf described in detail the conversation between the two passengers, as well as their being intoxicated. Police quickly linked the crime to Wheatley because of the report a few days earlier. Late Sunday night, they took Roy Frondorf to the Hancock County Jail, where he positively identified Wheatley as the man who was in his cab. Columbiana County Coroner Ernest Sturgis filed murder charges against Wheatley in East Liverpool Municipal Court the next morning. Sturgis called the crime, *"The worst example of a sadistic crime I've ever seen."*

Ohio authorities wanted to avoid a lengthy extradition process. They began working in conjunction with Hancock County, West Virginia officials, and on Wednesday, May 29th, they traveled with Wheatley to Wheeling, West Virginia. Wheatley had already waived his extradition rights and agreed to answer the complaint. Even though he had done this, the Circuit Court in Wheeling had to clear the custody of Hancock County Court. With that piece of legal *"red tape"* cleared away the group returned to East Liverpool in the late afternoon. Wheatley was arraigned before Judge Frank Grosshans on a charge of first degree murder, *"while in the act of rape or attempted rape."* Sheriff George Hayes then escorted Wheatley to the Columbiana County jail in Lisbon, Ohio.

For the next couple of months, the wheels of justice slowly ground on until it was announced on August 8th, that Wheatley would have his sanity investigated. He was sent to the Asylum for the Criminally Insane in Lima, Ohio to be diagnosed. The county court had placed him there for 30 days. Wheatley was returned to the county jail in early September and was ruled to be sane and able to stand trial. He was indicted by the Grand Jury for first degree murder on September 16th. The defense entered two pleas, not guilty and not guilty by reason of insanity.

Testimony began on November 19, 1946, before Judge Joel H. Sharp and a jury of four men and eight women. County Prosecutor Frank Springer led with the gruesome crime scene photos, to which Defense Attorney Robert Kapp objected, but was overruled. Kapp contended the pictures could have been altered. Photographer John Horsley testified that the photos were unaltered. Later, the fishermen Leo Payne and John Merriman testified to finding Mrs. Barrett's body.

Mr. William Barrett, husband of the victim, testified that he last saw his wife at 6:40 a.m. on May 23, 1946, when he left for work. Upon returning after work he found that she was gone, and reported it to the police. Under cross examination by co-defense counsel Louis Tobin, Barrett admitted he had looked in several downtown taverns for his wife. *(* He had actually waited about 36 hours before reporting her missing.)* Mrs. Louise Bratt testified about driving Mrs. Barrett downtown and paying her six dollars.

On day two, the prosecution called Roy Frondorf, the taxi driver, who testified about the pick up and the ride to the murder scene. He also related going to the funeral home and identifying Letha Barrett as the woman he had taken to the murder site. Then the Newell service station owner, Clarence Neese testified about the Wheatley's bizarre behavior and confession the night of May 23rd. Squire John Talbott testified of the shooting incident and subsequent arrest. One of the men who Wheatley met on the bridge, Lawrence Drumm, testified of the odd conversation that he and a friend had had with Wheatley on the bridge.

Dr. A.P. Faulkenstein was the pathologist for the Salem and Alliance, Ohio hospitals. He had performed the autopsy, and listed the cause of death as being due to shock following a diffuse hemorrhage, compound fractures of the facial bone structure, and exposure. After several other witnesses, mostly officials, testified as to their role in the investigation, the state rested.

The defense began on Thursday November 21st, with the defense attorneys introducing several witnesses who called into question the character and reputation of the victim. Prosecutor Springer objected, contending the victim was not on trial; however, Judge Sharp allowed the testimony. Other witnesses testified to helping subdue Wheatley the night of the murder, and how he *"had an odd look in his eyes."* On Friday, the defense called Doctor Robert Owens, a psychiatrist from Youngstown, Ohio, and began laying the groundwork for an insanity case. Owens testified that although Wheatley did not appear to be insane, he in fact had the intellectual capacity of a *"dull normal person."* He continued saying Wheatley had a recent period of memory lapses and latent epileptic tendencies which caused dizziness, but without loss of consciousness or convulsions. The doctor added that a person seized with an impulse of a primitive nature is incapable of direct planning, so the crime would not be premeditated. On the cross examination, Owens stated the type of amnesia coupled with that condition is caused by the person doing something that he could not bear to remember.

Judge Sharp asked Doctor Owens, *"Would a person be able to tell anyone about the crime if suffering from this type of amnesia?"*

Owens replied *"No, that would be contrary to the conception of amnesia."*

(* Doctor Owens was the third psychiatrist to have examined Wheatley. State psychiatrists from the Massillon and Lima Asylums had both found him to be sane.)

Wheatley then took the stand in his own defense. He testified that on the day of the murder, he had been drinking heavily and blacked out, not remembering anything until he *"came to"* in jail. He said he remembered drinking with his co-worker Emmett Howell, and to buying two bottles of brandy and a box of cartridges. He also remembered that he planned to go fishing later that evening. After that everything was blank. Prosecutor Springer asked him, *"When you are drunk, your mind doesn't go blank does it?"*

Wheatley replied, *"I wouldn't say that."*

The defense then called a surprise witness, Doctor James Fisher. Fisher was a general practitioner from New Cumberland, West Virginia. He had attended to Wheatley in the Hancock County Jail, the night Wheatley was arrested. Fisher stated that he had been a member of the Hancock County Mental Commission for the last 18 years. He testified that Wheatley's illness took the maniacal form of a manic-depressive. Defense co-counsel Louis Tobin asked Doctor Fisher, *"What does that mean?"*

Fisher replied, *"A person with that disease is inclined to be boastful, egotistical and has delusions of grandeur. Wheatley was ordering the sheriff around, and acting as if he were a king. He was unreasonable, obscene, and very excited."*

Under cross-examination by Prosecutor Springer, Doctor Fisher was asked, *"Do you agree with the state doctor who declared Wheatley sane?"*

Fisher replied *"Yes I do. I said he was insane that night."*

The defense then rested. The prosecution then called Doctor R.E. Bushong, chief psychiatrist at the Lima State Hospital for the Criminally Insane, to the stand. He testified that the Wheatley family had refused to let them use a truth drug. He said that he could find no evidence of symptoms of epilepsy, or a history of that disease. He did have amnesia, as a result of intoxication. His actions in the Hancock County Jail the night of the murder were consistent with intoxication.

After the closing arguments on the afternoon of Monday November 25th, the case went to the jury. The jury delivered their verdict at 11:00 a.m. on Tuesday morning, after deliberating for four hours and 45 minutes. Lawrence Abraham Wheatley was found guilty of murder in the second degree. The verdict carried a 20 years to life sentence. He would be eligible for parole after ten years. It was reported that the jury stood at ten votes for manslaughter and two for murder in the first degree at the end of Monday's deliberations. The murder in the second degree verdict had been a compromise.

In early December, the defense team filed for a new trial, but was denied by Judge Sharp. A few days later, Wheatley was transported to the Ohio State Penitentiary in Columbus, to begin his sentence.

Wheatley's wife Mary divorced him during his imprisonment and moved on with her life. Wheatley was eligible for parole in 1956, but was denied. He was serving his time at the Prison Farm in London, Ohio, when he was granted parole four years later. He was set free on August 26, 1960. He returned to Hancock County West Virginia, and remarried in 1963. He later moved to Weirton, West Virginia, where he lived the rest of his life, passing away in 1996 at age 76.

(*This is a cautionary tale of a person putting themselves in a situation they could have easily avoided. Letha Barrett should have never have got into the taxi or later gotten out of it. She should never have agreed to go with Wheatley, although the testimony showed that they knew each other, and may have done so before. Nevertheless, she certainly did not deserve to be brutally murdered. Lawrence Wheatley was probably an ordinary workingman, who allowed his addiction to alcohol to cause him to do things he would never have done without it. Unfortunately this type of story is all too common. What makes this story different than all the others? Letha Barrett was my paternal grandmother's older sister.)

Chapter 18
Fields of Flame

Oil and Gas Accidents in 1877- 1899

Starting around 2010, the oil and gas industry began to move into eastern Ohio and the surrounding area. They are drilling wells deep into the earth to tap the riches of the Marcellus and Utica oil shale. This, however, was not the first time oil men have drilled here. A walk through the farmland of this area will reveal the old wells, some of which are still producing.

Natural gas was first discovered in East Liverpool in the 1860s. Before long the town's streets were illuminated by gas street lights along with businesses and private homes. Local potteries drilled wells to tap the free energy for their kilns. Many times, the drillers found oil along with the gas. Even before the invention of the gasoline combustion engine, oil was valuable. The country was switching over to kerosene lamps to light their homes instead of whale oil. So when oil and gas was discovered here, men jumped at the chance to become millionaires. However, there was a certain amount of risk involved. A financial risk, and risk to life and limb.

The Island Run Disaster August 13, 1877

The Little Beaver Creek joins the Ohio River close to the Ohio – Pennsylvania border, about a quarter mile east of the city limits of East Liverpool. A short distance up the creek it turns west, leaving Pennsylvania and entering Ohio. Not much farther upstream, the creek again turns east into Pennsylvania, and then turns sharply west again, re-entering Ohio just east of Grimm's Bridge. On this bend, a small tributary known as Island Run enters from the east near a small island in the creek. In the 1870s oil was discovered along Island Run.

In August of 1877, William L. Rayl had a crew of men drilling a new well on a bench of land, above the stream. Rayl was a 57-year-old oilman known to some as Colonel Rayl. His crew included his son John Rayl, Charles Ammon, Bill McCready, and John McClinton and his young son. McClinton worked for the Jefferson Iron Works, of Steubenville, Ohio. He was there helping to set up the drilling rig.

Around 2:00 p.m. on Monday August 13th, the well came in. A powerful gush of gas shot oil high into the air, covering the men with the black sticky substance. A blacksmith forge was located about 100 feet away and the fire was burning. The men felt the forge was located at a safe distance. They were wrong.

Within an instant, the air became saturated with gas, and exploded into flames. The workmen had no way of escape, as the flames engulfed them. Charles Ammon whirled and ran stumbling down the steep rocky hillside trying to reach water. By the time he reached the creek his clothes were burned away, and he fell into the cooling water. Other men working at nearby wells raced to help the stricken men. Some men smothered the flames and cared for the injured, while others set about containing the burning well.

When rescuers reached Ammon, he was conscious but in terrible pain. He begged the men; *"Oh! Please kill me! Drown me, shoot me!"* The rescuers did neither. Ammon lingered in terrible pain for several hours before he died at around 11:00 p.m.

The explosion claimed another life around the same time, when William Rayl also passed away. He had been severely burned around his face and upper body. The other workers were also badly burned, including Rayl's son John, but they all would survive.

John Rayl would stay in the oil business and become a wealthy man. He would, however, carry the scars of those burns and the memories of the day he saw his father die on Island Run.

The Rayl-Karns Oil Well Disaster
September 23, 1899

The old Ridinger farm along the west side of the Lisbon Road (St. Rt. 45,) was part of an active oil field just outside of Wellsville, Ohio. The land was owned by Mrs. Slaughter of Allegheny, Pennsylvania. She leased the land to Vance Todd and J.H. Johnson of Wellsville. They in turn leased it to John Rayl of Wellsville, Harry Karns of Pittsburgh, Pennsylvania and S. Adams.

John Rayl was a wealthy long time oilman, who was well known in the area. He had seen "oil booms" before and was excited to be in on this new opportunity. The new field was quickly expanding with two active wells already in operation nearby.

The crew built a derrick 52 feet high and began drilling. They had picked a spot about 50 feet south of the successful 100 barrel Larson #2 well. The Rayl-Karns #1 well would prove to be the best in the field at 125 barrels a day.

On Saturday, September 23rd, the men had the feeling that they were getting close. Gas pressure built up about every twenty minutes, expelling a gush of oil. The men wanted to get the well under control quickly so they could "shoot it." This meant that they would lower explosives into the well and explode them so the rock would fracture and the oil flow better. They decided to drill just a little deeper and then they thought they would be deeper into the oil. But now they were at a standstill. The steam boiler that had been supplying the power to them and the Larson well had broken down and was being repaired. Rayl and his team were anxious, unwilling to wait for the repairs. They decided to start up their own boiler. No one thought there was any danger even though the boiler was only twenty feet from the well head.

They had placed a blowout preventing device known as an "oil saver" on the well, so everything would be okay. Rayl had just lighted the boiler when Charles Wilkerson noticed that the sand plug around the drill pipe was being forced up the shaft. He stepped onto it to try to hold it down and yelled to Rayl, *"Put out the fire."* It was too late. The enormous pressure forced the plug out, filling the air with oil and gas.

The oil shot about 75 feet higher than the derrick, and within seconds everything within an area of about an acre was covered with oil. The gushing oil was being pushed into the air by a powerful flow of natural gas. Before anyone could re-act, the gas was ignited by the nearby boiler located just a few feet away. Within an instant, the whole area exploded in flames.

Fortunately, a rope perimeter had been established to keep the many onlookers at a safe distance. A group of around one hundred people had come to watch the "shooting of the well." They scattered in every direction when the well exploded.

The oil workers, however, had nowhere to go. They were all engulfed in flames and began to run. Harry Karns was able to run a short distance and jump into a water tank. John Williams tried to run to nearby Little Yellow Creek, but he became confused from the shock. He ran twice around the nearby Ridinger house. Then he ran up a nearby hill before falling to the ground. He finally rolled down the hill and onto the roadway. Rescuers rushed to him and extin-

Scene of the disaster

guished the flames. He had been horribly burned and, sadly did not survive his injuries, dying at 9:00 p.m. that night.

Charles Wilkinson also ran up the hill, falling at the top and rolling all the way to the road. Somehow, he regained his feet and staggered against a fence, where he died. John Rayl and Charles Rogers were caught by nearby oil workers who smothered the flames, saving their lives.

The Wellsville Fire Department was soon on the scene. Along with a number of civilians, they extinguished the fire with their Babcock chemical fire extinguishers. They were in great danger, for the well could erupt again before they brought the flames under control. Workers from the Larson wells quickly contained flow of oil and piped it off.

During the early stages of the disaster, H.B. Luntz had his wagon of nitroglycerin standing by, waiting to "shoot the well." He immediately went and drove it away from danger. If not for him, the resulting explosion could have also destroyed the Larson well, killing those men as well.

The Rayl-Karns well rig was destroyed. Only the metal parts remained; the loss was at least $500. The fire had spread to the Larson #2 well, but it was only slightly damaged. An area of about 150 yards radius was burned.

All day Sunday, great crowds of spectators arrived by streetcar from East Liverpool and Wellsville. An estimated crowd of seven or eight thousand people came walking up the dusty road carrying children and pushing baby carriages. Everyone had to see the great disaster. One enterprising man set up a concession stand selling sandwiches and soft drinks. He did a brisk business.

John Williams, age 35, had lived in East Liverpool with his wife and is buried in Georgetown, Pennsylvania. Charles Wilkinson, age 21, was from Jewett, Ohio. He was living in Wellsville at the time of his tragic death. The three other injured men were all badly burnt on their upper bodies, but they would recover. The men were sent home since there was no hospital in the area.

Without a doubt, as John Rayl laid suffering from his painful injuries, he had vivid memories, of an earlier time. Memories of a hot August day, twenty two years earlier. He probably thought back, to that time when he was working at the well at Island Run. To a similar accident that had killed two men including his father. How could he ever forget? After all, he had long carried those horrible scars from that dreadful day.

By the next day, this disaster was no longer news-worthy, but for the victims their lives would never be the same. The well was soon back in operation, hardly missing a beat. It was after all the best well in the field.

Chapter 19
The Old Mill is on Fire!
The Rock Springs Park Tragedy
June 5, 1915

It was a warm Saturday evening, on June 5, 1915, and nearly 10,000 people had crowded into the park to enjoy the beginning of the summer recess. The public schools of East Liverpool and Wellsville in Ohio and Chester and Newell in West Virginia had sponsored their annual school picnic at the Rock Springs Park in Chester, West Virginia.

The Rock Springs Park had developed into a favorite destination for young and old in the tri-state area. For many years it had been just a pleasant picnic area. In 1897, a bridge over the Ohio River was

The Old Mill at Rock Springs Park

built, linking East Liverpool to the fast growing community of Chester, West Virginia. The bridge carried streetcar tracks, and the owner of Rock Springs Park quickly developed his property into a "trolley park." Trolley parks were amusement parks that were springing up across America in the late 1800s. They were located at the end of a streetcar line to take advantage of the extra leisure time and money many Americans now enjoyed.

The park first opened on Memorial Day in 1897. It really began to develop after 1900, when C.A. Smith bought the property. Smith was also the owner of the streetcar company that serviced the park. By 1915, the park included a merry-go-round, roller coasters, the chute-de-chutes ride, a swimming pool, a lake and a large ballroom. One of the most popular rides was the Old Mill Ride. Built in 1903, it was located near the front entrance of the park. What may have been called a tunnel of love, it was a boat ride that traveled through darkened passages connecting with three buildings.

Large three seated boats holding up to nine people traveled with the current along a canal 1500 feet long. Seven lighted rooms, each painted with historical murals were connected by darkened passageways. A large millwheel provided the current to propel the boats though the ride. The wheel was turned by an electrical dynamo or (generator.)

Just before 7:00 p.m., a total of five boats were inside the tunnels, when flames suddenly erupted at the entrance to the ride. The generator stopped, the water quit flowing and the lights went out. Two men, John Hughes and Andrew Biaschak, jumped into the canal and waded into the dark tunnel on the exit side. Once inside they found a stalled boat filled with children, and they pulled it through the exit doors to safety. They tried to go back in, but the flames had now engulfed the entire end of the frame building, blocking both the entrance and exit doors. Four boats remained inside the structure. By now the frantic mothers and fathers were beginning to panic. Men, brave and willing, broke the windows, and called out to the trapped riders. When they heard the frightened cries for help they broke down doors and even pulled the siding from the building to allow rescue. The occupants of three more boats were pulled from the blazing structure. All this happened within only a couple of minutes as hundreds even thousands of park goers began to descend on the Old Mill. Meanwhile, park employee Robert McElravy had rushed to a telephone. He made a call to the Chester Volunteer Fire Department but got no answer. He then called the East Liverpool Fire Department.

There was one final boat holding seven children still inside the building. While some people were being rescued, and phone calls to the fire department were being made, this boat slowly made its way toward the exit. The front seat held two boys; in the center seat were three girls; Hyacinth Mackey, Eva Dales, and Glenna Stout. Two boys occupied the third seat. Twelve-year-old Albert Rayner was one of the boys in the boat, but which seat he sat in is unknown. As the boat made its way slowly toward the flames, people were yelling out for the children to get out of the boat, and go back. Whether they became confused or did not understand is not known. People watched in horror as the boat slowly entered the inferno. Shrieks of horror filled the air, and women fainted as the children were snatched from the flaming hulk, their clothes ablaze. The flames were quickly smothered, but four of the children were horribly burned. The stricken children were quickly placed in waiting ambulances and rushed to the

Engine Company 1, East Liverpool Fire Department

small hospital of Doctor Wentz, in Chester. A man wrapped his coat around the burned body of Albert Rayner, and carried him to the ambulance. Albert handed the man back his coat saying, *"Goodbye, I guess I won't be seeing you again."* When his parents reached the hospital, Albert's face brightened and he said, *"Hello Daddy, Don't you worry Daddy I'll be alright. Hello Mother dear I love you. Daddy I love you. Mother I love you. Don't you worry, I'll be alright."* The brave boy would die at ten o'clock that night.

The East Liverpool Fire Department received the call at 7:08 p.m. and responded immediately. Chief Arthur Aungst took two men in his automobile and headed across the bridge. He was followed within a minute by Engine Company 1, from Central Station. Arthur Aungst had been the fire chief for the last three years, since being lured away from the Alliance, Ohio fire department. He was a proud, confident professional. He had brought many improvements to the East Liverpool department, but had rubbed many the wrong way. He was a man who was used to giving orders, and was used to having them obeyed. Upon arriving at the scene of the fire, Chief Aungst quickly assessed the situation. The children had all been rescued from the building, and a quick check revealed that there were no more victims. A hose line was put into service, and the firefighters went to work trying to save the remaining two sections of the ride.

Fire Chief Arthur Aungst

A few minutes later, the Chester Volunteer Fire Department arrived at the fire. The Chester men had had trouble finding a team of horses to pull the fire wagon. With thousands of people crowded around watching, the situation became tense. Headed by Chief Eugene Arnett, the Chester department had been in existence for only eighteen months. Their equipment was poor and their training not too much better, but they were proud men. The Chester men tapped into the park's water system, and began to spray water onto the blazing first section of the Old Mill. This, however, cut down the water pressure considerably. Chief Aungst went to them and told them to shut down these extra hose lines so the pressure in the East Liverpool line would be restored. After a minute or two delay, the Chester department complied with Aungst's order.

Chief Arnett then had his men hook their hoses to a hydrant on Carolina Avenue outside the park. However, they did not have enough hose to reach the fire, so they borrowed 500 feet from the East Liverpool truck. This was unknown to Chief Aungst. Once again they turned their attention to the first building. Chief Aungst, by this time, had given up on that structure and was concentrating on saving the other sections. Once again the East Liverpool chief went to the Chester men and gave them orders on how they should fight the fire. This time the Chester chief Eugene Arnett refused to listen. A turf war erupted. Arnett told Chief Aungst, *"Go back to East Liverpool and mind your own business. We are running things here."* Not wanting to get into an argument during the fire, Aungst returned to his own force, which included several Chester volunteers. Advancing their hose line through the canal, the East Liverpool force managed to bring the blaze under control.

With the fire now under control, Chief Aungst gave the order for the East Liverpool firefighters to gather up their equipment and get ready to leave. Going over to Chief Arnett, Aungst told him to move his hose line to the hydrant East Liverpool had been using and to return the hose they had borrowed. Arnett exploded. Shouting at Aungst he said, *"If you disconnect that line I'll have you arrested."*

Becoming more abusive, Arnett wanted to fight Aungst. It took direct orders from Chief Aungst to keep some of the East Liverpool firefighters from obliging him. Looking sternly at Arnett, Chief Aungst said, *"I'll give you five minutes to disconnect that line."* The hose line was disconnected and the East Liverpool men returned to Ohio.

The Chester firefighters remained at the park far into the night. As Chief Arnett was surveying the scene, he approached a group of men which happened to include a reporter from the *East Liverpool Morning Tribune*. Grasping at a chance to tell his side of the story, Arnett began to lament over his troubles. *"The Rock Springs Company will pay well for this night,"* he said. *"This is outside our limits. We didn't have to come to this fire."* Opening up his rubber fire coat he exclaimed, *"See, I've ruined a thirty dollar suit of clothes."* Now on a roll, Arnett switched to his fight with Arthur Aungst. *"He tried to order me around. I wouldn't stand for that. I told him where he could get off. I told him to mind his own business. He didn't have any right being here anyway. The park company should have called us in the first place."* Then with a triumphant air, he declared *"Chief Aungst better not come to Chester again or he will get his head punched."*

One of the other men from East Liverpool stood up for Chief Aungst, protesting vigorously. The conversation began getting tense and the man decided to withdraw. A Chester volunteer firefighter then said to the reporter, *"The first I knew of the fire was when I saw the East Liverpool truck go past my house."*

The cause of the blaze was never determined; however, owner C.A. Smith thought a discarded cigarette had sparked the deadly $12,000 blaze. A number of other people felt that the fire started in the room with the dynamo.

Meanwhile, seventeen-year-old Glenna Stout of Newell had suffered terrible burns to her face and upper body, as did fourteen-year-old Eva Dales, also from Newell. Stout would succumb to her injuries just before midnight, but Dales would linger another twenty-four hours before she too passed away. With the death of Albert Rayner, that left only Hyacinth Mackey still clinging to life. Miss Mackey was thought to be the least injured of the four victims; she remained in serious condition at the Wentz Hospital.

Before the ashes had time to cool, the Chester city government was in action. Mayor M.M. Swearingen apologized to the East Liverpool fire chief, Arthur Aungst. The mayor, along with the city coun-

Ruins of the Old Mill

cil, also called for an investigation into Chief Eugene Arnett's actions at the fire.

Interviewed by the local newspapers, park owner C.A. Smith had nothing but praise for the East Liverpool Fire Department and for Chief Aungst. Smith said, *"I am heartily disgusted with the treatment given to Chief Aungst and his men."* He went on to say, *"It was proper for East Liverpool to be in charge since they had much more experience, and the majority of people in the park were from East Liverpool. We called them. It is our property and as it is outside the Chester limits, we have a right to call who we please."*

East Liverpool Mayor V.A. Schreiber weighed in, saying, *"This is not the first time there had been trouble between the two departments. And as of right now no alarms in Chester will be answered by the East Liverpool department. This will end when the members of the Chester department start treating the East Liverpool department with the courtesy due to human beings."*

On Tuesday, June 8th, the Chester City Council announced that it would be conducting a probe into the actions of the volunteer fire department during the fire. The mayor and some councilmen felt they may have to dissolve the existing department and form a new one. However, the council was not united in their efforts. Councilman J.C. Cunningham, himself a volunteer fireman, stated that he did not think the Chester firefighters had done anything wrong. His only criticism was that he felt Chief Arnett had acted *"too hastily."* He was also critical of the East Liverpool department, saying, *"They did things they had no right to do."* Cunningham continued, *"The Chester Volunteer Fire Department was organized and incorporated under the laws of the State of West Virginia. I don't think the mayor or council has the legal power to dissolve it."*

Chief Eugene Arnett released his statement the next day. In it he was the model of cooperation and professionalism, in the face of an overbearing Chief Aungst. He said that Aungst was lying about what had happened. His statement passed without comment.

At the inquest on June 15th, Chief Arnett requested that the probe of the fire department be postponed. He wanted actual charges to be filed. The rules governing the Chester Volunteer Fire Department stated that the position of fire chief was regulated by the membership and not the city. William Hocking, the manager of Rock Springs Park, asked if a private citizen could file a charge. Mayor Swearingen said he thought so, although he was not sure the city had the power to conduct a trial.

Two days later, East Liverpool Mayor V.A. Schreiber, issued orders to Chief Aungst to refuse to answer any alarm in the city of Chester until this situation was satisfactorily resolved.

That same day, Chester Mayor M.M. Swearingen and city council passed an ordinance dissolving the current fire department and forming a new one. The new department was required to work under and take orders from any fire official from the city of East Liverpool. It passed a first reading by a 3-2 vote. Councilmen W.L. Smith, James Paisley, and Freshwater voted in favor, with I.N. Owen joining Cunningham in opposition. It would require passage at two more sessions. Chief Arnett and several of the volunteer firefighters vowed to fight this ordinance.

Hyacinth Mackey lost her struggle for life on June 20th. Doctors thought the sixteen-year-old girl had been improving slightly over the last few days. However, she took a turn for the worst and passed away at 8:00 p.m. Sunday evening, bringing the death toll to four.

The new fire ordinance finally passed on July 1st, and Chief Arnett struck back two weeks later. He served a writ on the mayor and city council, requiring them to appear in the Chancery Court in Wheeling on July 27th. After serving the writ, Arnett asked Councilman Smith if it would be all right if he took the fire wagon to an alarm if needed. Smith replied that no one would stop them but that the city no longer recognized their department. He also said that the street commissioner, Mr. Martin, had the city's team of horses locked in the stable. Arnett replied, *"It would be no problem to break the lock."*

Councilman Freshwater angrily shot back, *"It would be your responsibility if you do that. Your department no longer exists as a city department."* With the conversation growing more heated, Mayor Swearingen adjourned the meeting.

A temporary restraining order was issued on July 27th, returning things to the "status quo," while the case was decided. The "status quo" would continue well into the new-year, as no one seemed to be in much of a hurry to resolve the issue.

As with many political struggles, the vote of the people brings a settlement that the courts sometimes do not. East Liverpool mayor V.A. Schreiber lost reelection and was replaced on January 1, 1916 by W.F. Orr. Mayor Swearingen of Chester was replaced by W.B. Dalrymple in April. Only James Paisley continued as a Chester councilman, as all the others either lost or decided not to run.

On July 5, 1916, Mayor Orr decided to end East Liverpool's involvement by ordering that no fire calls be answered in Chester. An agreement had been worked out where Chester would pay for fire protection, but they never did. The ban was extended to all areas outside the city limits two days later. This caused a number of property owners to enter into private contracts with the city of East Liverpool, for fire protection. These contracts remained in force for many years.

Although the court in Wheeling had still not rendered its decision, the new Chester city government had cooled to the whole mess. Most of the city officials probably felt it was not their fight. So on July 12, 1916, after several weeks of behind the scene debate, the Chester city council and the Chester Volunteer Fire Department came to an agreement on all past grievances.

A few weeks later Chief Arthur Aungst decided it was time to move on. A mover and shaker in the fire protection business he was always looking for greener pastures. The fact that the new mayor had cooled toward him also may have played into his decision. Aungst resigned on August 2nd to accept a position with the Chalmers Motor Car Company in Cleveland. He would soon leave there and return to the firefighting profession in Pennsylvania, and later in South America. Assistant Chief Tom Bryan was promoted to fire chief on August 28th, a position he would hold until his death in 1940.

The last of the major players to leave the stage was Chester fire chief, Eugene Arnett. Arnett had remained as chief although his term should have expired. In those days the chief held a one year term. However, with the lawsuit and temporary injunction in place, his term was continued. That came to an end on December 4, 1916 when Arnett resigned. He had accepted a position as a special policeman with the Crucible Steel Company in Midland, Pennsylvania. He planned to move to that nearby community.

With that the court battle just disappeared, and the Chester Volunteer Fire Department continued as before. They have been serving the city of Chester for over 100 years. The turf battle that took place so many years ago was tragic, but it played no part in the horrible deaths of those four children. That part of this story was completed before either fire department arrived to fight the blaze. The working relationship between East Liverpool Fire Department and the surrounding volunteer fire departments has had its ups and downs throughout the years. And although there have been disagreements, none have ever reached the magnitude of the fight the day the Old Mill burned.

Chapter 20
Poison for Medicine!
The Strange Life of Laura Christy - 1879-1937

William Christy arose early on January 11, 1926 and ate a hearty breakfast with his new bride. Although they may not have thought about it, today was their anniversary of sorts. They had been married a full week. The couple ate pancakes and fried eggs and drank coffee that morning. An ironing board was the main topic of conversation, and William said he would go to town to buy one.

It had been a whirlwind relationship, although it could hardly be called a romance. The couple had met one another for the first time on the evening of January 4th, only a week earlier. They were married the next morning.

The 56-year-old Christy had been in town just a few weeks, although he had lived in East Liverpool at one time. He was known to be a peddler by trade; however, during the last few years he had turned to the ministry. He had been living in Akron, Ohio with his adult children since his wife had passed away. There he and his sons started a ministry known as the United Christian Missionary Workers of the United States of America, with headquarters in Akron. Organized on a military basis, Carl Christy was listed as the General-in-Chief, while his father William was a Brigadier General. Another son, A.W. Christy was the National Treasurer. William was ordained as an Elder in the organization in late 1922.

During the Thanksgiving holiday, William was visited by an old friend from East Liverpool, George Crawford. The two had met several years ago when William was plying his trade as a peddler in the East Liverpool-Wellsville area. At the time of Crawford's visit, the ministry was beginning to expand out of Akron. Carl was planning to travel to St. Louis, Missouri to operate there. Perhaps that is why William decided to return to the East Liverpool area. What is known is that William Christy returned to East Liverpool shortly after his visit with Crawford, and purchased a small house on December 4th. The house was a two room structure on Flint Street in the East End section of town. Located on a parcel of land rented from the Laughlin Pottery Company, it was not much more than a shack. Christy paid fifty dollars for the house. One month later, on January 4, 1926, Christy was visiting at the home of George Crawford. He told Mrs. Crawford that he would pay her twenty-five dollars if she would find him a wife. Mrs. Crawford immediately thought of her recently widowed cousin, Laura Ebert.

Returning to the Crawford home that evening, William met Laura for the first time. Laura was a very plain looking, heavyset 48-year-old woman, who was blind in one eye. After talking a short time, Christy proposed marriage and Laura consented. The next morning the couple made a trip to Beaver, Pennsylvania, where they were married. They returned to the two-room shack on Flint Street and began their marriage. Christy's son Carl was staying with them, but after a couple of days he departed for St. Louis, leaving the newlyweds alone.

Laura Christy's life had not been an easy one. It could best be described as tumultuous. She was born on April 9, 1879, the second child of Jacob and Emma Whippler in Steubenville, Ohio. Her mother Emma died in 1882. Jacob was unable or unwilling to care for his three young children, so he sent them to live with relatives. Four-year-old Laura, at least, lived with her maternal grandparents, Mr. and Mrs. Moses Bennett. "Coal Oil" Bennett as he was known, was a disciplinarian whom Laura clashed with from the very beginning. The more he punished her the more she fought back. Defiant and willful, Laura refused to go to school, and after enduring brutal punishments which did nothing to break the rebellious spirit within her, she finally left home at age fourteen.

Completely incorrigible, her life continued to spiral down. Laura became a regular in some of the most depraved dives in East Liverpool. Her older brother Charles tried his best to change her lifestyle but was unsuccessful, and finally even he gave up on her.

Laura's antics finally landed her behind bars in 1898 or 1899. She spent about a year in the workhouse in Canton, Ohio on a charge for disorderly conduct. Sometime after getting out Laura married for the first time. Laura was around twenty, and her husband, Jesse Sears, was at least twenty years older than her. Sears was a night watchman at the Louthan Company stilt works in East Liverpool. The couple lived on a houseboat, one of many that used to be tied along East Liverpool's riverfront. On the evening of May 5, 1907, Sears dropped dead on his way to work. He was believed to have died from a heart attack. No wife came forth to claim his body. His funeral expenses were paid for by his employer and friends.

A few years later Laura married Charles O'Neal (O'Neill) and the couple moved to Cincinnati, where Charles found work as a teamster. Within a few days Charles' family in East Liverpool received word that he had died. A family member left at once to help Laura in this time of grief. Upon arriving in Cincinnati, they found Charles alive and well. Laura laughed it off as a misunderstanding and a joke. The O'Neal family was not amused. Two weeks later a second letter was received from Laura stating that Charles was dead, and she was bringing his body back to be buried in East Liverpool. When Laura arrived with her late husband's body, his family requested an autopsy. Laura became very agitated, saying he had died from pneumonia. When the family insisted on an autopsy, Laura flew

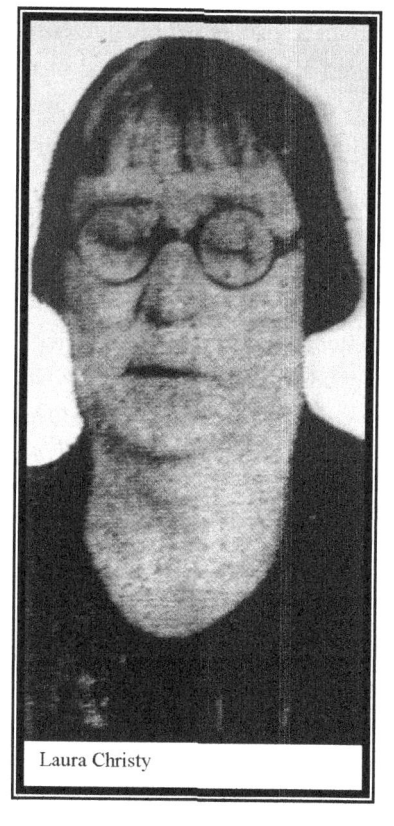

Laura Christy

into a rage, insisting that she had already had Charles embalmed. The family relented, and Charles was buried in the Spring Grove Cemetery.

Laura was a free woman again, but that would not last. Over the next fifteen years men came and went; some she married and some she just lived with. Many times they were bigamous relationships. There is no evidence the men ever knew about each other.

Laura married a man named George Holt and lived with him about a year when he suddenly died. Laura later said he had been injured at work but had died of typhoid fever. A marriage to an unidentified Steubenville man ended with her arrest on a bigamy charge, which resulted in a short prison sentence.

Once released, Laura resumed her pursuit of the opposite sex. She married Charles Graham, a pottery worker who lived on Dresden Avenue. They had been married only a few days when Charles became violently ill. Charles became suspicious of his new wife, and left her. After a few days without her loving care, he was feeling better. He never returned to her. *(*He went on to live a long and for most part, heathy life. Apparently free from the pneumonia, typhoid fever, heart attacks, or whatever else that seemed to plague Laura's husbands.)* Undeterred, she met Jacob Barnhart, and they lived together for a time. Laura later claimed they had gotten married, but soon separated. After the breakup Jacob committed suicide, that is, according to Laura.

Laura soon met another man who was not identified in Hannibal, Ohio. The couple lived for a time in Sistersville, West Virginia before coming to East Liverpool. They finally settled in Newell, West Virginia where they lived together although they were never married. Before too long, the man was declared to be insane. He was taken to the West Virginia State Hospital for the Insane in Elizabeth, West Virginia where he would die. His name was never released. *(*It just makes you wonder.)*

Eventually, Laura married Fredrick Harmon in Athens, New York. The couple lived together happily for a few years, according to Laura. That is until Laura began having trouble with her sisters-in-law. During one argument, Fredrick's sisters revealed the fact that they were all first cousins. This must have been a shock to the happy couple. Why Fredrick and Laura did not know this was never explained. *(*Perhaps they had missed the family reunions.)* Laura and Fredrick split up, but they were never divorced.

(*It is impossible to keep a chronological record of these marriages and various other men in Laura's life. The record keeping was very poor in those days. Much of this came from Laura's own testimony, and she sometimes even confused herself.)

After a time, Laura met and married John F. Ebert, a 65-year-old widower. The couple settled down on Harrison Street in Newell, West Virginia. They lived together for a while *(*Laura later told the police it was years. However it was a much shorter time.).* Around Halloween of 1925, John became ill. Doctor C.R. Campbell made three or four house calls to the Ebert home and diagnosed the problem to be congestion of the lungs, and mumps. John responded well to Doctor Campbell's treatments, and after his last visit the doctor told Laura he did not need to return. He told her to keep giving him the medicine and he should make a full recovery. John died suddenly on November 7th, and Laura had him buried the next day. Doctor Campbell was shocked when he heard of the death.

Two months later the grieving widow married William Christy, and the newlyweds moved into their honeymoon home on Flint Street. After eating his breakfast that cold January morning, William went downtown to buy the ironing board. He returned home about 10:00 a.m. complaining of an upset stomach, and not feeling very well. Laura helped him into bed and applied a hot water bag and heated plates to his stomach. He continued to suffer from severe stomach pains and after a while, he asked for something to relieve the pain. Laura gave him a dose of baking powder on the end of a knife along with a glass of water. As the day went on, William's pains grew worse, and he began to vomit. Laura later said she tried to get a doctor but could not find one. At about 3:00 a.m. Wednesday morning Laura talked to the night watchman at the nearby Laughlin No. 1 Pottery, who called the Sturgis Funeral Home ambulance, which transported William Christy to the hospital. Christy arrived at the hospital about 4:30 a.m. and Doctor Albert J. Michels began to treat him. Christy grew worse throughout the day; he was unable to hold anything in his stomach, vomiting up everything they gave him. At 6:20 p.m. Wednesday, January 13th, William Christy died. Doctor Michels was immediately suspicious and called the police.

Laura had not gone to the hospital with her stricken husband, but had, instead, taken care of some business. Early that morning she went to the bank and withdrew $200 dollars from their account. She then traveled downtown where she rented a room in the Gilbert Boarding House on W. 6th Street. Around 9:00 a.m. she made her way to the hospital to briefly check on William's condition, but did not linger. Laura then went on a shopping spree, purchasing a trunk for $15, a travel bag for one dollar, silverware for $10 dollars, clothes and shoes for around $50 dollars, a $3.50 bracelet and some other items. Later that day, after hearing of Christy's death, she gave orders to have the body taken to the Miller Funeral Home to be embalmed. Laura then returned to Flint Street to finish packing. She had decided to go to Cleveland.

Because of Doctor Michels' suspicion, the police ordered the body to be held and not embalmed. The police also began searching for Laura Christy. Police Chief Hugh McDermott, along with Captain Mason Conley and Patrolman Lister began searching the city. At nearly midnight, Officer Lister found Laura near the Newell Bridge, and placed her under arrest. Taken to the women's cell of the jail at City Hall, Laura was locked up for the night.

Police Chief Hugh McDermott

The next morning, Columbiana County Coroner J.M. Van Fossen arrived at City Hall to help question the woman. The police had quickly gathered information on some of Laura's previous marriages.

As soon as the news of William's death got out, relatives of her previous husbands began calling the police.

Sobbing heavily, Laura answered Chief McDermott and Coroner Van Fossen's questions. She admitted she had been married to Jesse Sears and John Ebert, and that both were now dead. She also admitted she had married her cousin Fredrick Harmon in the state of New York.

"Do you know that Mr. Christy died from the effects of poison?" asked McDermott.

"No sir, I do not. Oh I'm sorry but I'm not to blame. I ate the same food and some of the pancake batter is still in the house," exclaimed Laura.

"You married John Ebert even though you knew you had a husband in New York," asked Van Fossen.

Laura replied, *"Yes I did but I didn't know it was against the law."*

The questioning was suspended about noon, and an autopsy was performed that afternoon on William Christy's body. Chief McDermott announced that Laura would be held on charges of suspicion until the cause of William Christy's death has been determined.

The autopsy was performed at the Miller Funeral Home, by Coroner Van Fossen. He was assisted by Dr. Albert Michels and City Health Commissioner, Dr. John Frasier. The doctors removed Christy's heart and stomach which they sent to the laboratory at Ohio State University for chemical analysis. They also sent a sample of his blood.

Chief McDermott had already made up his mind. He told the *East Liverpool Review-Tribune*, *"Mrs. Christy has the brains of a child. This is shown in the purchase of a necklace, a bracelet, silverware, a trunk, and other items on Wednesday, while her husband was dying in the hospital. It will not take long for a lunacy commission to judge her mentally unbalanced. She should be committed to the State Hospital for the Criminally Insane."*

Meanwhile, more information was coming into police headquarters about the many men in Laura's life. A Mrs. Densmore, an aunt of Charles O'Neal, revealed the strange tale concerning *his* death in 1911. Police interviewed George Crawford in the hospital where he was recovering from being accidently poisoned in his work place. Crawford revealed how Christy had paid his wife to find him a wife. He told police he suspected something when he heard that Christy was dead. *"That woman has been married six or seven times and most of the men died suddenly or died under mysterious circumstances."* However, Crawford denied ever hearing Laura Christy make threatening statements as was being reported.

The police continued to interrogate Laura about the suspected poisoning of her husband. Finally exhausted, she broke down and admitted she had given him arsenic. She said she had given it to him because he asked her to. She claimed he had told her that he had taken small doses of arsenic before, to alleviate pain. However, as the questioning continued, her story began to change. Laura finally confessed that she had given Christy three doses of arsenic, starting at 10 a.m. when he returned from shopping, then again at around 5 p.m. and later, around 10 o'clock that night. Laura was sobbing heavily when she blurted out, *"I have told you everything, do whatever you want with me!"* She was taken back to her jail cell.

The East Liverpool police searched the two-room shack on Flint Street, looking for the box of rat poison that the woman said she used. They did not find it. Later Laura told them she may have burned it up by accident. They did confiscate the trunk and other items she had purchased the day her husband died.

On Friday, one of Christy's daughters arrived in East Liverpool to claim her father's body. It was then that the family was told of the suspected murder. Christy's body was taken back to Akron and buried next to their mother.

Columbiana County Prosecutor Robert Brookes led the interrogation on that same day. The goal was to wring a confession out of her that she gave Christy the arsenic without his knowledge. Brookes first questioned her about her previous husbands, trying to fill in the many gaps in the unfolding story.

Then with a hardened gaze Brookes said, *"You gave him the poison without his knowledge!"*

Laura cried out, *"I gave it to him because he asked for it."*

"You gave it to him telling him it was baking powder and it would relieve his pain" said Captain Mason Conley.

"No! No! He made me give it to him. To get me into trouble," she sobbed.

"Did you kill Ebert?" one of the men asked.

"No I didn't," she cried. *"Dr. Campbell gave him medicine that didn't agree with him."*

"Where did you get the arsenic?" Brookes demanded.

"I bought it at a drug store in the Diamond, from an old man." Laura said.

The druggist was sent for and Laura identified him, but the druggist denied ever selling her the arsenic, or even having ever seen her before.

Brookes and Chief McDermott then took Laura into another room and continued to question her. After a while they took her next door into Municipal Court Judge Jesse Hanley's office. Judge Hanley read the charge of murder against her. He asked her, *"Are you guilty or not guilty?"*

"I don't know what to say. I have never been in trouble before," she said. *"I didn't mean to poison my husband."*

Judge Hanley told her, *"You can plead not guilty and let the Grand Jury investigate your case."*

Laura replied, *"Well I guess that will be alright."*

With that, Laura was removed from East Liverpool, and taken to the county jail in Lisbon, Ohio.

Word was received on Saturday morning from the chemist at Ohio State University. He told police officials that he would not perform any tests on the organ and blood samples. He said there was not sufficient interest in this case to warrant a chemical analysis. Prosecutor Brookes was livid. He authorized East Liverpool Health Commissioner Dr. John Frazier to demand that the tests be performed at once. The officials at Ohio State reluctantly agreed to conduct the tests, saying they would report the findings.

Laura received no visitors over the weekend, and appeared nervous to her guards. She, however, had no loss of appetite eating her meals with "apparent relish."

Charles Whippler was called to the police station on Sunday to answer questions about Laura and her past. The story he told was one of despair. Her older brother told of her being a willful, troubled child, unlike either him or their younger sister, Anna. He said that Laura was completely incorrigible and had left the family at the age of fourteen. He said that she had sunk into such depravity that he and other family members refused to allow her into their homes. Charles said, *"Several times when I would see her I would remonstrate with her, but all in vain."* He told the police about all the men in Laura's life that he knew about, adding one or two to the list.

Charles continued, *"My sister is as good as dead to me. I will engage no attorney to defend her. If she has done wrong she should be punished. Of course I feel sorry for her but I washed my hands of her years ago."*

Laura herself was talking to the authorities, adding to her list of husbands which by now had reached at least eight, along with three or four men she just lived with.

On Monday, January 18th, the case broke. During an afternoon session with Prosecutor Brookes, Police Chief McDermott, and Sheriff George Wright, Laura confessed to both the murders of William Christy and John Ebert.

"Mrs. Christy, we want you to tell us the truth," said McDermott. *"You have told us several stories and none of them agree. Be truthful this time and you'll feel better after you make a clean breast of everything. Did you poison Ebert?"*

Laura began to cry and buried her face in a handkerchief. *"Yes I did. I gave him arsenic because he was mean to me."*

"How many doses did you give him?" asked McDermott.

"Only one," she said.*"He was taking capsules from Dr. Campbell. I emptied one and filled it with arsenic. He died a few days later."*

McDermott pressed on, *"You told us a few days ago you gave Mr. Christy arsenic because he asked for it. Is that true?"*

"No he didn't ask for it. I gave it to him telling him it was baking powder, and it would help his indigestion. Oh! I didn't think it would kill him, I thought it would make him real sick," she said.

The men then asked about her other deceased husbands.

"Did you kill Jesse Sears? "No I did not," she replied.

"Did you kill Charles O'Neal?" "He died of pneumonia. The rest of that story is lies," Laura insisted.

"Did you kill Jacob Barnhart?" "He committed suicide after we separated," she said.

"Now we believe you killed George Holt!"

Laura then began to talk. *"No, I didn't. He died a natural death. I then married Charles Graham. But I didn't live with him very long. I then went to Athens, New York and married Fredrick Harmon. Then I found out he was my cousin. I returned to East Liverpool and married John Ebert. About four years ago."*

"Ebert beat me often, and made life miserable. I gave him poison but I guess I did not think what I was doing. He had a little over $300 in the bank, and no insurance. I paid the burial expenses and had about $200 left. I spent it before I married Christy."

In explaining how she and William Christy got married, she said, *"Mrs. Crawford came to my rooming house one night and told me about Christy, who wanted a wife. I met him at the Crawford home on Monday, January 4th, and he proposed marriage. I consented and we* went to Beaver the next day, where the marriage was performed. We started housekeeping in the two room shack which Christy had been living in near the Laughlin Pottery. He made life unbearable for me, and after his son John left for St. Louis, we were alone."

"On Tuesday, January 12th, he came home suffering pains in his stomach. I had arsenic in the house which I purchased for rat poison. I gave him a dose of this, telling him it was baking powder, and it would relieve his pain. Later in the day I gave him two more doses and early the next morning sent him to the hospital."

A photograph of Laura Christy ran in the Tuesday edition of the *Review-Tribune*, as well as newspapers statewide. After seeing the photograph in the Coshocton Ohio *Tribune*, Mr. Isaac Randles, a farmer from nearby Layland in Coshocton County, Ohio, came forth, claiming he also was married to Laura Christy. Randles produced a marriage license that showed they had been married on March 30, 1925. Using the name Elsie (maybe her middle name) May Harmon, they were married by Rev. C.J. McGee in the United Brethren Church. The couple had met through a matrimonial service. Elsie/Laura left on June 16th, saying she was going back to Athens, New York to see about some furniture. She was also going to pick up some money she had inherited from an aunt. She never returned, and two other husbands were now dead.

With her confession of the murder of John Ebert, West Virginia authorities began the process of exhuming his remains for the purpose of toxicology testing. Authorities in Ohio also were beginning to think about digging up some of her other dead husbands.

By now, Columbiana County and East Liverpool authorities were in agreement that Laura Christy was insane. An Affidavit of Lunacy was signed by Sherriff Wright and Prosecutor Brookes, and at 1:00 p.m. Wednesday, January 20th, a lunacy panel made up of Dr. C.H. Bailey and Dr. Albert Michels met in Probate Court in Lisbon. The doctors found that Laura Christy was insane, and Judge Lodge Riddle sentenced her to the State Hospital for the Criminally Insane in Lima, Ohio. The next day Sheriff Wright and others transported Laura to the asylum by automobile. Sheriff Wright told the press, *"I don't believe she realizes what's being done with her."*

When Laura was committed, the State of West Virginia stopped their procedures, agreeing to work with Ohio authorities. They did reserve the right to prosecute her for the Ebert murder if she was ever released from the asylum.

The East Liverpool police shipped the trunk and other items Laura had bought to the asylum by train, along with the $37 dollars they had found on her. Upon her arrival, Laura was again searched by hospital staff who found $120 dollars in her possession. The money was held by the superintendent for Laura's use in buying items not provided by the hospital. She was placed under close observation for a period of four to six weeks. If the staff found that she was sane, she would be sent back to Columbiana County to stand trial for murder.

Nothing more was heard of Laura Christy until late October 1926. At that time the *Review-Tribune* printed a story that was written by Dan Gallagher, a reporter for the *Cleveland News*. Gallagher had covered the story back in January and had found out that the laboratory tests had found no trace of poison in the organs and blood of William Christy.

(*This is not really surprising, for modern medicine now tests the hair and fingernails of arsenic victims. These have the longest window of viability of up to a year. Urine and blood have a much shorter span of viability; a matter of 24-48 hours. The reluctance of the laboratory in conducting the tests probably eliminated any chance of finding a positive result.)

Gallagher went to the asylum and conducted an interview with Laura. In it he said that Laura should not have confessed since the State had no evidence and their case would have fallen flat. He spoke with Superintendent Dr. Charles Clark, who said that he did not think Laura was truly insane. While she was certainly *feeble-minded,* he felt she had been wrongly institutionalized. He went on to say that she was forced, due to her confession and commitment, to mingle everyday with truly insane women. He felt she should be placed in a home for the feeble minded instead.

Gallagher had heard her confession nine months earlier, and he thought she should have been given an attorney to keep her from talking. She had admitted to buying the rat poison, but the druggist denied selling it to her, or ever having seen her before. When no arsenic was found in the test samples, Gallagher felt she should be set free regardless of her confession. He said that the State could have never found her guilty. Gallagher met with Laura near Pavilion #20, where she lived with twenty or so other women. Female attendants were always on duty, watching and listening.

Laura spent her days working in the laundry and now denied her confession. She insisted that Christy had wanted to take the arsenic as medicine.

Gallagher asked her, *"How are you getting along?"*

"If I can't go free I'd just as soon be here as in some other institution," she replied.

Gallagher asked, *"Would you wed again if given your freedom?"*

"Well I might if I could find the right kind of man," she said. *"I might say I still have hopes in that direction. That is if they only let me out of here. My eyesight is bothering me. I busted my horn rimmed glasses. But other than that I feel fine. And I'll look just as nice as ever when I get my new teeth. I haven't a tooth in my head right now. I've had them all pulled."*

Gallagher told Laura about Isaac Randles, the farmer from near Killbuck, Ohio coming forth to claim her marriage to and later abandonment of him in 1925. Laura exclaimed, *"That isn't true. If he says I married him he is mistaken. I was never in Killbuck in my life. I don't know anyone having that name. He's away off when he says I'm the woman he married."* Gallagher ended his interview there.

Gallagher remarked in his story that, *"Laura may have been attractive in girlhood, but such was not the case now. She is of tremendous girth. She does look better than when I interviewed her at Lisbon last January. But how she won husband after husband is quite beyond me."*

Laura Christy, guilty of murder or not, insane or not, spent the next eleven years keeping herself ready just in case she found the *right kind of man*. She never got the chance. Laura died in the asylum on September 1, 1937. She was 57 years old.

Chapter 21
East Liverpool is Burning!
Major Downtown Fires

The downtown section of East Liverpool has been struck by fire many times over the years. Two of the worst fires were the Dry Goods Fire of 1892, and the Diamond Fire of 1905. Both of these have chapters dedicated to them. The three fires covered in this chapter rank closely behind them in severity.

The Walls Came Tumbling Down!
Milligan Hardware Fire
February 22, 1925

East Liverpool had bounced back following the devastating fire of 1905. The burned out buildings had all been rebuilt on an even grander scale, and business was booming. The Milligan Hardware Company building had been totally destroyed in 1905. The firm now occupied a new six story building, that was built on the same lot. They rented space on the first floor to the National Wholesale Millinery & Fur Company, and to the National Clothing Company. Both firms had storefronts on E. 5th Street and storerooms on the second floor. Milligan Hardware occupied the rest of the building with first floor access in Crook Alley.

Jacob House was a night watchman for the Merchants Association. He was walking his beat along 5th Street, when at about 1:44 a.m. on Sunday morning, flames broke out in the Milligan Building. House saw flames on the second floor above the National Wholesale

Millinery & Fur Company. He rushed over to the First National Bank where he telephoned the fire department.

Assistant Fire Chief Elmer McMillan and the crew from Central Station were soon on the scene. The men were quickly joined by Chief Tom Bryan and other firefighters. Several hose lines were put into service, but by now the lower floors were a mass of flames. Within minutes the fire breached the partitions between the National Clothing Company (a men's clothing store), and the rest of the building. The greedy flames were soon consuming stocks of oils, paint, grease, and ammunition. The super-heated air traveled up the wooden stairways and the elevator shaft bringing, the flames to the upper stories.

East Liverpool's ten firefighters were aided by many civilian volunteers in manning the several hose lines that were pouring thousands of gallons of water onto the growing disaster. Men raised fire hoses onto the roofs of nearby buildings, such as the Exchange Building. The two story Exchange Building was located on the east side of Crook Alley, next to the Milligan Building.

Chief Bryan quickly realized that the fire was beyond their control, and called for help. Chester, West Virginia sent their truck and twelve men. Wellsville, Ohio and Newell, West Virginia went on standby alert. Even Salem, Ohio, twenty seven miles north of East Liverpool, sent a truck. However, due to the foggy weather it would not arrive in time to be of assistance.

When the fire breached the roof of the six story Milligan Building Chief Bryan began to worry about the walls. The chief remembered that the buildings had collapsed back in 1905. Bryan began to see signs that it was going to happen again. He ordered the men off the roof of the Exchange Building and out of Crook and Diamond Alleys. Firefighters moved to safer but less effective positions. Within a few minutes the Chief was proven right when the eastside wall buckled and fell. The massive wall came crashing down onto the roof of the Exchange Building. The tons of bricks smashed through into the interior of the building. Along with the bricks came burning debris, and within an instant this building was also burning fiercely. Tons of debris filled Crook Alley, burying and cutting three desperately needed hose lines. Several gas lines also were severed allowing pockets of gas to build up and then explode.

The Exchange Building at 5th Street and Crook Alley was of a unique construction. It was essentially two buildings joined together by common front and back walls. Dividing the buildings was an interior hallway. Known as a "blind alley" it was about four feet wide with doorways that allowed access. The western half of the building was occupied by the Lewis Brothers Furniture Store, while the Woolworth 5&10 Store occupied the eastern half. Firefighters entered the 5&10 store and fought the fire by way of the interior alleyway. Through their efforts the Woolworth store was saved, with only minor damage.

Shortly after the eastern wall fell, the western wall also collapsed. Next door was the three story Wasbutzky Building. Tons of flaming debris and bricks literally crushed the smaller structure. All three floors were breached, and the Moyer Brother's Star Bargain Store simply vanished in the flames. Several smaller structures in Diamond Alley were also badly damaged. Paul Hune lost both his home and his confectionery store. Bert Gillespie's Diamond Café and Bar was also

Ruins of the Exchange Building

badly damaged when the Milligan Building collapsed. The intense heat wave that occurred when the Milligan Building collapsed broke nearly every window of the seven story Crook Building on the south side of 5th Street. In less than an hour, two large buildings had been totally destroyed and another had been severely damaged. Other smaller structures had also been damaged. Several families had been forced early on to evacuate apartments in the fire zone. Although they lost everything, no one was injured.

When the fire was at its worst, another fire was reported in the kiln shed of the Standard Pottery on Broadway. Assistant Chief Elmer McMillan along with firefighters George Metsch and Earl Fenton sped to the scene. The building's sprinkler system held the flames in check until the firefighters arrived and extinguished the blaze. The men soon returned to the Milligan Building. Fires had broken out on the roofs of several buildings in the business district. This was caused by hot embers landing onto them. These were extinguished by civilian volunteers.

The large W.L. Thompson Building, next door to the Wasbutzsy Building was saved by the use of cooling water being sprayed onto it, and a strong firewall. In the end, a repeat of the disastrous 1905 blaze had been averted.

Although a few of the firefighters sustained minor injuries, there had also been several narrow escapes. Firefighters continued to wet down the ruins throughout the day and into the night. Broken gas lines were allowed to burn until the gas company employees could shut the lines down. 5th Street was blocked by rubble. Streetcar traffic on 5th Street had to be diverted. Over the next few days the remaining ruins were razed for safety reasons, and the city tried to return to normal. Once again the buildings would rise from the ashes. Milligan's would lead the way with two three story buildings built end to end on their large lot. Later, the Wasbutzky Building would again stake its place on E. 5th Street. The destroyed portion of the Exchange Building was not rebuilt. In its place, a five story building was built which for many years was occupied by the J.C. Penney Company. The cause of the $750,000 fire was never determined.

A Long Cold Sunday!
The Diamond Fire
of March 3, 1968

It had been many years since the downtown business district was struck by a major fire. That would come to end on a cold late Sunday afternoon.

Roy Watson of the LaCroft section of town parked his car at 5th and Market Streets about 4:30 p.m. As he exited his car he saw smoke coming from the Siff Shoe Store building in the Diamond. Watson opened the door leading to the second floor and went upstairs. He had not reached the second floor when he saw that the hallway was full of flames. Racing back to the street level he stopped a passerby, and asked him to call the fire department. The man replied, *"I don't carry a phone in my pocket!"* (* *Too bad that guy was not an inventor, considering today's world.*) Watson then entered the New York Restaurant on the opposite side of the street. He was again unable to place a phone call because someone was talking on the only phone in the place. Watson then gave up and went outside and waited. (* *Central Fire Station was only two blocks away.*) After a few moments he heard sirens, and then a waitress came outside and told him the fire department had been called.

Several other people would relate their own experiences in discovering the fire. David Sakol had been in the American Legion Post #4 on the second floor earlier that afternoon. He said there was a strange odor, but he did not know what it was. He also said the door leading to the third floor was always padlocked since it was unoccupied. That day, however, it was standing open when he left.

It was just after 5:00 o'clock when Firefighter Dolph Knott received the call at Central Station. The A-Shift was on duty, led by

Assistant Chief Frank Butler. Butler, along with firefighters Ralph Chapman, Clarence Snediker, and Knott were quickly on the scene. The men from the Northside Station, Lew Hood and Russ Dray, were also on their way. Chief Butler saw heavy smoke curling from the eaves of the four story building when he arrived. While his men were busy laying out the fire hose, Butler tried to go to the second floor to investigate, but was met with intense heat and smoke. He could see the tell-tale glow of flames rolling along the ceiling through the smoke. Knowing that he needed more help, he called out additional alarms, bringing firefighters Jim Miller and Ralph Wood from the East End and Ed Greenwood from Pleasant Heights Stations. All the off-duty men from B & C Shifts were also recalled.

Assistant Chief Frank Butler

The initial attack was slowed somewhat due to the nearest fire hydrant at 6th & Market Street being frozen. At least two other nearby hydrants were also frozen. The Water Department was called and they used blow torches to thaw them, while the firefighters used more distant hydrants. Even though thousands of gallons of water were being sprayed onto the fire, the greedy flames continued to grow. The off duty men were now beginning to arrive and more equipment including the aerial ladder was put into service. Fire Chief Alfred Van Dyne was now on the scene conferring with Butler and the other officers. The specter of 1905 loomed heavily on the minds of Van Dyne and his assistants. They feared the blaze would spread into the nearby buildings. Chief Van Dyne called for more help. Mutual Aid calls brought the Chester and Newell departments from West Virginia. Midland, Pennsylvania sent its aerial ladder, which was badly needed. Before the battle was won firefighters from Liverpool Township, Calcutta, Glenmoor, and Lawrenceville, West Virginia would join the fight. Even Boardman and Minerva, Ohio sent aerial trucks, but they arrived too late to be of assistance.

The Siff Shoe Store building was originally known as the Smith Fowler Building. Brothers David and Lawrence Siff of Akron, Ohio now owned it, and leased the first floor to the Gilbert Shoe Company Inc. with William McWhorter as the manager. The store carried the name Siff Family Shoes. The other portion of the first floor held the Robert's Jewelry Store. Robert Schlang and his family operated this firm. The American Legion Post #4 occupied part of the second floor along with several operations of the Junior Achievement group. Junior Achievement made decorative items from metal, and there were lathes, saws and drill presses in their rooms. The third and fourth floors were currently vacant.

The entire Siff Building was a mass of seething fire; flames could be seen on the roof of the Grand Opera Building on E. 6th Street. That building abutted the Siff Building on the northeast corner. The old Grand Opera Building had been built around 1880 as a 2,000 seat theatre. Over the years it had changed; now it was a commercial building on the first floor with apartments and storage space on the upper two floors. Harold Bricker had his Isaly's Store and cafeteria at the eastern end of the building, at Crook Alley. Sanford Weiner's Outdoor Army Store occupied the center room and the western end storefront was vacant, although the

Battling the Blaze

Bendheim Shoe Store had been the last occupant. Two apartments were occupied on the second floor above Bricker's Cafeteria.

The fire quickly spread across the roof and penetrated into the third floor space. As more firefighters reached the scene, they were deployed to this new front. Manning the rooftop of the American Theatre on the east side of Crook Alley, firefighters worked to cut off the spreading flames.

On Market Street, next to the blazing Siff Building, were two narrow buildings, the closest being the Gaston Building, lately owned by Paul Braslawsce. He operated the Paul Arrow Pant Shop on the first floor with the three upper floors being vacant except for some storage for the men's shop. An old building, it had been the sight of a severe fire back in 1909, when the Diamond Hardware Company had been the occupant. An extra floor had been added following that earlier fire. Next to the Gaston Building is the four story Lowe Building owned by Frank Diamond who operated the Frank Diamond Men's Store, on the ground floor. Firefighters kept heavy hose streams on these two buildings to prevent them from catching fire. On the corner of 6th & Market Street is the ornate J.C. Thompson Building. Good fortune was with this structure since the fire passed it by, moving behind it into the Grand Opera House.

Along with the 140 firefighters fighting this massive blaze were dozens of other people working where they could. Mayor George Wilshaw and a city councilman helped with traffic control. Other councilmen assisted the Street Department crews in spreading salt on the icy streets and sidewalks. Temperatures had fallen into the mid-twenties during the night. Once again groups of concerned citizens patrolled nearby rooftops to guard against fires being started by hot embers landing on them. They had to extinguish a fire on the roof of the Farnsworth Television Store.

The streets and alleys provided fire breaks that held the fire in check. Slowly the flames began to die down as the firefighters gained the upper hand. By 10:30 p.m. most of the neighboring firefighters had returned to their own communities, with the grateful thanks of city officials. East Liverpool's twenty-nine exhausted firefighters remained on duty throughout the long cold night and into the next day. While some guarded against a rekindle of the blaze, most were busy putting the equipment back in service. After any large fire, trucks had to be reloaded with dry hose, and all the small equipment sorted, cleaned, and put back where it belonged. A reporter asked Assistant Chief Butler, *"How are you doing?"* Speaking for all the firefighters he smiled, his face streaked with soot, and said *"I'm tired."*

The fire had taken a huge toll. The four-story Siff Building was completely destroyed, its towering walls buckled and leaning. The interior of the building was completely gutted, a total loss. The Gaston Building had been saved with only smoke and water damage. Later it was determined that the wall abutting the Siff Building had been damaged, which resulted in the top two floors being removed. Frank Diamond's Lowe Building had water in the basement, as did several other businesses along Diamond Alley. The heavily damaged Grand Opera Building was left standing without a roof. The third floor was gutted and the bottom two floors were ruined by the massive amount of water that was poured onto the flames.

Chief Alfred Van Dyne ruled that the dangerous Siff Building must be razed immediately. In the coming days, the wrecking ball brought down the building. During the operation, a time capsule was found. It contained newspaper accounts of the 1905 blaze that had destroyed the previous building sixty-three years earlier. In the next couple of years a new two-story business building known as the Blair-Morse Building was constructed on the sight. It was also necessary to remove the top two floors of the Grand Opera House, leaving it a one story building. The top two floors were also removed on the Gaston Building. Soon the businesses in these buildings reopened and things returned to normal. The cause of the $900,000 dollar blaze was never determined. Chief Van Dyne theorized unofficially that perhaps a vagrant had gained access to the upper floors of the Siff Building through the unlocked door, and started a fire to keep warm. There is no way to know.

Fire and Ice

The Washington Street Fire

January 8, 1974

Rapport Building

It was bitterly cold on that Tuesday morning. East Liverpool police officer Tom Edgell was driving on Market Street, when two ladies in a car flagged down his patrol car. They told him there was a fire a couple of blocks away. He quickly drove to the corner of E. 6th & Washington Street. Heavy smoke was pouring from the basement of the Rapport Building. He called the police dispatcher who then called the fire department. The time was 4:42 a.m., and the temperature was eight degrees.

The A-Shift under Assistant Chief Frank Butler rushed the one block to the scene. Upon their arrival they found the basement of the Rapport Building engulfed by flames. The first floor was also burning and heavy smoke blanketed the area. Firefighters fought to gain entry into the first floor, but were quickly driven from the building by the intense heat and flames. They began to set up their hose lines on the street and prepared for a long fight.

The Rapport Building was a three-story brick structure which had been built in the early 1880s. The original owner was Frank Stewart, who had rebuilt this building following the terrible fire which destroyed his original wooden building in February of 1881. That fire had claimed the lives of eight people. *(*See Chapter 2)* It held several storefronts on both Washington Street and E. 6th Street. It originally was the site of a hotel on the top two floors, but now the second floor was vacant and the third was rented to the Ogilvie Department Store who used it for storage. On the first floor facing Washington Street were two businesses. The corner was occupied by Clark and Edna Geer, who ran the Geer Office Machine sales and repair shop. Mrs. Geer was also a realtor with Bondy Realty, and had a branch office in the store. The other Washington Street business was the Come Together Boutique. Larry and Vickie Stiteler ran this clothing store for *"hip younger crowd."* Along 6th Street were three storefronts. Mrs. Edith Connell

Washington Street

ran her candy and confectionary restaurant in one. Optometrist Doctor Earl Voegtley's office and the U.S. Army Recruiter occupied the other two. This building, now owned by Mr. Maurice Rapport, had been extensively remodeled in 1952.

Assistant Chief Butler had by now called for additional alarms, bringing all thirty-four of East Liverpool's firefighters to the scene. The hungry flames continued to eat their way upward, defying all efforts to stop them. The second and then the third floors became roaring infernos, and at about 5:30 that morning, the flames burst through the roof. The aerial ladder truck was positioned in front of the Rapport Building on Washington Street, and was pouring water into the upper floors, to no avail. The frigid temperatures had turned everything on the outside of the building to ice. Ice covered the streets and sidewalks, along with the trucks and other equipment. The heavy firefighting coats of the men were frozen stiff as were their hands and faces. Maintaining their footing was difficult for the men manning the powerful hose lines. Men from the Street Department were kept busy spreading salt on the icy streets and sidewalks. Mutual aid calls had been sent by Chief Alfred Van Dyne, and units from Liverpool Township, Calcutta, and Wellsville were at the scene. The aerial ladder truck from Midland, Pennsylvania was positioned on E. 6th Street to stop the fire from travelling toward the Diamond.

Chief Alfred Van Dyne

When the flames had burst through the roof of the Rapport Building, flaming debris began to land on the roof of the Heddleston Building next door. Within minutes the roof of that structure was ablaze. The three story brick business building known as the Heddleston Building was part of an estate controlled by the Heddleston family.

The only occupant on the ground floor was the Heimie's Cigar and Magazine Store. This business was owned and operated by East Liverpool mayor Norman Bucher. The upper two floors were rented to the D.M. Ogilvie Department Store, and were used as a stock room. With the roof of the Heddleston Building aflame, the fire jumped to the roof of the Knowles Building at the corner of Washington Street and Diamond Alley.

The three-story brick Knowles Building had two first floor occupants. The Allen Shoe Store was operated by Mr. Dayton Allen. The Associates Finance & Loan Company was the other tenant. On the second floor, a covered walkway crossed Diamond Alley, and connected with the second floor of the Ogilvie Department Store. Ogilvie's maintained their toy, furniture and small appliance departments on the second floor of the Knowles Building. On the third floor the department store had offices, the advertising department and display workshop. The third floor connected through into the Heddleston and Rapport Buildings, and was used as a stock room. Fire doors separated all three buildings, and it was thought that all were closed. However, firefighters did close and secure both fire doors on the

Truck 1 frozen in place

walkway over Diamond Alley. This protected the main Ogilvie store from loss, except for some minor smoke and water damage.

The roof finally collapsed on the Rapport Building at 6:00 that morning. The roofs of the other two buildings also collapsed about an hour later. The third floors were all burning fiercely and totally destroyed. Thousands of gallons of water poured down into the second floor area, destroying whatever the fire missed. Eventually, the massive weight caused the third floors to collapse, and in the end, so did the second floors of all three buildings. Each floor "pancaked" onto the floor below, leaving only burned out shells where three fine business blocks had stood.

Amazingly, due to a quirk in construction, the Heimie's Cigar and Magazine Store did not burn; nor was it crushed. During the worst of the blaze it was still possible to enter it. In the end, however, what the flames failed to accomplish, the smoke and water did. The store and its stock was ruined.

By late morning the worst was over. All that remained were huge piles of smoking rubble within the blackened ice covered walls. The neighboring departments all packed up and returned to their own communities with the grateful thanks of East Liverpool. Chief Van Dyne quickly determined that the buildings must be razed as soon as possible. He was fearful they might collapse onto the streets at any moment. The entire fire scene was a frozen wonderland. Ice covered the buildings, along with the streets and sidewalks. The aerial ladder truck was encased in ice and frozen in place. Much time and effort was required to chip the ice away from the ladder rungs and pulleys so the 75-foot ladder could be retracted. Once that was accomplished it was taken back to Central Station to thaw out.

Total damage was estimated to be at least one million dollars. Aside from a few minor injuries no one had been hurt. Chief Van Dyne knew that the fire started in the basement of the Rapport Building. However, until the rubble was cleared away, no cause could be determined. The wrecking crews began work on Wednesday and soon the walls were down. The site was cleared by January 25th, and the final rulings were released. The investigation by Chief Van Dyne and officials from the State Fire Marshall's office ruled that the fire had started in the basement area of the Come Together Boutique. Mr. Stiteler told the investigators that he had a space heater in the area where the fire started, although he was certain it was not plugged in. The exact cause of the fire is unknown. Chief Van Dyne also said the fire had spread so quickly because the automatic fire doors that separated the buildings had failed to work. The loss was now estimated to be at least $1,311,500. Insurance would not cover the entire amount. The D.M. Ogilvie Company estimated their loss to be $250,000.

The buildings would not be rebuilt this time; the empty lot would eventually become a parking lot. Most of the affected businesses never reopened. The decline of East Liverpool's once thriving business district had begun.

Postscript

Every time fire strikes the congested downtown business district of any town, there is great danger of it spreading. This has happened numerous times in East Liverpool over the course of its history. The various fires that have been covered in this book are a testament to that danger. They represent some truly dark days in East Liverpool.

Chapter 22

"A Wild and Treacherous Man"

The Life and Death of "Crip" Cain
<u>1895-1905</u>

Milo Cain was born around the year of 1874 where his family lived, in the west end of East Liverpool. As he grew he became a wild and unpredictable young man. He was quick tempered and prone to violence. The local police were well aware of Milo even at a fairly young age. Perhaps he became this way as a result of his being handicapped from birth. This resulted in his being given the derogatory nickname of "Crip."

"Crip" was not an easy man to get along with, even for his family. For example, on May 7, 1895, he and his brother Louis got into an argument at the kitchen table. It quickly escalated into a full scale "donnybrook." The two brothers tore viciously at each other, overturning the table. They then began using dishes and eating utensils, whatever they could find, as weapons. Mrs. Cain began screaming for the police. Even though the men knew it would be awhile before the police could reach the area, it caused them to break off the fight and flee the home. Their mother's kitchen was in shambles.

A little more than a month later on June 16th, "Crip" was hanging around the streetcar trestle that crossed over Jethro Hollow in the West End. He was there with a gang of thugs. The gang soon noticed Theodore Aurochs, known as "Rocky" who was sitting on a large rock near the east end of the trestle. It was around 2 o'clock in the morning and "Rocky" was waiting on his friends. His companions had gone up the road to a notorious house operated by a woman named Caroline. Aurochs did not have much money, so he decided to wait at the trestle for his friends. He was soon approached by two of the gang members, whom he recognized; one of the men was "Crip" Cain. They demanded all his money, and one of the thugs menaced him with a rock he held in his hand. Aurochs said he did not have any money, but just then the man threw the rock which struck Aurochs just above his right eye, knocking him to the ground. Within an instant, the two thugs were upon him, punching and kicking him into unconsciousness. They then began to rifle through the victim's pockets. They found 65 cents and a pocketknife, and one of them even took Aurochs's necktie. The victim was left lying on the edge of the trestle.

About then, another of "Rocky's" companions happened along. George Flowers, known as "Posey," was stopped by the gang and told, *"Give us your money!"* "Posey" told them, *" No!"* Cain said *"I'll go right through you!"* To which Posey said *"You will like -----!"* It was about then that someone hit "Posey" in the neck. "Posey" however, was made of sterner stuff. He put up a lively defense, but the odds were against him. After a few moments he managed to break free and ran across the trestle. He passed by the rumpled form of his friend, but did not stop.

After this skirmish, the gang called in reinforcements and now stood at four. They did not have to wait long as James Mullens, the last of Aurochs' companions came down the road. The routine was the same, except by now "Crip" had found a piece of iron which he swung at Mullens' head but missed. Mullens escaped, running across the trestle. The gang decided to cut their losses and vanished into the night. When Mullens got across the trestle, he found his friend Aurochs standing hanging onto the railing. Along with "Posey" who was hovering nearby, they took their friend home and called a doctor.

The next day Theodore Aurochs hobbled into the police station looking as if he had tackled a tornado. His head and face was heavily bandaged, and he had several cracked and bruised ribs. He was in a lot of pain. He did however, manage to tell his story and identify Milo "Crip" Cain as the leader of the gang. Two policemen went at once to the Cain residence to bring "Crip" in. Mrs. Cain however, refused to let the cops in without a warrant. After a rather lengthy discussion the police entered the home. The officers found "Crip" sleeping soundly in his bed. He was rudely awakened and dragged off to the "slammer."

Cain was a frequent "guest" in Mayor Addison Gilbert's court, *"due to his capacity for liquor and his proclivity for fighting once that capacity had been exceeded."* He was charged with highway robbery and assault.

Court was held on Wednesday June 18th, and Aurochs was the first to testify. At first all the victims were hesitant to admit that they were at Caroline's but finally told the story. When various members of the gang were called, some odd testimony came out. One man said he did not like the victims because they were stingy, only buying drinks for themselves. They all had alibis, although they were poor ones. When questioned, gang member Joe O'Brian testified, *"I don't know any more about de case dan a big dog goin to eat a big elephant."* (* Whatever that means.)

In the end, only Milo Cain could be positively identified. The mayor bound him over for the Grand Jury, setting bail at $500 on each charge. Since "Crip" did not have $1,000 in his pockets he went back to jail. A few weeks later, he was found guilty and sentenced to four years in the penitentiary. Cain would not serve the full sentence; nor was he rehabilitated.

On May 31, 1898, the police were called to a restaurant on 6th Street, where they found "Crip" in the process of *"cleaning the place out."* He was on his last opponent when the cops arrived. Cain had come in dead drunk wanting something to eat. He was refused service and told to move along. That started the fight. He was fined $6.60 by the mayor.

Later that summer a strange occurrence happened. It seems that a man who gave his name as Cain entered into a restaurant on 6th Street around 3 a.m. on July 25th. The man's face was covered with blood. He had been shot in the head, with the bullet just creasing his scalp. After washing his face and bandaging the wound, Cain got something to eat. He then went to see Doctor W.A. Hobbs, who used several stitches to close the wound. He told the doctor that he was about to enter a house near the West End Trestle when a woman shot him from a window. When the doctor was done, Cain left. The next day police searched the area but found no one willing to talk about it. *(* This may not have been "Crip" but it sounds like his normal behavior.)*

The arrests continued. On August 10, 1899 he was arrested for trying to sell a "suspicious" gold watch. On October 7th he was drunk and disorderly at the home of Mrs. Victoria Fortner in Dew Drop Alley. On December 23rd he was again in Dew Drop Alley, and was again drunk and disorderly, acting according to the neighbors like, *"The Wild Man from Borneo." (* Dew Drop Alley is now Green Lane)*

On February 2, 1900, he was again terrorizing Mrs. Fortner. Arrested for tearing her place up, he was sentenced to six months in the Canton, Ohio workhouse and fined fifty dollars and costs. In August he was out of the workhouse and arrested again for abusing Mrs. Fortner.

"Crip" was a restless man who would disappear from East Liverpool for months at a time. It was reported that he had made himself known in many places between Pittsburgh, Pennsylvania and Wheeling, West Virginia. He may have also have been locked up in these cities as a result of his visits. East Liverpool, however, was his home.

The on-again off-again relationship with Mrs. Fortner continued through the year of 1901 and into 1902. "Crip" also spent a portion of 1902 in the workhouse. It was during 1902 that his affections appear to have changed. A new lady friend began to draw his attention. Bessie Hughes also lived in Dew Drop Alley. This new relationship would be just as stormy as the last one.

On the night of January 3, 1903, the police were called to the home of Bessie Hughes. It seems that "Crip" had come calling, drunk as usual. On this night, however, Bessie denied him entry. The fight was on. Bessie locked the door, and "Crip" tried to break it down. Bessie began to fear for her safety and called the police. "Crip" after hearing that the cops were on the way decided to leave. Officer Bill Ruhe arrived, and a badly shaken Bessie told him the story, pointing out the direction "Crip" had gone. Ruhe was actually a firefighter. In those days the firefighters also served as part time police officers. Ruhe decided to go after Cain because he feared that Cain would cause trouble wherever he went. The trail led along the railroad spur known as the Horn Switch, past several potteries and run down houses. He finally caught up with "Crip" near the West End Ball Field. *(*The area of Westgate School today.)* Ruhe shouted at Crip to halt, that he was under arrest. Cain complied at once. Ruhe slowly approached his prisoner. The police were always wary around Cain, not because he was a great fighter or a large man, but because he was so devious and was willing to go to any extreme to escape. He would attack without warning, using whatever he could find as a weapon.

William Ruhe

Ruhe had his man, but they were all alone in the dark. The nearest place where Ruhe could summon help was a grocery store that had a police call box located in front of it. But that was a few blocks away. Ruhe made the mistake of not handcuffing him as he walked him toward the call box. Suddenly "Crip" began to run. He had the reputation of being as fast as a deer, but Ruhe could run too. Seeing that he could not outrun the officer, "Crip" whirled around, and attacked Ruhe like a wild animal. The two men were locked in a vicious hand-to-hand struggle, both *giving as good as they got.*

This went on for what seemed several minutes. In reality it was a much shorter time. Finally, Ruhe managed to get hold of his night stick, and clubbed Cain to the ground. Standing over his fallen opponent, Ruhe began to yell for help. Someone heard him and notified the police station. Officer Henry Aufderheide caught a streetcar which let him off near the scene of the battle. Cain started to struggle again, but the vigorous use of the club calmed him down. By now the Patrol Wagon had arrived with two more firefighters, Tom Bryan and Pat Wood. Cain was thrown unceremoniously into the back of the wagon by the officers. Aufderheide climbed in the back with the prisoner, but Ruhe declined the ride. He was battered and bruised, and his uniform was torn and dirty. He said he would walk back so he would have time to collect himself.

During the slow ride back to City Hall, "Crip" sat against the bulkhead, and Aufderheide sat at the open end of the wagon. Cain was carefully watching for his chance. Steeling himself, he suddenly sprang forth as if shot from a cannon. Henry Aufderheide was a large tough man, and as Cain sprang at him he unleashed a massive left hook which connected solidly with Cain's jaw. The punch knocked "Crip" out, and broke a bone in the policeman's hand. Arriving at City Hall, Cain was dragged from the patrol wagon and thrown into a jail cell. Cain was a mess; his jaw was broken as were several fingers. He was bloodied and bruised, and his clothing was in tatters. *The Evening Review* said he looked as if he had been through a threshing machine. Doctors were called to treat the injured men; Doctor W. A. Hobbs treated Aufderheide, and Doctor C. B. Ogden tried to patch up Cain. The next day the mayor and police chief wanted to send Cain straight to the workhouse over in Canton, Ohio. The officials at the workhouse however, refused to accept him. They did not want to take him because he was handicapped, and would not work. He was also in no fit condition, and would not be for several weeks.

Henry Aufderheide

Mayor Davidson charged Cain with malicious destruction of property and resisting arrest. The only option left was the Columbiana County Infirmary. Cain was transported there, but the mayor would be happy if he just went away. "Crip" spent the next couple of weeks healing up, until on January 22nd, when he just walked out of the infirmary and disappeared. The officials at the infirmary quickly contacted the East Liverpool police, telling them that Milo Cain had escaped. Officials at the infirmary also said they would not search for him as they did not want him back. The superintendent said Cain was the worst inmate they had ever held, and they would not take him back.

The next day "Crip" surfaced in the West End, declaring that he would kill every policeman in town. He vanished before carrying out his threat. He may have left town for a while to finish recuperating from the fierce battle. Fit again, he reappeared on March 31st, drunk as usual and trying to break down Bessie Hughes' door. Once again the police arrived after he had fled, but this time they could not find him. Mayor Davidson issued orders to arrest him on sight.

Once again, the police were called to Bessie Hughes' house on August 31st. "Crip" was in a drunken rage and was smashing against the door while screaming and cursing at his lady friend. This time the police caught him and tossed him into jail. The next day the mayor was contemplating on just letting him go once he sobered up. No institution, short of the penitentiary, would take him and he could not stay in the city jail. However, before the mayor could act a new complaint was filed. Mrs. Hugo Stahl had come to East Liverpool with her two small children in search of her wayward husband. She had not found him, and not wanting to be dependent on the city, she went to work as a laundress. She also made friends with Bessie Hughes who rented three rooms in her house to her. Mrs. Stahl said when she arrived at her new home she discovered that Cain was also living there. It seems that Cain had left town for a while until things "cooled down" and then had slipped back into town, taking up residence at Bessie's about ten days ago.

Mrs. Stahl said it was like a living hell in the house. Cain was always intoxicated and treated Mrs. Hughes badly. He was always demanding money and threatening the women. He told Bessie if she did not do what he wanted he would kill her and bury her in the cellar. Mrs. Stahl said a couple of days ago the threats became so violent that, fearing for her life, she got a gun, and would have shot him if he had not run away. It was the following day when the police arrested him. She said Cain had told her that he had committed enough crimes to be imprisoned for the rest of his life. He said the mayor was not slick enough to catch him. Now the mayor had him, but what could he do with him?

For reasons never explained, before long Cain was again free. Officer Bill Ruhe captured "Crip" on October 24th, and hauled him before Mayor Weaver's court. Cain expressed surprise when he was told that several outstanding charges were lodged against him. Told he could face serious jail time, maybe even a return to the penitentiary, Cain implored the mayor to pass judgment on him, and not send him to the county court. However, Mayor Weaver did hold him over for the county court. Cain was gone from East Liverpool for the next several months, some of it spent in jail. He returned, and on March 31, 1904, he was again harassing Bessie Hughes and Mrs. Stahl. The police were issued another arrest on sight order. For the next year Cain virtually vanished from the streets of East Liverpool.

Word of him surfaced again on October 19, 1905. A telegram was received at the police station saying that Milo Cain had been severely injured in a railroad accident in Bellaire, Ohio. It requested his family (a brother and sister) to come to his aid. It also requested that Bessie Sheets be notified. Cain's sister was married and living in town and his brother was also working full-time on the new Ohio River dam being built between East Liverpool and Wellsville. Neither responded to the telegram.

It seems that "Crip" had been up to his old ways in the river town of Bellaire opposite of Wheeling, West Virginia about 60 miles downriver from East Liverpool. Highly intoxicated as usual, he apparently crawled under a railcar to escape the rain and to sleep it off. Before daylight, the railroad workers arrived to shift the cars on the siding. They did not see Cain asleep under one of them. When they moved that car, it pinched Cain under the steel wheels. The brakeman heard his screams and stopped the car. He had been caught on his right side by the wheels. Workers carefully removed him and he was taken to the City Hall in Bellaire. The town did not have a hospital, so two doctors came to care for him at the police station. They determined that his back and right arm were probably broken, also the right side of his chest was crushed. With severe internal injuries, there was little they could do. Cain was conscious and told them that he was thirty-one-years old and of his family in East Liverpool.

Because the family did not come to his aid, Cain was left to the mercy of the police department. The officers obtained a cot which was set up in the hallway and brought a blanket to cover him. "Crip" lay there all day in severe pain. The city of Bellaire refused to pay for his care because there was no money allocated to help in these kinds of cases. They said it was out of their jurisdiction. East Liverpool authorities also refused to accept responsibility. Finally at 6:00 p.m. Bessie Sheets arrived by train. She immediately took control of this deplorable condition. She ordered that Milo be transferred to the North Wheeling Hospital, and paid all his expenses. Mrs. Sheets, however, refused to tell the police what her relationship was to the victim. She accompanied him to the hospital and then left a short time later.

Milo "Crip" Cain succumbed to his injuries shortly before midnight October 19, 1905. He died alone in the hospital. He is buried in the Mt. Calvary Cemetery in Wheeling, West Virginia. Mrs. Sheets paid for everything.

A couple of days later, Mrs. Bessie Sheets arrived at the office of Mayor W.A. Weaver. The mayor was talking with police chief John Wyman when the lady came into the office. Mrs. Sheets told them the story. She said Milo was in jail when she arrived in Bellaire. She immediately paid for him to be taken over to Wheeling and placed in the hospital. His back was broken and his chest was crushed. There was nothing the hospital could do, and he died a little while later.

Mrs. Sheets said she had come to see the mayor to thank him for all he had done for Milo, when he had been arrested for some wrongdoing. To further show her appreciation, the woman got down on her knees at the mayor's desk. She then opened her purse and took out a $10 dollar bill which she gave to Mayor Weaver. She *said " I have a considerable amount of money saved up and for a long time I have wanted to make you a present to show my appreciation."* Continuing she said, *"I also have a fine set of china dishes that I want you to have."*

Stunned, the mayor politely declined both the money and the dishes. Mrs. Sheets then thanked both men again and quietly left the office. *(* I do not know if Bessie Sheets and Bessie Hughes are one-and the same woman. Perhaps "Crip" had found a new love in his life.)*

Despite his handicap, Milo "Crip" Cain was a thoroughly dangerous and treacherous young man. He was an alcoholic and a criminal, an ill-tempered man who was the equal of any two men in a fight. Milo was born with a palsied and withered right arm, which hung essentially useless at his side. "Crip" Cain was a one-armed man.

Chapter 23
The Exploding Lamp!
The Hazlett House Fire
June 3, 1905

It is East Liverpool's misfortune, indeed every town's misfortune to be struck by what is called in the fire service a "working" house fire. These are the fires that usually do not make headlines or at least do not hold them for long. However, to the firefighters these fires are the most dangerous part of the job.

The firefighters rush into the smoke-filled house trying to extinguish the fire before it grows. Outside, the people on the street cannot see what is going on so they decide nothing is happening. Many times this could not be further from the truth.

The most frightening thing to face a firefighter upon arriving at a fire is to be told *"There is someone trapped inside."* In my years on the East Liverpool Fire Department, I was confronted with this numerous times. Fortunately most of the time it proved to be a false report. In most cases, the occupant had already escaped or was not at home. Rarely is there a victim for the firefighter to rescue from the flames. When there is a victim, too often it is too late to help. For this reason I chose to include this small but tragic incident.

In the early 1860s, Preston Parker built a wood frame building at the northeast corner of 5th Street and Jackson Street. The building became known as the "Swiss Cottage" and was occupied by a beer garden. Today the lot is occupied by the old Martin Funeral Home.

After many years the Hazlett sisters, Eleanor and Mary purchased the building and remodeled it into a duplex residence. They occupied the western half of the building and rented the eastern half to Charles Ulser and his family. Mrs. Ulser's Grandmother, Louisa Webber, also lived with the family. Mrs. Webber had been born in Germany and had come to America at a young age. She had lived in East Liverpool for the last twenty five years. She was 72-years-old. For the last few years Mrs. Webber had been crippled by severe rheumatism.

At about 8:30 p.m. on Saturday evening June 3, 1905, Mrs. Webber's son-in-law, William H. Bloor, came to check on his mother-in-law. Bloor was 58-years-old and was a well-respected potter from a pioneering pottery family.

Once inside Mrs. Webber's rear bedroom, he somehow knocked over a kerosene lamp, which exploded into flames when it hit the floor. Mrs. Webber was trapped in her bed. Bloor began yelling *"FIRE"* and ran out onto the porch.

There he met Mrs. E.L. Trimmer and Eleanor Hazlett. Mrs. Trimmer had been visiting Eleanor Hazlett and had heard the commotion. Bloor quickly told the women what happened and told them to call the fire department. He then ran back into the house to rescue Mrs. Webber.

Mrs. Trimmer would later tell a reporter from the *Morning Tribune* that she could see all the way into the rear bedroom. She saw Bloor lift Webber from the bed and try to carry her out of the burning room. However, he soon was overcome by the smoke and heat and fell to the floor. Mrs. Trimmer said the flames enveloped the poor souls, and she could hear their pitiful cries as she stood helpless on the front porch.

Just then the fire department arrived after a fast run of several blocks by the horse drawn apparatus. The Rev. Father T.J. Mahon of the St. Aloysius Catholic Church told the firefighters where they could find Mrs. Webber. Father Mahon had made numerous visits to the bed-ridden woman. He knew the home well.

Doing what he had done many times before Chief H.C. Morley entered the structure as heavy black smoke poured from the door. His only thought was to rescue the victims. As Morley found the helpless pair Bloor cried out to him *"Pull us out."* Morley grabbed hold of

Bloor and began to pull but he could not move them. Bloor was holding onto Webber. Morley's grip failed and he fell backwards through a screen and into another room. Nearly overcome by the dense smoke he staggered from the building and collapsed exhausted in the side yard. Firefighter Pat Wood then rushed into the house and found the victims. He managed to pull Bloor out of the house with his last ounce of strength. Wood was a small but strong man, yet he was nearly asphyxiated by the dense smoke. Bystanders carried Wood into the side yard. There Dr. George P. Ikert went to work to save his life. The *Morning Tribune* reported that for fully fifteen minutes Wood's life hung in the balance. Meanwhile, other men picked Bloor up and laid him in the street. Bloor was horribly burnt, and his clothes were burned away.

While this was going on, Firefighter Tom Bryan decided to try once more to rescue Mrs. Webber. Finding the woman lying flat on the floor, he managed to drag her lifeless body from the burning house.

This entire rescue operation would have taken maybe two or three minutes. This was long before firefighters had any special equipment to allow them to breath in smoke-filled structures. In those days, a firefighter took pride in being known as "*leather lungs.*"

In 1905 there were no ambulances in town except for the city Patrol Wagon. The Patrol was operated out of the fire department by firefighters while performing police duties. While it was mainly used to haul prisoners to jail, it was also used as an ambulance. The problem was, it was already in use transporting Pat Wood to the hospital and then to his home. This left no way to transport William Bloor.

By now hundreds of spectators had arrived to watch the fire. Many had come from a carnival that was operating nearby. Although the police had cordoned off the street with a rope, that did little to hold back the mob.

Bloor continued to lay suffering terribly as hundreds of thrill seekers stood staring at his nude burned body. Doctors attended him as best they could but the crowd was a huge problem. Some people began to request that he be carried into a house or taken to the hospital. The police told them they could not move him because of the dense crowd. Finally someone took control and found a cot upon which Bloor was placed. The police at last were able to clear a path through the crowd as several men began to carry the man to the hospital several blocks away.

When they had nearly reached their destination, the patrol wagon came along. It was returning from taking Pat Wood home. How they managed to get him through the crowd was not reported. The men carrying the cot, however, decided to continue carrying Bloor.

Once at the hospital, the doctors and nurses worked for two hours to dress and care for his burns. The shock began to wear off and it was only with injections of morphine that they could keep him quiet. There was little hope. His wife Annie was comforted by family and friends at the hospital. Just before the end she was permitted to enter her husband's room. At 12:50 a.m., Bloor lost his fight to live. Annie Bloor had lost both her mother and her husband this awful night.

The fire itself was stubborn but unremarkable. The fire department managed to keep the flames confined to the eastern half of the duplex. The four-room apartment was gutted by the blaze. The Hazlett sister's residence had only minor smoke and water damage. Property damage amounted to about $1,800, a fair sum in those days, but really quite ordinary.

The death of two people, however, is never ordinary; nor is the courage of those whose job it is to risk their lives to make a difference.

This story is also one of those mysteries of history. I have always tried to get as many sources as possible to give the reader as clear a picture as I could. Most of the time newspaper reporters differ only in small details. However, this time is different.

The rescue details above come mostly from the *Evening Review* with additions from the *Tribune.* However, the *Tribune* story tells only of Firefighter Pat Wood and his rescue of Bloor. It also says that Mrs. Webber's body was found after the fire was out by police officer Clifford Dawson and Father Mahon. The *Tribune* reported that her mutilated body was taken from the doorway of her bedroom.

Both of these accounts cannot be accurate. I tend to believe the report of the *Review* since it is entirely within the character and past and future actions of the men in question. Unfortunately the official records of the East Liverpool Fire Department are of no help since the record consists of a single line entry in a logbook. Regardless, in my experience the fire department would have not allowed others to search a burned out structure for victims, especially a civilian such as Father Mahon. I guess it is up to you to decide.

Chapter 24
The Wrong Man?
The Murder of William Hyatt
February-March 1923

Edward Johnson was born on January 2, 1901 in Greenville, South Carolina. His family soon moved to the nearby town of Greer, were Edward spent his childhood. He was one of a family of ten children whose father worked as a carpenter and a Baptist Minister.

At age 22 he decided that he needed to leave home and travel north to find a job. Eventually he made his way to Homestead, Pennsylvania on the Monongahela River, near Pittsburgh. There he could find a job in one the many steel mills.

For some unexplained reason however, Johnson found himself in Wellsville, Ohio on the night of February 17, 1923. He was playing poker in an illegal gambling club operated by Alvin Smith. Smith's club operated with the full knowledge of the police.

Johnson was angry, he was losing. Worst of all, it had nothing to do with his skill or luck. He was being cheated, and he knew it. But what could he do about it?

Edward Johnson

After a while he left the club, but soon returned, and held the place up at gunpoint. He took over one hundred dollars from the four card players and then fled. He made no attempt to conceal his identity. That night he stayed at a boarding camp, and made his way back to the Pittsburgh area in the morning.

Alvin Smith and his cohorts were not about to take being robbed lying down. They were supposed to have protection. They reported the robbery to the Wellsville police, giving them Johnson's name and a full description. Police Chief John Fultz alerted his men to be on the lookout.

On Saturday February 24th, just a week after the robbery, word came to police headquarters that Johnson was back in town. Fultz quickly mobilized his forces. Because the Wellsville police department was small, Fultz swore in a number of volunteers to back them up. One of the posse members was 53-year-old William T. Hyatt. Hyatt was born in Baden, West Virginia on December 8, 1870. He was a railroad inspector for the Cleveland & Pittsburgh Railroad at the Wellsville railroad yard. He was the foreman of a crew that inspected the railcars for damage or thefts. He and his wife Alice had several children.

Meeting with his posse, Fultz assigned them to strategic positions around town. Hyatt was assigned to patrol along the railroad at Boring's Crossing, an area in the far western end of the city. Hyatt was well acquainted with this area. (*Today this area is part of the Columbiana County Port Authority, Wellsville Terminal.)*

Later that night, at around 8:00 o'clock, Hyatt confronted someone and a gunfight occurred. Hyatt was shot twice in the stomach and then apparently two more times after he had fall-

Police Chief John Fultz

en. Hyatt was able to fire two shots of his own. The gunfire alerted two railroad workers who were working on an engine nearby. Hearing the shots they rushed to the scene. There they found Hyatt unconscious, but still alive. His assailant, however, was long gone.

Hyatt quickly regained consciousness and remained awake all the way to the hospital in East Liverpool. He said that he was sure he hit his assailant at least once in the back. At the hospital, doctors rushed Hyatt into the operating room and went to work trying to save his life. The wounds, however, were too severe. William Hyatt died at 1:00 p.m. Sunday afternoon.

Meanwhile, Chief Fultz had tightened his dragnet around the city. Johnson seeing that the streets were full of armed men decided that he had better get out of town fast. He managed to hop a west bound freight train and slipped out of town. Police quickly sent Johnson's description to nearby cities, and early on Sunday morning it paid off.

A railroad policeman in Alliance, Ohio was checking a train that had just arrived at the station. He saw someone hiding in a boxcar. It was Edward Johnson. He was taken into custody, and turned over to the Alliance police, who contacted Wellsville. Officer H.E. Castleberry traveled to Alliance to take custody of the prisoner. Castleberry loaded Johnson onto an interurban streetcar and headed for Salem, Ohio. There, Castleberry was met by several sheriff deputies and Wellsville officers. They then traveled by automobile to Wellsville.

Back in Wellsville, a large, angry crowd had gathered around City Hall. Tensions were running high, and police feared that Johnson, a black man, could be lynched if they were not careful. Upon reaching City Hall the police were able to sneak Johnson into the jail, through a back door. Once he was safely in the jail, he was booked for the murder of William Hyatt.

Interrogation known as the "third degree," started immediately, Johnson, however, steadfastly maintained his innocence. During William Hyatt's funeral, Chief Fultz took Johnson from his cell, and took him to the funeral home. Fultz dragged Johnson up to the bier, and shoved his face into the casket nearly, touching noses with the dead man. Fultz snarled, *"Now tell me you did not kill that man!"* Johnson calmly replied, *"I never saw that man before."*

Meanwhile, the police were busy gathering evidence. Within a couple of days they had enough to present their case to the Grand Jury. Twenty four witnesses gave testimony. The police also had found a revolver and fifteen cartridges in the home of another black man, who lived just north of Wellsville. They speculated that Johnson had left them there during his escape. The Grand Jury had heard enough, and returned an indictment for first degree murder.

Johnson was removed from the Wellsville lockup and taken to the County Jail in Lisbon, Ohio by Sheriff Gomer Lewis. County Prosecutor Jesse Hanley promised a quick trial. He was a man of his word. The trail began on March 26th, just a month after the murder.

A visiting judge, Fred Wolf from Wauseon in northwest Ohio, was named as the presiding judge. Prosecutor Jesse Hanley represented the people and the court appointed Attorney Ben L. Bennett and Attorney Blaine Cochran to defend Johnson. A jury of ten men and two women would decide the case.

In his opening statement, Attorney Bennett accused the police of giving Johnson the brutal "third degree" treatment. He also said that the police in Homestead, Pennsylvania had arrested another man for the murder. They had beaten a confession to Hyatt's killing out of the man. He said it was evident that Johnson was innocent of the murder, and that the police had the wrong man.

County Prosecutor Hanley produced a great many witnesses. Charles Weis testified that he had seen Johnson hanging around the railroad yard. Fred Cornell and Harold Cosgrove said they were sure Johnson had followed them as they walked up McClain's Run Road, late on the night of the murder. This, however, was not near the railroad. George Seeley testified that it was Johnson whom railroad police had arrested that Sunday morning in Alliance, Ohio.

Doctors J.S. McCullough and H. C. Fraser testified about Hyatt's wounds, and their attempt to save him. Alvin Smith, the owner of the gambling house, identified Johnson as the man who had robbed him on February 17th.

It was not all good for the prosecution, however. Charles Brinkley, one of the gamblers, said that the revolver (State Exhibit C,) was not the gun that Johnson had used on the night of the holdup. John McSwaney said he had been getting a shoeshine when Johnson came into the Smith's club. McSwaney said he had not seen any gun. The prosecutor speculated that Johnson could have thrown his gun into the river. With that, the State rested.

The defense began with Attorney Bennett taking the stand. Attorney Cochran questioned him about the fact that the police denied the defense team access to potential witnesses that they had in custody.

Later, Johnson took the stand in his own defense and calmly related his story. He said that he had been playing cards in Smith's club and had been given a "raw deal." Johnson said they used a "cheater's deck," on him, and he did not like it. He admitted that he had decided to get even. Johnson admitted that he had robbed the club on February 17th. He said he had stayed the night at a boarder's camp and then left town in the morning, travelling back to the Pittsburgh area.

Johnson said he did not have a gun when he left town, and had not thrown a gun into the Ohio River, as the prosecution was claiming. He did admit that he had four pairs of dice on him when captured in Alliance. He also admitted that two of the pairs were crooked. At that the Defense rested.

Throughout the trial, Edward Johnson had remained remarkably calm and deliberate in his demeanor. He appeared nonchalant while maintaining a slight grin on his face.

The jury began deliberations on Monday, April 1st. After fifteen ballets the vote was tied six to six. At that, they broke for the night. After breakfast, the jury began deliberating again. Just before noon they sent word to Judge Wolf that they did not think they could come to agreement. Judge Wolf told them to keep at it. Lunch was served in the courtroom, and at 1:00 p.m. the jury was sent back to work. At 3:45 p.m. the jury finally reached a verdict. The courtroom quickly filled as Johnson was led in by Deputy Sheriff George Wright.

Judge Wolf asked if the jury had reached a verdict and the foreman answered, *"Yes your Honor."* Johnson stood calmly smiling as the verdict was read. *"We the jury, find the defendant,* guilty *of murder in the second degree."* At this Johnson let out a long audible sigh. Judge Wolf thanked the jury for their service, and immediately sentenced Johnson to life imprisonment in the State Penitentiary in Columbus, Ohio. As Sheriff Gomer Lewis led Johnson from the courtroom, he still had the grin on his face. People in the crowd speculated that Johnson must have been smiling because he had escaped a death sentence. Judge Wolfe then left for Salem, where he caught the evening train for Wauseon.

Johnson arrived at the prison in Columbus at noon on April 5, 1923. Did he kill William Hyatt? Who knows? The evidence was pretty weak. There were no eye witnesses, and the police had no murder weapon. So the question remains.

Did they get the wrong man?

Chapter 25
Pursued by Misfortune
The Laird Family
1903-1911

Neil Laird left his home in Scotland at a young age, enlisting in the British Navy. *(*Some said it was the army.)* Laird spent several years in the service of The Crown, spending much time in the Far East. Once he left the service he joined with his two brothers and immigrated to America. The brothers settled in Pittsburgh, Pennsylvania and found work in the steel mills. It was there that Neil met Mary Grammell. *(* This may not have been her last name.)* Mary had grown up in nearby Canonsburg, Pennsylvania. The two were married and soon started their family. The Laird family grew quickly with the births of three children. The Laird's had lived in Pittsburgh for several years when tragedy struck. They lost, possibly their first son, in a streetcar accident. *(* This was reported in later news accounts, however, I was not able to confirm it.)*

Around the year 1893 the Laird's left Pittsburgh and moved to East Liverpool. Neil found work in the potteries as the family continued to grow. However, all was not well with Neil Laird. He began drinking heavily. This caused his work to suffer, and holding down a steady job became difficult for him. He also began to make himself known to the police. On October 24, 1898, he was arrested at his Franklin Street home on a charge of fighting and being drunk and disorderly. He was hauled into jail, probably after being roughed up by the police when he resisted arrest. The next day Mayor Charles Bough fined him twenty five dollars and costs. Unable to pay the $29.60, he was sent back to jail. The mayor indicated that he might send Laird to the workhouse in Canton, Ohio if the fine was not paid.

Mary Laird appeared before the mayor the next day, pleading for mercy. It must have worked because Laird was released with the promise to pay the fine in installments.

Laird was back in trouble again on May 19, 1900. He was arrested by Police Chief Thomas Thompson on a charge of theft. Laird was accused of stealing dishes from the Burford and Vodrey potteries. Facing Mayor William Davidson, Laird confessed and was sentenced to fifty days in the Columbiana County Jail. He was also fined $29.05. Mary Laird appealed to the mercy of the city to help care for her four children.

Once he was released, Neil seems to have changed his rowdy ways. He quit drinking, and tried his best to hold a steady job. He was not having much success, however, and was growing more depressed with each passing day. By late 1902, Neil Laird had been sober for nearly two years, but was in poor health. Some of his old friends convinced him to drink some hot toddies, saying they would be good for him. Unfortunately, being an alcoholic, once he began drinking he could not stop.

Early on the morning of December 29, 1902, Neil Laird got ready to leave his home to look for work. He dressed in what would not be called his best clothes, and left all his valuables behind. He had been drinking heavily through the holidays, and was very depressed. However, today he seemed to be perfectly sober. It had been difficult for the Laird family with him being out of work. He hoped today would be different. Laird had heard that the Buckeye Pottery might be hiring, so he was going to talk to them. Mary Laird bid her husband goodbye and good luck. She pressed a nickel into his hand for the streetcar ride, and then he was off. Neil Laird never returned. When he failed to come home that evening, Mary began to search for him. She was pregnant again with what would be their sixth child, and was quite worried. Inquiring at the Buckeye Pottery, she was told that her husband may have come that day, but they had no openings. His friends had not seen him; neither had the police. She began to think that he may have joined the United States Navy. After several days she contacted his two brothers in Pittsburgh, to no avail; they said they had not heard from him for some time. As the weeks passed, rumors began to circulate that Neil was living in New Cumberland, West Virginia. A search there turned up nothing. Nearly destitute, Mary gave birth to their sixth child, whom she named Annie, in late February. On March 6th, as soon as she was able, Mary started work at the Brunt Pottery for two dollars a day. She had many little mouths to feed.

Shortly after 7 a.m. on March 7th, Water Superintendent Phil Morley and a couple of his men were making an inspection around the city reservoir on Thompson Hill. They noticed something dark floating just under the water. It had not been there the night before when the second of the twice daily inspections had been made. The men put together a crude raft and paddled out to retrieve this unwanted object floating in the city's water supply. When they reached the object, they were astounded by what they saw. *It was a body!* The men pulled it to the edge of the tank and carefully lifted it out. The body was in bad shape, and had evidently been in the tank for some time. The victim was a fully clothed adult male. The outer layer of skin peeled away and the remaining skin had blackened. The corpse was transported to the morgue at the McQuillkin Funeral Home, where an investigation was performed. Meanwhile, Superintendent Morley ordered the flow of water to be shut down and the reservoir drained.

At the funeral home officials determined that it was the body of a Caucasian male, five-feet-eight-inches tall and about 140 pounds. The victim had black hair and wore a small mustache. He also had several gold teeth. They also noticed that, although worn, the clothing was of good quality. Upon removing the clothing they found that the victim was heavily tattooed. Considering the condition of the body, the tattoos were still very evident. On the victim's chest was a large crucifix about ten inches long. An image of a woman holding the British flag, a large eagle, several hearts, and the heads of oriental women adorned other parts of his body.

The search of his clothing did not reveal any identifying papers. In his pockets, there were, however, two pipes and a small amount of tobacco, two large handkerchiefs, and a nickel. All morning people paraded through the morgue to view the corpse. Finally, one of them said, *"That looks like Neil Laird."* Mary Laird was sent for at once. Upon arriving at the funeral home, Mary Laird asked a newspaper reporter, *"Is Neil dead?" "Yes",* said the reporter. When Mary was taken in to view her husband's remains she nearly collapsed, having to be supported by two men. *"My God! My God! It is Neil",* she exclaimed." Staggering against a table she cried, *"This is terrible. What did he do it for? What did he do it for?"* Collecting herself she said; *"Yes, he is dead. Yes, he is dead. This will kill me."*

Mary was allowed to rest for a few minutes before the police and city officials began to question her. She told the authorities about his leaving that December morning in search of work. She said, *"He had been out of his mind for several hours before he went away. He didn't know what he was doing half the time."*

Once the reservoir was drained the only thing that was found was the victim's hat. It was thought that the body may have been held under the water by a piece of debris; although nothing was found. The official cause of death was ruled to be suicide as there were no wounds on the body or any evidence of foul play. A water employee by the name of Brooks related that several weeks ago he had seen a man climb over the wire fence and crouch beside the reservoir, putting his hands into the water. Brooks said he was too far away to get a good look. He looked away to tend his business, and when he looked back, the man was gone. He now thought this must have been Laird.

Due to the suicide, Neil Laird is buried in the Spring Grove Cemetery, for he was denied burial in the St Aloysius Catholic Cemetery. With nothing left to do, Mary Laird returned home and was soon back to work. She had a large family to support. The generous nature of the people of East Liverpool was displayed by a relief fund which raised over $350 dollars for the Laird family.

Life went on for the Laird family. Mary continued to work at various potteries for meager wages. The family now lived in a two-room house on College Street and the older children were beginning to enter the work force. However, nothing much was heard from Mary Laird and her children until May 11, 1907. It was early Saturday morning, just 5 o'clock, when a weary Mary Laird pulled herself from her bed. She started a fire in the stove to cook breakfast, but she was tired and the children were still asleep. Mary decided to lie down for just a few more minutes, not expecting to fall into a deep sleep.

G.H. Craven lived next door to the Lairds, and was eating breakfast when he noticed smoke coming from his neighbor's house. He ran to the house and looking through a window, saw the flames beginning to grow. Joined by other neighbors he broke the window and climbed through. Craven groped his way through the dense smoke until he located one of the beds. Struggling mightily, Craven managed to get three of the children (George, John, and Annie) out of the burning structure. Margaret, the oldest child, managed to escape the flames without help. All of these children suffered minor burns and singed hair. Mary Laird was awakened by the yelling and breaking glass. Feeling her way through the suffocating smoke and finding a window, with her hair and clothing beginning to catch fire, she flung herself through. Landing heavily, she severely injured herself.

About now the fire department arrived. Chief H. Clinton Morley and others crawled into the burning building, hugging the floor to stay below the smoke and flames. Within a few moments the firefighters found the lifeless bodies of seven-year-old Leo, and five-year-old Ruth. Their small bodies were burnt badly, but firefighters felt sure that they had succumbed to the smoke before the flames had reached them.

Once the blaze was extinguished, firefighters discovered that a tall dresser had fallen across the bed where the children had been sleeping. Although the children were found away from the bed, Chief Morley thought that it might have caused them to become disoriented, resulting in them not finding a way out. What caused the dresser to fall was not determined; perhaps the rescuers had knocked it over. Who knows? The home was a total loss, and the suffering family was now completely destitute. Caring neighbors quickly took the shocked family in, nursing their injuries and trying to console them in this time of devastating loss. The two small bodies of the children were taken to a local funeral home to prepare them for burial. They are buried in the St. Aloysius Catholic Cemetery.

Mrs. Laird remained bedridden for several days. For most of that time her oldest daughter Margaret was also confined with her, suffering from severe shock. Meanwhile, the *Evening Review* started a relief fund; unfortunately it did not raise much money. Perhaps people remembered the previous Laird family relief effort, and decided that they had already given enough.

Once Mary had recovered from this tragedy, she made the decision to return to her home in Canonsburg, Pennsylvania. By this time the three oldest children were all old enough to be on their own. They decided to stay in the East Liverpool area, so Mary and Annie bid them farewell and left for Pennsylvania. Margaret, the oldest, eventually married and lived her life in Wellsville, dying in 1973 following a long illness. She had no children. Her brother George worked in the local potteries and never married. He was living with his sister Margaret when he passed away in 1937. The last brother, John "Jack," married and survived his wife by two years, dying in 1968. He was living in Salem, Ohio at the time.

Mary Laird probably added her maiden name when she returned to Canonsburg. She was known there as Mary Laird Grammell. *(*There is no evidence that she remarried, so the name Grammell must have been her maiden name.)* She worked in the Canonsburg Pottery to provide for herself and young daughter Annie.

The Morgan Opera House on Pike Street was a landmark in Canonsburg. On August 26, 1911, a crowd of at least 600 packed in for the early show. The second floor auditorium was filled with a crowd of mostly women and children. The show that Saturday was a live vaudeville act, followed by a motion picture called *"A Little Child*

Mary Laird

Shall Lead Them." As the film was running, the highly flammable cellulose nitrate film caught fire. *(*This was a very serious and all too common occurrence with this type of film.)* The fire was confined to the asbestos cabinet that encased the projector, and the operator, John McCullough quickly extinguished the fire. While this was happening the large audience was blissfully unaware of any danger. Then the unexpected happened. As McCullough opened the door, the odor of smoke drifted into the auditorium. A man in the audience suddenly stood up and yelled *"FIRE!"* The crowd exploded from their seats as if they were one entity. Panic stricken, they rushed into the narrow eight-foot wide hallway that led to the stairway. As the front of the human wave reached the top of the stairway, those in the rear began to push forward. People began to fall, tumbling down the stairs. The pile of people grew quickly as more and more unfortunate victims fell head first down the stairway. Those who remained on their feet began to climb over the pile, compressing it ever more tightly. Adding to the confusion was the large crowd waiting to view the late show. Almost at once men on the outside rushed in and tried to pull people free. One young man was successful in pulling a couple of people from the pile, but was caught in the mass, and lost his own life. Outside the theatre, the scene was one of mass hysteria. As emergency personnel reached the theatre they were impeded by the crowd. The fire chief had to order fire hoses be turned onto the crowd to disperse it.

Once the surviving crowd had made their escape, police and firefighters entered to untangle the mass of humanity. The terrible pile was wall-to-wall and seven to ten feet high. Over 100 people had been injured, with sixty seriously so. Most horrifying were the twenty-six dead bodies contained within the pile. These deaths were caused by suffocation and being crushed. Within this ghastly pile were the crumpled bodies of Mary and Annie Laird.

On August 29th, a funeral mass was held at St. Patrick's Catholic Church in Canonsburg. Afterwards, Mary and Annie were laid to rest in a single grave in the church cemetery.

An investigation determined that the theatre met all the legal requirements. The exit doors swung both ways and the narrow hallway was wide enough. The ruling was listed as *"accidental due to a false alarm of fire."*

In the end, the Laird family was truly *"Pursued by Misfortune."*

Chapter 26

A Mighty Deluge

The Reservoir Collapse
October 13, 1901

(*Newspaper reports are invaluable historical resources. However, reporters are human, and therefore sometimes make mistakes. These mistakes get into print and become historical facts. However, the fact that less water was involved does not change the magnitude of the disaster. It was truly "a mighty deluge.")

East Liverpool has always been blessed with an unlimited source of water. Early settlers drew water from the Ohio River or one of several small streams by the bucket full, and that met their needs. As the town continued to grow, many people dug wells and built cisterns to collect rainwater.

The town boomed following the Civil War. Several new potteries were built, and the water supply was inadequate for their operations. Fire protection was also nonexistent except for a bucket brigade.

During the summer of 1879, the city began work on a water system that would service the town. Work was carried on at a furious pace, and on November 5, 1879, water began to flow though the waterlines laid beneath the city streets.

The first system consisted of a pumping station located on the River Road, and a reservoir located on Thompson's Hill. The reservoir was located 320 feet above the river and gravity moved the water though the waterlines at a good pressure. The water was pumped from the river into the reservoir, and then it flowed into homes and businesses. There was no attempt to filter it in any way.

The existence of nearly a million gallon pool of water perched on a hill above the city has always had its dangers. In late June of 1893, water was found to be leaking through the reservoir's retaining wall. Actually, it was gushing from the southwest corner of the reservoir in an ever increasing stream. City officials and business leaders quickly investigated, and determined that the water pipe must be leaking. Mr. Harker of the Harker Pottery was especially worried. His pottery sat 287 feet below the reservoir. He feared his business could be destroyed if the reservoir failed.

On June 30th, the leak was finally found. A twenty-inch supply pipe had broken and the water was pouring freely from the fracture. The break was quickly repaired and the danger averted. However, many people still worried about the cracks in the hill that seemed to be the result of the ground slipping.

The Evening News-Review reported that people had been digging for clay in the old abandoned clay mines that ran under the reservoir. The city had to threaten prosecution to stop them. The newspaper speculated that the miners may have disturbed the ground.

On July 3rd, Water Superintendent Phil Morley reported that the broken pipe had been repaired. The reservoir had been drained and cleaned, and was in good shape. He said it was being slowly refilled, and that the danger was now over. However, he noted that it could happen again.

The city continued to grow. By the turn of the century, the water supply was again not meeting the demand. The answer was to build a second reservoir to increase the water supply.

The city purchased the land on May 26, 1899 for $8,500 from Eugene Bradshaw, and decided to build the reservoir at the cost of $32,000. Several contractors had submitted bids ranging up to $65,000. City officials thought these bids were too high. The city could build it themselves at the lower price, saving the taxpayers thousands of dollars.

Work began a few months later, but then the project languished for more than a year due to a lack of funding. During that time, the city newspapers and the public called for the work to continue.

The quality of the river water was atrocious, especially when the wickets of the Davis Island dam were lowered. *(*This needed to be done each year to release all the debris that had piled against the dam.)* Whenever this was done, the government required the dam officials to notify the towns along the river. When notified, towns would stop pumping until the "filth" had floated past.

East Liverpool, however, paid no heed to this warning and always kept right on pumping. Officials reasoned that if they stopped pumping, the city would run out of water. The current reservoir was just not large enough to meet the demand. It could not hold the two or three day's supply of water that was required. Clearly the new reservoir had to be completed as soon as possible.

The reservoir was 140 x 275 feet and 27 feet deep. The inner concrete wall was about two feet thick, reducing the depth to about 25 feet. *The Evening News-Review* reported that the reservoir would hold about 7 or 8 million gallons of water. When the reservoir was finished, river water would be pumped through a sand and gravel filter and then into the holding tank. The water would first fill the large tank, then flow into the old reservoir, and finally into the water mains. This would give the city a supply of water for about a week, allowing them to shut down the pumps when necessary.

The reservoir was finally finished in early October 1901. By 5:00 p.m. Sunday, October 13th, it had been slowly filling for a few days. The new vessel was at least twice as large as the old reservoir.

Superintendent Phillip Morley was watching as the tank was being filled; by early that evening he thought it was more than half full. Everything appeared normal to Morley and the few workers that were on duty.

Suddenly, there was the sound of stones falling and a loud hissing noise. The southwest corner of the earthen dike that surrounded the concrete tank had collapsed. The concrete inner wall held unsupported for a few seconds, then exploded outward with a loud crack that would be heard a mile away. Tons of water rushed under immense pressure from the tank.

A gaping hole some twenty-feet wide and about thirty-feet deep had opened up in the southwest corner to the reservoir. The water rushed from confinement with the force of a tidal wave. Sweeping all before it, the wave uprooted trees and anything else in its path.

Morley and others stood thunderstruck, eyes wide and mouths open. The tank emptied within a matter of seconds. There was nothing the men could do to stop it or even sound an alarm.

The rushing water first struck a makeshift shanty in which several Italian laborers had been living. The structure was blasted to pieces. Luckily, no one was in it at the time. It was the first of many close calls. There was also a group of children playing in the water's path. Hearing the noise, the children became frightened, and ran to safety just as the wall let go.

The wave quickly reached the edge of the steep hill. The drop was over 300 feet to the level of the river. For a few seconds it must have looked like Niagara Falls. The wave crossed Pennsylvania Avenue, and then plunged over the hill, taking tons of dirt and boulders and all matter of debris with it.

The Cleveland & Pittsburgh Railroad ran along the bottom of the hill. A freight train had just passed through the area only a few minutes before the disaster. The train would have been destroyed if it had been hit by this wave. The water deposited tons of mud and debris upon the tracks, and then swept on, making for the river.

Standing between the tracks and the river was the Harker Pottery Company. Fortunately, it was Sunday, an off day at the pottery. On a normal day, dozens of workers would have been in harm's way, but now there was only the watchman.

The wave shoved tons of mud into the pottery, nearly filling the basement work areas. The first floor was also badly damaged by the flood. Three kilns filled with ware waiting to be fired in the morning were destroyed. The frame kiln shed was nearly washed away.

Also in the path of the deluge was the water pumping station for the city. Located along the River Road, it was about a half a mile from the reservoir. Again, good fortune or Divine intervention kept the disaster from growing. The wave hit the pump house, but much of its force had been blocked by the buildings of the pottery. The lower floor was flooded, and a lot of mud and debris was piled in and around the building. However the pumps and engines were undamaged and kept operating. This allowed water to be pumped directly into the water mains, thus keeping the city supplied.

The wave swept over the tracks of the streetcar company's East End line and spent itself into the river. It was over in the matter of a minute or two at the most. A small stream of water continued to drain from the tank for several minutes, but the danger was over. There were miraculously no deaths or injuries at all.

The reason for this was there was a man with nerves of steel. Car #16 was westbound, speeding along on the East End line, under the control of Motorman Thomas Hendershot and Conductor George Ferguson. On board were several lady passengers, and a reporter for the *Evening News-Review*. Hendershot saw the fast approaching wall of muddy water heading directly for them. He stopped and told Ferguson they needed to reverse the car. He removed the control handles and began to walk calmly to the rear to attach them on the rear control station. By this time the lady passengers saw the danger and pandemonium broke out. It took all Ferguson could do to stop them from jumping off the car. It would have probably meant their deaths if they had done so. Hendershot reattached the levers and applied the power and the car shot back the way it had come. The wave hit just seconds later. It would have swept the car into the river if not for the actions of this calm and decisive hero.

Interesting is the fact that the *Evening News-Review* had called for Hendershot to be fired a few months earlier. He was driving a streetcar that jumped the rails crossing the Yellow Creek Bridge in Wellsville. The car hung suspended over the side of the bridge. Hendershot, it was said, was so frightened that his grip had to be pried loose from the car. The paper believed he had been traveling too fast. There were no serious injuries except to Hendershot's reputation. Perhaps he had redeemed himself.

Now it was a matter of cleaning up the mess. Railroad traffic was at a stand-still. The 6:25 p.m. eastbound passenger train was stopped at the depot near the foot of Washington Street. The 7:48 p.m. westbound passenger train stopped first in the East End. Some passengers got off and caught streetcars to travel around the landslide. Most stayed aboard and traveled as far as the water pumping station. From there they walked, carrying their luggage nearly a half a mile through the pitch dark debris field. Railroad personnel guided them by lantern light through knee deep water holes and mud. Once on the west side of the slide, they boarded streetcars and rode the short distance to the depot. There they boarded the eastbound train that had been waiting for them. Once all were aboard, the train backed down the track all the way to Steubenville, Ohio, nearly thirty miles. There the passengers made new connections.

The westbound passenger train at midnight stopped in the East End and unloaded the passengers onto streetcars which took them to the depot. There a special train made up at the Wellsville, Ohio yard took them to Steubenville.

The 4:56 a.m. eastbound passenger train managed to get through after only a half an hour delay. The line was open both directions by early morning, and by midafternoon the trains were back on schedule.

To accomplish this herculean feat, about 100 men worked through the night assisted by a steam shovel that was brought in from Bellaire, Ohio by train. The tracks were covered by tons of debris ten feet deep for over a hundred feet. Lesser amounts extended a like distance. The tracks, however, were not damaged.

The streetcar tracks were also covered, but not as badly. Four or five feet of mud covered a space of fifteen to twenty feet. A large crew of men labored for several hours, clearing them by ten o'clock that night. Again, the tracks were undamaged.

Mr. H.N. Harker was returning from the Buffalo Exposition, and was in Pittsburgh when he heard of the disaster. He hurried home and was shocked by the damage to his pottery. The force of the water had ripped doors from their hinges, and the first floor and basement of the main building were nearly destroyed.

Machinery and equipment was badly damaged or destroyed. Worst of all was the mud. It was everywhere, several feet thick. The basement was filled nearly full. Kilns and ware had been lost, and 150 people were out of work. Undaunted, company officials employed a large force of men to dig out the pottery. Working with shovels and wheelbarrows, it would take several days. Initial estimates put the loss at between twenty and thirty thousand dollars.

Breach in the Reservoir

By the end of the next day thousands of people had come to see the muddy disaster. Soon, people began to blame the city for the way the reservoir was built. The city had not bid the project. People thought the piping tunnel through the retaining wall had not been properly constructed and had been the source of the collapse.

Superintendent Phil Morley said he felt the cause of the collapse was a leak in the piping of the old reservoir. He thought water had seeped through the ground and undermined the retaining wall, causing the failure. He said the failure had occurred several feet away from the pipe tunnel.

A hydraulic engineer was called in from Philadelphia, Pennsylvania to inspect the reservoirs before any repair work was done. In the meantime, both reservoirs were out of service, the old one was being drained for a badly needed cleaning. The pumping station, however, was on-line pumping directly into the water mains.

A few days after the disaster, Water Department Clerk J.W. Gipner told the *Evening News-Review* that the city was not worried about lawsuits. He believed that the Harker brothers would be reasonable.

On October 18th, Mr. J. W. Hill, a hydraulic engineer from Philadelphia, arrived to inspect the reservoir. Mr. Hill said it would require several days to make his conclusions. He made a lot of notes but kept any criticism to himself. The *Evening News-Review* did report that he had called the reservoir a thoroughly scientific job. Superintendent Morley was still searching for the leak in the old reservoir piping that he felt was the cause. So far he had not found it.

Nearly a month passed with no report from Mr. Hill, and patience was wearing thin. On November 12th, Mr. William R. Hill, the chief engineer of the Aqueduct Commission of Brooklyn, New York, arrived to inspect the reservoir. After his inspection, he reported the break was caused by trying to fill it too quickly. He thought the pressure at the bottom of the tank would have reached 1050 pounds per square foot. He further stated that the construction was good, but the retaining wall was of poor material.

Repairs began at once. Soon a layer of solid rock was found by digging seven feet deeper. Concrete was poured onto this rock layer for the new base of the retaining wall.

In early December the Harker brothers submitted their bill. The first reports of twenty to thirty thousand dollars damage proved to be high. They gave the city a bill of $10,000 for their loss. The city rejected that and requested an itemized bill. After a careful review, the Harkers came back with a bill of $10,968.35. City officials came back with their own offer of $8,000, which to the Harkers, was unacceptable. The two parties finally settled for $8,500 to be paid over a period of three years. Damage to the reservoir itself came to $4,000.

Later in December, Morley reported that water was being pumped into the old reservoir for the first time since the accident. Up until now the pumps had been working nonstop, keeping water flowing in the city.

On January 13, 1902, several men were inspecting the empty reservoir. They saw a new crack in the concrete inner wall. The crack was in the southeast corner whereas the break had been on the southwest corner. New fears about safety ran through the city. Local engineers felt the reservoir would never be usable. Water Department Clerk J.W. Gipner called the crack an expansion joint that would allow the reservoir to expand and contract with the weather. The public was doubtful.

On January 22nd, the *Evening News-Review* broke the story that the Philadelphia engineer J.W. Hill had told city officials that the reservoir was badly located. He thought the construction was faulty, and the walls would never hold the pressure. Work on the reservoir came to a stop as further inspections were needed. Bad weather also intervened.

In late March, work resumed on repairing the breach in the wall. On April 25th, *The Evening News-Review* reported that the repairs had nearly been completed. Another coat of concrete was being added to the floor due to damage from freezing winter weather.

On May 16th, the reservoir began to be filled. Water was let in at a very slow rate, so it would take several days to completely fill with water. Before the water was turned on, workmen had applied four coats of soap and alum to the concrete walls. Three hundred pounds of castile soap and two hundred pounds of alum were worked into all the little crevices to prevent water from damaging the concrete.

By the end of the month the reservoir held nearly twenty feet of water. The water from the tank was being fed into the city's water mains and its long history of service began. The reservoir was in service into the 1970s with annual cleaning and service during which a liquid cement solution known as gunite was sprayed onto the concrete walls, filling any cracks. Today there are no open reservoirs. All have been replaced with steel tanks.

Postscript

On August 1, 2013, I had an opportunity to interview Robert Disch, the superintendent of the East Liverpool Water Department. I asked him about the newspaper report that the reservoir would hold several million gallons. He told me that there was never a reservoir in East Liverpool that could have held that amount of water. He said the two Thompson Avenue reservoirs held about three million gallons combined. The first reservoir had a capacity of about 900,000 gallons. The new reservoir that had failed was at least twice as large. Disch said that in 2013 the water storage capacity of East Liverpool is less than seven million gallons.

Chapter 27
The Death Badge

The Death of James McCullough
May 13, 1913

James McCullough was born in Walton, Massachusetts on March 3, 1861. At sixteen he decided to leave home, and seek his fortune farther west. McCullough arrived in East Liverpool in 1876, at the time when the Ohio River town was beginning to boom. Over the next several years he vanished from the historical record, but in the mid 1880's the young man resurfaced.

In January of 1885, the fire department acquired its first horses. Two good-sized horses were bought and placed under the control of the fire committee. Since someone would need to feed and care for the animals every day, it was decided to hire a full time employee. That man was Henry Clinton Morley, and he was given the title of hostler. Morley was a member of the volunteer fire department, and the brother of the chief. It was his job to feed and clean the horses, to train and keep them exercised, ready for any fire alarms.

This proved to be such a success that within a few months the volunteer fire department

James McCullough

purchased a third horse. Around this time the city council voted to hire a man to work on the town's streets. At that time all the streets were dirt, so when it rained they became a muddy quagmire. This street man would smooth out the ruts and clean up from the many horses that traveled the streets. It is unclear if the city bought a horse and wagon for the use of the street man or contracted with the fire company to provide this service. In any case, the horse was kept with the fire horses, and by June of 1887, the man doing the job was Jim McCullough. The following year, when Clint Morley was reelected hostler, Jim McCullough was elected as assistant hostler. Morley and McCullough would become lifelong friends.

McCullough's personal life changed in 1891 when he married Miss Emma Deacon on March 3rd, his thirtieth birthday. Their union would produce three daughters.

East Liverpool would continue to grow throughout the 1890's. With that growth came several disastrous fires. As a result of these fires the city would be forced to improve the fire protection. The "China Works" of Knowles Taylor & Knowles Pottery Company was totally destroyed in November of 1889. This resulted in the purchase of the Silsby Steam Fire Engine, *(* It is now in the Lou Holtz Upper Ohio Valley History Museum on E. 5th Street in East Liverpool.)*

The "Dry Goods District" was consumed by fire on March 3, 1892, McCullough's thirty first birthday. April of 1893, saw the "Dresden Works" of the Potters Co-Operative Pottery destroyed in a massive blaze. These disasters resulted in many improvements to the fire department. The city bought a building to be used as a new fire station, new equipment and more horses. Council also hired three full time firefighters in December 1893. Although Morley and McCullough had been on the payroll for several years they technically were not full time firefighters. Clint Morley was named captain and was second in command to Chief Bart Adam. Jim McCullough was named as driver of the hook & ladder wagon, and Joshua Curfman was the engineer of the Silsby steam engine. The duties basically remained the same except now McCullough no longer cleaned the streets. This organization remained in force until May of 1896. Due to the continued growth of the city, a full time fire department was organized, and the old volunteer department was disbanded.

Melvin Bart Adam, the former chief declined the new position due to the requirement of living at the firehouse. H. Clinton Morley was named as the new chief and he quickly elevated his old friend Jim McCullough to the position of assistant chief. Serving as part time police officers was part of the duties of the new department. The firefighters were issued badges, revolvers, night sticks, and handcuffs. They operated the patrol wagon (paddy wagon) because the horse that pulled the wagon was kept with the fire horses. Jim McCullough answered many of these police calls, fighting drunks, hauling prisoners to jail, and making arrests. He also fought nearly all the fires that occurred, including the disastrous Diamond Fire of 1905.

McCullough continued to serve as assistant chief until tragedy struck on September 3, 1907. Chief Morley suffered a heart attack at the scene of a fire at E. 8th Street and Dresden Avenue. He was helped onto a nearby porch, but within minutes he died. Jim McCullough was now the acting fire chief. However, he had lost his best friend. City Council took their time in naming a permanent replacement for Morley. They finally settled on Jim McCullough who began his new duties on October 17th.

During Chief McCullough's tenure, he would oversee the building of a fourth fire station and the expansion of the manpower of the fire department. He also shepherded the department's fire horses through a strange debilitating disease in 1909. The disease left horses throughout the county weak, and unable to stand. Several of the fire horses were affected, and McCullough worked very hard to combat this disease. He arranged for the sick animals to spend time on a farm in hopes that a full recovery would be made. Sadly, the affected animals never fully recovered and had to be replaced. This caused some city officials to start thinking about the new technology of gasoline powered trucks.

Three years later, in 1912, Dr. Robert J. Marshall was elected mayor of East Liverpool. He came into office on the platform of reforming and modernizing city operations. One of the areas that the new mayor was interested in reforming was the fire department. Mayor Marshall wanted to motorize the fire department, and needed a chief that was like minded. Jim McCullough was clearly not that man. McCullough had probably never driven a gasoline powered vehicle, and may have never even ridden in one. He was a man of the past, and Mayor Marshall needed to replace him if his plans were to work.

On February 9th, Chief McCullough suspended Captain Pat Wood for conduct unbecoming of an officer. The Chief charged that Wood was intoxicated on his day off. It would seem that Mayor Marshall saw his opportunity in this event. It is quite likely that Marshall had a conversation with Captain Wood, who was probably not McCullough's biggest fan. Wood may have told the mayor about other firefighters who disagreed with the chief. *(*This of course is all conjecture, but to be possibly proven by later events.)*

The next day, the mayor walked into the Central Fire Station and summarily fired Chief McCullough. Marshall charged him with incompetence, gross neglect of duty, intoxication and allowing the intoxication of others. He was also charged with failing to obey the orders of his superior officers, (the mayor and safety director). Chief McCullough vehemently denied these charges, and vowed to fight for his job and his reputation. Later that day, the mayor revoked the suspension of Captain Wood and returned him to duty.

It seems that the new mayor was not the only person that was ready for a change. The editor of *The Evening Review* ran a scathing editorial saying the fire department was in serious need of a "house cleaning." The newspaper was in complete support of Mayor Marshall. Jim McCullough hired two attorneys and began his defense. For the next couple of weeks McCullough weighed his options as Assistant Chief Tom Bryan ran the department. In the end however, he began to see that he was not going to win. Deciding to make the best of a bad situation, McCullough requested a meeting with the mayor. Meeting with Marshall and Safety Director Joe Wilson, the former chief dropped his lawsuit and requested to be reinstated as a regular firefighter. In those days there was no pension plan, and at his age he was in no condition to start over. Being a firefighter was the only thing he could do, so he was willing to accept the demotion, and vowed to make no trouble. Mayor Marshall accepted the offer and reinstated McCullough as a rank and file firefighter. Jim McCullough returned to work on March 1st, and was assigned to the Northside Station.

Arthur S. Aungst would be the new fire chief. He was currently serving as the chief of the Alliance, Ohio Fire Department. He was a young man, just thirty-five. He was innovative and progressive thinking, and perhaps the youngest full-time professional fire chief in the country. Mayor Marshall was able to lure him away from Alliance with the offer of more money. Alliance could not match the offer, due to a city ordinance that prohibited a pay increase until after his present term expired. Several members of the East Liverpool department filed protests because they were not allowed to compete for the job. A test was given and Aungst came in first, defeating two "unnamed opponents." He was named as the new fire chief on May 9th. He immediately set about reorganizing and modernizing the fire department; some of his innovations are still in practice. Meanwhile, Jim McCullough served quietly at the Northside Station following the many new rules and keeping his opinions to himself. After a few months, Chief Aungst purchased the first fire department badges and issued them to the men. Due to his seniority, Jim McCullough was issued the first badge, which for some reason started with the number "12."

On Friday night, May 9, 1913, McCullough was on duty at the Northside Station when he noticed some dirt on his uniform coat. While using his hand to brush the coat clean his left thumb was cut, when it stuck the edge of his badge. McCullough did not think too much of it, he just wrapped a piece of cloth around it and kept on working. Later, as he was washing and brushing the fire horses, the cloth either fell off or he took it off. Over the weekend his hand became red and began to swell due to an infection. At home, McCullough's condition continued to deteriorate until a doctor was called on Sunday. Doctor Clyde Larkins took one look, and knew it was a case of septicemia. *(*Commonly known as blood poisoning, it is caused by bacteria entering into the blood system.)* McCullough was now confined to his bed with a high fever and severe pain in his arm. By Monday evening, his left arm was badly swollen and beginning to turn black. Doctor Larkins pronounced his condition as being "very precarious." Fearing he was missing something, Doctor Larkins called in another physician. Doctor W.A. Hobbs joined the struggle to stop the spread of the deadly infection. The two doctors did everything short of amputating his arm, but were fighting a losing battle. There were no antibiotics in those days. The doctors thought some foreign material had entered the wound after the bandage had been removed. This had caused the infection.

Assistant Chief Tom Bryan and Captain Bill Ruhe stood by their comrade's bedside throughout the struggle. The end came at 5:22 p.m. on Tuesday, May 13th, when Jim McCullough passed away at his home on Lincoln Avenue. He was surrounded by his family and friends. Just four days had passed since the incident had occured.

McCullough's body was laid out in his home, and grieving firefighters stood as an honor guard around the clock. A firefighter's funeral was held on Friday, with the ringing of the fire bells. The hearse passed in front of Central Fire Station where the horses stood hitched to the fire apparatus and the firefighters stood to attention. Six of his closest friends served as his pallbearers; three firefighters and three police officers. The hearse then made its way up St. Clair Avenue to the Riverview Cemetery, with the firefighters marching behind.

(*Many years later, Fire Chief Charles Bryan, the son of Assistant Chief Tom Bryan, created a file for each man that had served on the fire department. Although it was compiled from memory and the scant records available, it is informative, if not completely accurate. The entry for James McCullough has a personal notation which reads; "In my mind Chief McCullough did not have this coming (his dismissal). It was a dirty rotten trick on the part of the Mayor and Safety Director at the time [and] the three men who testified against him at his trial. All died with cancer of the throat and tongue." In the files of Captain Wood and two others, Chief Bryan made the notation that they had died of cancer of the throat or tongue.)

Postscript

Sixty two years passed, and now it is 1975. I am a rookie firefighter for the City of East Liverpool. One day after returning from a fire alarm, I noticed that I had a splinter in my thumb. Lacking anything else, I removed my fire badge, and used the pin to dig out the splinter. As I was engaged in this operation one of my fellow firefighters said *"Hey, some guy died on here doing that."* I replied *"Who? When? Where? How?"* He did not know; he just knew someone's badge had killed him. I thought to myself, what a great story.

Always being eager to perpetuate a great story, I also began to tell it. The use of your badge pin as a tool was not an entirely uncommon practice, and it usually came with the warning. It was usually accompanied with the grim humor common to firefighters, about being a witness for *"line of duty"* death benefits.

Badge Collection

Several years later, I became interested in delving into the department's musty logbooks. Looking through the daily record for 1913, I found the badge incident in a log entry written by Chief Aungst.

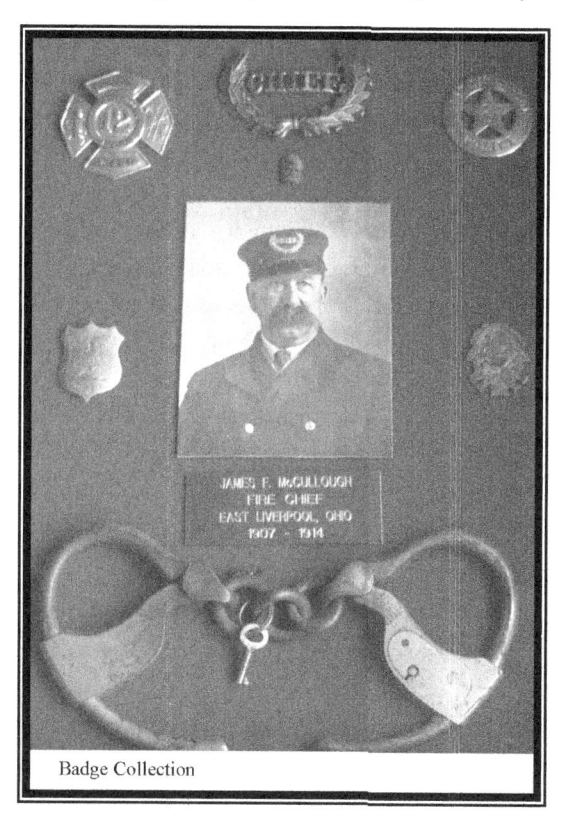

Then, in the late spring of 2001, Fire Chief Jerry Barcus called me into his office, and handed me a letter he had just opened. It was from Mr. James Warrick of Lancaster, Pennsylvania. Mr. Warrick stated that he was the grandson of Chief James McCullough. Mr. Warrick was requesting information about his grandfather. Mr. Warrick was in his 80's and had never known his grandfather, only his grandmother. He was requesting any information we could provide. I sent him a letter with some information, (not about his demotion or strange death) and Xerox copies of a couple of photos. Soon he wrote back thanking me and revealing that he also had some memorabilia from his grandfather. Oddly enough, my family and I were planning a summer vacation to the Amish Country around Lancaster. We would also be visiting friends while there. I asked Mr. Warrick if we could arrange a meeting while I was there. He agreed, and several weeks later my wife Laure and I went to the Warrick home for the meeting. After a few minutes of small talk, I gave him some more information that I had brought with me. He then began to show me his artwork. He was an excellent wood carver. He carved historical scenes in three dimensions, some of which had won first place in the Florida State Fair. They were mostly Egyptian scenes, pyramids and the like. Finally, I was able to switch the conversation back to his grandfather. After a little while, he went into another room and brought out some items, including a great photograph of the East Liverpool Fire Department lined up in the Diamond. The timeframe is from about 1891. Then he handed me something in a picture frame, and I was blown away. There was a collection of his grandfather's badges and handcuffs grouped around a photo of the chief. In the upper left corner was badge #12, *"the death badge."*

I told him how surprised I was to see it, and then related the story, which he said his grandmother had never talked about. I also told him about the department's legend surrounding the badge. Mr. Warrick chuckled. As my wife and I were leaving, I knew I had to request the badge for the Fire Museum. Mr. Warrick told me he would probably give it to his grandson. I told him I completely understood that it should remain in the family, but the museum would love to have it if he changed his mind.

Shortly after returning to East Liverpool, I received the first of many letters from Jim Warrick. He would write to me just as if I were related to him. He told me about his daily activities, his aches and pains, and about various family members. Some of the letters told of he and wife's trips to Florida for the winter. The letters would continue to come quite often for the next couple of years. I always answered his letters, never quite knowing what to say.

On August 16, 2001, I was off duty when Chief Barcus called my home to tell me that Jim Warrick was at the station and wanted to see me. His wife Betty, still had family in the Glenmoor section of town, and they had come for a visit.

I hurried to meet him, and showed him around the station and the Fire Museum. He seemed pleased with what he saw. When we were finished, I walked with him back to his car, and he reached into the trunk and took something out. It was the badge collection, including #12. He said, *"Put this in your museum. That is where I want it to be."* I gratefully accepted.

Jim's letters continued to come for a couple of years, but his health faded and finally the end came. It is sometimes strange how things turn out, how a lost badge and an old legend brought two men together as friends.

The Death Badge

Chapter 28
A Degenerate!
The Adamant Porcelain Murders-Arson
February 7, 1918

The young stranger arrived in the village of Lisbon, Ohio on Monday, February 4, 1918. There was something about him that just seemed out of place to those who noticed him walking the streets. Before long, a police officer noticed him and asked for his identification and selective service card. There was a war on, and young able-bodied men ought to have been in the army. The stranger produced his draft card, but could prove no visible means of support, so he was taken to jail, where he spent the night. The next morning, he claimed that he just wanted a job. The police took him up on that. They took him to the American Sewer Pipe Plant in town, where he was hired as a laborer.

For the next two days he worked as a pipe hauler, working from 7:00 a.m. until 5:30 p.m. When his shift ended on Wednesday, he got cleaned up and left the flop house where he was staying with other plant workers. He was going out on the town; they thought.

The interurban streetcar coming from Youngstown on the Y & O Line made a stop at West Point about 6:30 that evening. The West Point station was several miles southeast of Lisbon. There the young stranger got on for the trip into East Liverpool. The conductor took a long look at this young man. There was something about his eyes, a kind of wild look that made the conductor uneasy. The car arrived in the "Diamond" at 7:10, and the young man got off and disappeared into the crowded streets.

The Adamant Porcelain Company was located at 442 W. 6th Street, on land that is now part of the highway interchange. It was typical for potteries in that era. A two-story brick building 275 feet long and 115 feet wide, encompassing five kilns made up the major portion of the plant. About one hundred employees were busy producing porcelain insulators for the United States government. Company President Harry Peach and Secretary Treasurer George Reed had procured the wartime contract and were eager to keep the orders filled. However, they had a problem; the war had brought with it numerous shortages, and natural gas was one of them. The plant was ready for operation, but the kilns were idle until the gas could be turned back on.

In the very early hours of Thursday, February 7th, night watchman David Mumaw was in the engine room of the plant when someone pulled the door open. The young stranger stood in the doorway, each man surprised to see the other. The stranger asked Mumaw if he could "flop" there for the night. Uneasy, Mumaw told him *"No, get out of here."* The stranger left but stayed close, watching. A few minutes later he sneaked into the plant. Seeing a hatchet lying on a work bench he picked it up, and began to stalk the night watchman. Soon he found the sixty-year-old Mumaw near one of the kilns. He was bent over looking at something and never heard the stranger coming. Sneaking up from behind, the man raised the hatchet and stuck. The ghastly deed was done. Quickly the young stranger gathered up paper and other flammable material, piled it up against a clay bin, and set it on fire.

At around 3:40 that morning, Tom Hester was awakened by an odor of smoke. Hester lived next to the plant in a company-owned house on 7th Street. Hester looked out his window into the cold night, but saw nothing amiss. About an hour later the same thing happened to Mrs. Henry Hancock. She smelled smoke and at first thought her house was burning. The Hancock family lived in another company house located at the southern end of the plant. Mrs. Hancock searched her home but found nothing wrong. As she was about to go back to bed, she looked out her back door, just as the flames burst into view.

Quickly she awakened her husband and they contacted the night watchman at the nearby West End Pottery, who called the fire department. Meanwhile, streetcar motorman William Bailey saw the flames erupt from the plant as he was crossing the West End Viaduct. The viaduct passed over the southern end of the pottery. Bailey also contacted the fire department.

Fire Chief Tom Bryan and the crew from Central Station were soon on their way. As the trucks passed through the Diamond the firefighters could see the bright orange-red glow in the night sky. Flaming embers filled the air as the firefighters arrived on the scene. One end of the plant was fully engulfed by flames, and the heat was intense. Working quickly, the firefighters soon had hose lines in action pouring thousands of gallons of water onto the flames. Within minutes, the Northside and East End fire companies were on the scene, and now the entire East Liverpool force was battling the blaze. Bryan quickly saw that trying to save the pottery was useless; the fire had gained too much of a head start on them. He gave orders for the exposures to be protected. The two wood frame houses located at either end of the doomed plant were also burning, but the firefighters worked like demons, trying to save them. In the end it would prove to be impossible; both homes were completely gutted by the flames. Located over the southern end of the plant was the West End Viaduct. This streetcar bridge extended from the western end of 6th Street downhill to the flat land near where the Westgate School is now located. During the height of the blaze, the wooden railroad ties became overheated and caught fire. Firefighters were concerned that if they sprayed cold water onto the bridge the steel rails might warp. Instead, the men used firefighting chemicals to extinguish the burning ties. Though scorched and slightly charred, the bridge was saved and was relatively undamaged. The cooper shop, which occupied a separate wood frame building, was the only portion of the plant to escape the flames.

It was a long four-hour battle before the fire was declared to be under control, although it would continue to smolder for several more hours. A large number of people had braved the cold night to watch this desperate struggle, including a wild-eyed young stranger who stood in the shadows, smiling.

During the blaze, Chief Bryan had been told that the night watchman was missing. However, there had been no way for the firefighters to enter the building to search for him. Before long, the chief was informed that a second man, Joseph Cannon, may have been in the pottery, and he too was missing.

Joseph Cannon was a fifty-five-year-old potter from Wheeling, West Virginia. He had been sleeping in the pottery for the last several nights, and had been seen there by relatives at about nine o'clock last night.

Fire ruins

By mid-morning the rubble had cooled enough to conduct a search for the missing men. At 11:00 a.m., Chief Bryan and Firefighter Clyde Supplee discovered a badly burnt body near the ruins of the #3 kiln. It was barely recognizable as being human. The headless, limbless trunk was first thought to be that of David Mumaw, the night watchman. About thirty minutes later a second body was discovered near the #5 kiln. This body was also badly burned but a little less than the first. It was determined to be the body of Mumaw when the remains of the punch clock were found. It was attached to a piece of cord around what remained of the head and neck of the victim. The night watchman would punch the clock as he made his rounds. This meant that the first victim had to be Joseph Cannon.

Although the firm had been working on a government contract for the war effort, no thought of sabotage was entertained. *(* Strange as this may sound, German agents were at work sabotaging factories in the United States in an effort to hinder the Allied cause.)* The theory put forth of a gas explosion being the cause was quickly dispelled due to the gas being shut off because of the shortage. Chief Bryan said as a result of the severe damage, the exact cause of the deadly $100,000 blaze might never be determined. He thought the two victims probably died from being overcome by the heavy smoke. Company president, Harry Peach vowed to rebuild as soon as possible. They had a government contract to fill.

Fire ruins

Meanwhile, the young wild-eyed stranger returned to Lisbon early on the morning of fire. He slipped quietly into his place at the sewer pipe plant and worked all day. At the end of his shift, the stranger quit and asked for his pay. After drawing his pay he went into town and purchased a new suit; then he headed for East Liverpool.

On Friday, February 8th, Frank Stanley was the night watchman at the Kenilworth Tile Company, located on Third Street in Newell, West Virginia. He walked into the drying room at 8:00 p.m. Seeing nothing wrong, he punched his clock, and turned to leave. It was then that Stanley saw the stranger lurking in the shadows. Stanley ordered him to move on, so the stranger started up the path leading back toward town. Stanley did not think too much of it. Drifters often sought out potteries as someplace warm and dry on cold winter nights. The stranger did not go very far however; he hid along the path and watched as Stanley went into the outhouse at that end of the building. Then he crept past the watchman and went into the drying room. This area of the plant was heated by steam pipes fed from the boiler room, and was used to finish drying the ware. There were no open flames in this room. The night watchman left the outhouse, walked away from the drying room, and re-entered the plant.

The young stranger remained hidden until the watchman was gone. Then he went to work. Finding some paper and other debris, he piled it and soon had a nice sized blaze going. The young stranger then silently left.

About fifteen minutes past eight, Stanley began to worry. He could smell smoke. Rushing back along his route, he soon came to the drying room and found the single story frame structure ablaze. Stanley called the Newell Fire Department, and the East Liverpool department was also notified. Chief A.M. Fisher and the Newell Volunteer Fire Department arrived to find the building engulfed by fire. Meanwhile, Chief Bryan had gained Mayor Wilson's permission and was on his way. Bryan, along with firefighters Clyde Supplee, Bill Davis and Bill Fowler were soon battling the blaze beside the Newell volunteers. There was little hope of saving the wood frame portion of the plant, so most of the effort was concentrated on the brick section. Firefighters used five hose lines to bring the blaze under control at about 11:00 p.m. The blaze had fully consumed two thirds of the pottery. The office, kiln shed, and machine shop had been spared although these areas had some water damage. Volunteers had carried the company records and furniture to safety early in the fire. Seeing that there was nothing left or them to do, the East Liverpool men returned home around mid-night. The Newell department remained on the scene until dawn.

The plant was nearly destroyed, and about one hundred people were now out of work. Management placed the loss at $60,000. They vowed to quickly rebuild in hopes of filling their government contracts. With this second blaze in just two days, rumors began to circulate; maybe sabotage was being directed at the East Liverpool area.

The young, wild-eyed stranger may have spent part of the weekend in Midland, Pennsylvania, but he was back in East Liverpool by Sunday night. The stranger showed up at the home of Garfield Glenn, a slight acquaintance of his, who lived on W. 8th Street. It was nearly mid-night; he was hungry and wanted someplace to sleep. Glenn agreed to feed him, but would not let him sleep there. The man left the Glenn home at about 1:30 Monday morning.

Just before 2 o'clock Monday morning, February 11th, night watchman Frank Higgins was making his rounds through the darkened interior of the Thomas & Sons Porcelain Company. The plant was located on Baum Street in East Liverpool, just above W. 8th Street, and very near to the destroyed Adamant plant. As Higgins was passing through the slip house, something in the shadows caught his eye. Turning his flashlight in that direction he saw a man crouched beside a clay bin. The man looked like a wild animal about to pounce on its prey. The intruder started to move toward Higgins who quickly pulled his revolver and ordered the man to stop. The intruder whirled and began to flee, but then stopped. He lifted his hands and surrendered. Higgins marched the intruder upstairs at gunpoint. He kept him covered while one of the night shift kiln operators called the police. Captain George Toland and Patrolman Kinsvatter soon arrived and took the strange young man into custody. As Captain Toland slapped handcuffs on the prisoner he asked, *"What is your name?"* The wild-eyed stranger looked at him and answered, *"Willis Payne."* They took him to City Hall and locked him in a cell.

Payne was born on January 30, 1894, the son of Charles and Minnie Payne, in the small town of Proctorville, Ohio. Proctorville is located in the extreme southern portion of the state along the Ohio River, opposite of Huntington, West Virginia. His parents were first cousins; in fact what are called "double cousins." That is when two brothers marry two sisters. Consequently, their children are related by blood to both sets of grand-parents. They then have twice the normal blood relationship. Whether or not that fact had anything to do with it, Willis was a troubled child. Young Willis enjoyed fire. He liked to see fire and to set things on fire. In other words, he was a pyromaniac, *(* a person with a persistent desire to burn things.)* By the age of five he was accused of burning down a barn. At the time it was thought that it was simply the act a young child who had accidently set the fire while playing with matches. However, the suspicious fires continued, and Willis always seemed to be the main suspect. Those people who knew him best described him as a "dull child," and one who was easily influenced. A poor student, Willis quit school after the sixth grade.

In 1912, at the age of eighteen, his disturbing behavior had become too much, and he was committed to an asylum. For the next five years, Willis shuffled through life among the disturbed souls at the Ohio Institute for the Feeble Minded, in Columbus. In those days, places like this would have been little more than prisons. However, Willis was not destined to remain there. On January 8th 1917 he was released. He went back to Proctorville, but within a short time he was arrested in nearby Ironton, Ohio. After spending a little time behind bars in Ironton, Willis drifted to Western Pennsylvania. Trouble had not left him, for soon he was behind bars again. This time he was arrested for breaking and entering in Allegheny County and spent 30 days in the county jail. Once he was released, he became the guest of the Beaver County Jail. He had tried to run out on his boarding house bill in Midland, Pennsylvania. The Rochester, Pennsylvania police arrested him on December 28th, for failing to have a Draft Registration Card. He was sentenced to 30 days; he would spend his twenty-fourth birthday behind bars. A day or two after his release he was again arrested, this time in New Galilee, Pennsylvania, for breaking into a garage. He was quickly released and by February 4, 1918, he was once more walking the streets, this time in Lisbon, Ohio.

Willis Payne was a well-built young man with high cheekbones and straight black hair. Everyone who saw him would talk about that strangely wild look he had in his eyes. He was also a man with many vices. He drank alcohol and chewed tobacco. He also abused cocaine and morphine.

Once he was securely locked away in the East Liverpool Jail, the questioning began. Payne freely admitted to Captain Toland that he had been in trouble with the police over in Pennsylvania. Although his actions at the Thomas Porcelain Plant were suspicious, no connection to the other fires was evident. He was being held for only trespassing and attempted assault.

Police Chief Hugh McDermott arrived for work later that morning and was briefed about the early morning arrest and the suspicious character that was occupying a cell. McDermott took over the interrogation. In those days it could be fairly rough. With the police utilizing what was known as the "third degree," Payne refused to talk at first. He soon changed his mind, however. Chief McDermott's police dog "Turk" had been keeping a watchful eye on Payne, and Payne had been keeping his eye on the dog as well. Suddenly "Turk" lunged viciously at the prisoner, and the chief did very little to restrain him. Badly frightened by the dog, Payne began to talk. He quickly confessed that he had burned the two potteries, and was planning to burn others when he was caught.

The chief was soon joined by Fire Chief Tom Bryan, Mayor Joe Wilson, and City Solicitor R.G. Thompson. Payne began to weave several confusing accounts of his motives and actions leading up to the crimes; however, the details of the crimes remained constant. He readily admitted to murdering the night watchman David Mumaw at the Adamant Plant and stuck to it. The intense questioning went on for over two hours. At one time Payne said he did it because he could not get a job, and wanted to *"get even."* In another version, he said he was upset because Mumaw refused to let him sleep in the pottery. In still another version, he said the night watchman had let him *"flop"* there. He had set the fire and killed Mumaw because he *"had nothing else to do."* Payne said that a man in Midland, whom he named, had paid him two dollars to burn the Adamant Plant. Later he said the pay had been 50 cents.

The testimony went like this;

> Police: *Did your friend give you any cocaine that night before you went down there?*
>
> Payne: *I took a little bit of it.*
>
> Police: *How did you take it?*
>
> Payne: *With water.*
>
> Police: *Ever take it in your nose?*
>
> Payne: *Sure.*

Later during the questioning;

> Police: *Do you like to see fire?*
>
> Payne: *I like to see some of them.*
>
> Police: *What do you like to see about them?*
>
> Payne: *Like to see the firemen work. Like to see the*

> blaze. And if anyone is caught in them, like to hear the screams.

Police: How would you like to see those dead men now?

Payne: Sure. I'd like to see them.

That afternoon Chief McDermott and Fire Chief Tom Bryan took the prisoner to the site of the Adamant fire. The officers wanted to be sure that Payne was telling them the truth. Payne led the two chiefs to the exact location where the night watchman's body had been found. He told them how he had killed the man and showed them where and how he had set the fire. *(* During the investigation of the fire, firefighters had found a hatchet head beside the body of David Mumaw. Payne knew nothing about Joseph Cannon because he had not known Cannon was in the building.)*

The chiefs then took Payne to Newell, West Virginia by streetcar. When they got off the streetcar, the two officers pretended to not know where to go. Payne said to them, "See that cinder path?" Chief Bryan said, *"Yes, where does it go?"* Payne replied, *"Down to the fire."* Payne began walking down the path with the two chiefs following behind. Upon reaching the burned-out ruins Payne announced, *"See, there it is."* Frank Stanley, the watchman, was patrolling the plant when the officials walked down the path. Before anyone could say anything Payne said *"That's the man."* Chief McDermott asked Stanley if he had ever seen the prisoner before. Stanley identified Payne as the man he had talked to the night of the fire. Entering the fire ruins, Payne led them to the spot where he had set the fire. Stanley confirmed that that was where he had first found the fire. Confident that Willis Payne was both a murderer and an arsonist, the chiefs returned him to jail. Both men, however, were convinced that Payne was insane.

That evening the investigators were joined by two men from the Ohio State Fire Marshal's office. Joseph Hershberger and S.E. Hartman took part in questioning Payne. Telling much the same story while adding new some details and changing others, Payne held his audience's complete attention. Payne now said that an unknown man in a *"fur coat"* had induced him to burn the Adamant Plant. The officials suspected this unknown man might be a German agent, since both factories had been manufacturing items needed in the war effort. By Wednesday, February 13th, fearing that Payne might be a *"tool of saboteurs,"* investigators from the United States Justice Department joined the hunt for *"the man in the fur coat."* (* No connection was ever found.)

Charged with double murder and arson by Columbiana County Prosecutor W.W. Beck, Payne was photographed and then transferred to the county jail in Lisbon. Copies of the photograph were sent to various places where fires in factories had also occurred.

Payne was not without his supporters. Two laborers at the American Sewer Pipe Company told police that Payne had slept in the rooming house with them on the nights of the fires. Payne himself refuted that, saying he had indeed set both fires. Records of the sewer pipe company showed that Payne was at work at 6:50 a.m. on Thursday morning, while the Adamant fire was still burning. This would have made it difficult for Payne to have made it back to Lisbon in time for work. However, plant manager Ben Connors, told police that they did not have a time clock. He said the clerk starts work at 8:00 a.m. and then writes in the time that the employees tell him. This evidence showed that Payne would have at least an extra hour to get to work. Investigators also talked with Y&O streetcar conductor Coleman, who identified Payne as the strange man who boarded his car in West Point the night of February 6th. Mr. Garfield Glenn told police about feeding Payne, but denying him a place to sleep the night he was captured in the Thomas plant.

On Monday, February 18th, one week after being arrested, Payne was visited by members of his family. Joseph Payne, his uncle from Proctorville, came along with two cousins from Wellsville, Ohio. They spoke to Payne under the watchful eyes of Fire Chief Bryan and Prosecutor Beck.

Beck later announced that the state would not present the charges to the Grand Jury until the completion of the investigation. Although all the officials were satisfied that Payne was guilty, they were also sure that he was mentally unbalanced. He had told several versions of the crimes, including possible German sabotage, and all these trails had to be followed.

Over the next few weeks, the investigation continued without media attention. Finally everyone was satisfied that Payne had acted of his own accord. In late April, the Grand Jury found that Willis Payne was guilty, and also insane. They called for an Inquest of Lunacy to be held.

On April 25th, an Inquest of Lunacy was held before Probate Court Judge S.W. Crawford. The investigating panel consisted of Doctors Seward Harris and Hugh S. Maxwell. They found that Willis Payne was a young man of about 25-years-old. Although clean in his personal habits, he chewed tobacco and drank intoxicating liquor to excess at times. He also abused cocaine and morphine. They found that he sometimes had fits of violence. Payne demonstrated absolutely no remorse for the crimes he had committed. He spoke of them as if they were just ordinary occurrences. Payne also told the doctors that he had set several other fires.

The Court ruled that Willis Payne was guilty, but insane. He was sentenced to the State Hospital for the Criminally Insane in Lima, Ohio. Sheriff William Dalrymple transported him to the asylum on May 3rd, 1918. Payne would spend the rest of his life working in the leather shop, and shuffling through life along with other disturbed souls. He would set no more fires, but he would never be free from his desires.

Postscript

The journey into the dark past has been completed for now.

Although there have been some tedious and even frustrating times for me, four years of research and writing have been pleasurable for the most part.

I hope my readers have enjoyed these glimpses into our area's past, into some of the dark days.

Chapter Sources

Various newspaper sources were used in the research of this book. Over the years *the East Liverpool Review* has changed its name, numerous times. However, the name *Review* has always been a part of their title. As such, for this work, *The Review* alone will be used.

Chap. 1 *"Fire or Water!,"* The Winchester Disaster, February 23, 1866

Newspapers

The Union, Wellsville, Oh. 3-1-1866, 3-8- 1866

Ohio Patriot, Lisbon, Oh. 3-2-1866

The Republican, Salem, Oh. 2-28-1866

The Journal, Salem, Oh. 3-9-1866

The Herald, Steubenville, Oh. 3-1-1866

The Intelligencer, Wheeling, W Va. 2-24-1866, 2-26-1866, 2-28-1866

The Commercial, Pittsburgh, Pa. 11-6- 1865, 1-5-1866, 1-19-1866, 1-22-1866, 2-15-1866, 2-20-1866, 2-24-1866, 2-26-1866, 2-27-1866, 2-28-1866

The Gazette, Pittsburgh, Pa. 11-8-1865, 1-20-1866, 1-26-1866, 2-15-1866,

Other Sources

Way's Packet Directory 1848-1994, Compiled by Frederick Way Jr. Copyright 1983 / Revised Edition 1995, Published by Sons & Daughters of Pioneer River men

Chap. 2 *"Holocaust!,"* The Destruction of the Sloan Family, February 23, 1881

Newspapers

The Potter's Gazette, East Liverpool, Oh. 8-6-1878, 8-22-1878, 5-27-1880, 10-14-1880, 2-24-1881, 3-10-1881

The Tribune, East Liverpool, Oh. 8-6-1879, 8-22-1878, 2-5-1879, 7-5-1879, 1-31-1880, 2-26-1881, 3-10-1881, 4-9-1881, 8-31-1882

The Review, East Liverpool, Ohio 10-16-1880, 2-26-1881, 7-23-1901, 10-10-1894, 10-9-1901

Commercial Gazette, Pittsburgh, Pa. 2-24-1881, 2-25-1881

Other Sources

United States Census Records 1860- 1870- 1880

www find a grave. Com Hannah Sloan

Chap. 3 *"The Siren's Song,"* The Mysterious Death of Joseph Martin, December 7, 1918

Newspapers

The Review, East Liverpool, Oh. 12-7-1918

The Tribune, East Liverpool, Oh. 12-9-1918

Chap. 4 *"Hurtling to Destruction!,"* Stories of Terror on Streetcars

Newspapers

"Walking the Trestle"

The Review, East Liverpool, Ohio 12-1-1893, 12-2-1893

The Daily Crisis, East Liverpool, Oh. 12-1-1893, 12-2-1893

The Tribune, East Liverpool, Oh. 12-2-1893, 12-23-1893

"Trouble on Franklin Street"
"The First Trip was His Last"

The Review, East Liverpool, Oh. July 8, 1895

The Daily Crisis, East Liverpool, Oh. 7-9-1895, 7-10-1895, 7-12-1895, 7-16-1895

"Terror in the Afternoon"

The Review, East Liverpool, Oh. 10-18,1902, 10-20-1902

The Daily Crisis, East Liverpool, Oh. 10-18-1902

"Franklin Street Again"

The Review, East Liverpool, Oh. 1-11-1903

"Calamity on the Grandview Line"

"Four Winter Days"
Dec. 17, 1900 – Jan. 19, 1901 – Jan. 29, 1902 – Jan. 24, 1903

The Review, East Liverpool, OH. 11-10-1900, 12-17-1900, 12-18-1900, 12-19-1900, 1-19-1901, 4-6-1901, 1-30-1902, 1-11-1903, 1-24-1903

"Lisbon Street Hill"

"The Pleasant Heights Miracle"

The Review, East Liverpool, OH. 9-24-1902, 3-23-1903, 3-24-1903

The Daily Crisis, East Liverpool, OH. 3-23-1903

"The Final Run was Nearly the End"

The Review, East Liverpool, OH. 3-26-1903

"A Few More Rides"

"Over the Bridge!"

The Review, East Liverpool, Oh. 12-8-1906

"The Grandview Line Again"

The Review, East Liverpool, OH. 3-19-1915

"Autumn Leaves", **Oct. 27, 1902**

The Review, East Liverpool, OH. 10-27-1902

"Coming Home from the Dance"

The Review, East Liverpool, OH. 10-15-1910

Other Sources

Ghost Rails III, Electric, by Wayne A. Cole Copyright 2007

Chap. 5 *"Taken for a Ride!,"* The Roy Marino Murder, September 10, 1937

Newspapers

The Review, East Liverpool, OH. 8-21-1936, 11-21-1936, 7-27-1937, 7-29-1937, 8-2-1937, 8-3-1937, 8-4-1937, 8-6-1937, 8-10-1937, 8-23-1937, 8-25-1937, 8-26-1937, 8-28-1937, 9-2-1937, 9-

7-1937, 9-10-1937, 9-11-1937, 9-17-1937, 5-19-1938, 5-27-1938, 7-22-1938, 1-3-1957, 1-30-1958, 7-19-1958

The Herald –Star, Steubenville, OH. 12-22-1937, 12-23-1937, 12-24-1937, 4-9-1938, 4-11-1938, 4-12-1938, 5-18-1938, 5-19-1938, 5-20-1938, 5-25-1938, 5-27-1938, 6-9-1938, 6-10-1938, 7-12-1938, 7-22-1938

The Vindicator, Youngstown, OH. 9-10-1937, 9-11-1937, 9-12-1937, 9-13-1937, 9-14-1937, 9-15-1937, 1-11-1938, 4-9-1938, 4-10-1938, 4-11-1938, 4-13-1938, 4-15-1938, 5-17-1938, 5-18-1938, 5-19-1938, 5-20-1938, 5-21-1938, 5-22-1938, 5-23-1938, 5-24-1938, 5-25-1938, 5-26-1938, 5-27-1938, 6-8-1938, 6-9-1938, 6-10-1938, 6-11-1938, 6-12-1938, 6-13-1938, 6-14-1938, 6-15-1938, 7-11-1938, 7-12-1938, 7-13-1938, 7-14-1938, 7-22-1938, 7-23-1938, 11-2-1938, 1-8-1949, 1-3-1957, 1-29-1958, 7-18-1958

The Palm Beach Post, Palm Beach, Fl. 1-6-1966

The Miami News, Miami, Fl.   6-3-1967

Books

Crime town USA, The History of the Mahoning Valley Mafia, Allen R. May, 2013

Chap. 6 *"Ninety Minutes of Terror,"* The Dry Goods District Fire, March 3, 1892

Newspapers

Ohio Patriot, Lisbon, Oh. 3-10-1892

The Daily Crisis, East Liverpool, Oh. 3-3-1892, 3-4-1892, 3-5-1892

The East Liverpool Tribune, East Liverpool, Oh. 3-5-1892, 3-12-1892, 3-19-1892, 3-26-1892

Chap. 7 *"Something Terrible has Happened!,"* The Tweed-Morris Murders, July 31, 1973

Newspapers

The Review, East Liverpool, Oh. 7-31-1973, 8-1-1973, 8-2-1973, 8-3-1973, 8-4-1973, 8-7-1973, 8-8-1973, 8-9-1973, 8-30-1973

The Vindicator, Youngstown, Oh. 8-1-1973

Websites

www.reviewonline.com/ *A Look Back; Murders that Shocked the Community*, August 8, 2006, by Michael D. McElwain

Obituaries, Arthur L. Morris, August 24, 2010

www. ccfhv.com / 2011/06/documentary-details-ohio-cold-case-from-1973,html

www.post-gazette.com/ *Documentary Details Ohio cold case from 1973*, by Torsten Ove, Pittsburgh Post-Gazette

Documentary

759 Dresden, A David Dunlap Film, 2010 www.28 parallel.com

Chap. 8 *" Wrong Place at the Wrong Time,"* The Tragic Death of Herbert Sayre, Oct. 8, 1925

Newspapers

The Review, East Liverpool, Oh. 10-8-1925, 10-9-1925

Records of the East Liverpool Fire Department

Fire Alarm Book #3, Jan. 1923 – Dec. 1930, Entry for October 8, 1925- Run #149

Chap. 9 *"Death of a Firefighter,"* The Henry Avenue Tragedy, August 2, 1962

Newspapers

The Review, East Liverpool, Oh. 8-3-1962, 8-4-1962, 8-6-1962

Records of the East Liverpool Fire Department

Fire Alarm Book #7, Jan. 1961 – Dec. 1978, Entry for August 2, 1962- Run #163

Central Station Daily Logbook, Oct. 24, 1961- April 6, 1963, Entry for August 2, 1962- Pg. 79

Interviews

Asst. Chief Gerald Goodballet, Retired, June 26, 2012

Asst. Chief Carmen Perorazio, Retired, July 9, 2012 (by Telephone)

Firefighter Richard Bissell, Retired, July 6, 2012 (by Telephone)

Chap. 10 *"Shootout in Little Italy,"* The Jim Kenney Murder, May 17, 1926

Newspapers

The Review, East Liverpool, Oh. 3-21-1926, 5-1-1926, 5-3-1926, 5-17-1926, 5-18-1926, 5-19-1926, 5-20-1926, 5-25-1926, 5-28-1926, 6-17-1926, 6-22-1926, 6-29-1926, 7-19-1926, 7-23-1926, 7-27-1926, 7-29-1926, 7-30-1926, 8-9-1926, 8-23-1926, 9-10-1926,

The Review, Cont.   9-17-1926, 9-23-1926, 10-7-1926, 10-12-1926, 10-19-1926, 10-21-1926, 10-22-1926, 10-23-1926, 10-30-1926, 11-3-1926, 11-5-1926, 11-6-1926, 11-8-1926, 11-11-1926, 11-12-1926, 11-13-1926, 11-30-1926, 12-9-1926, 12-16-1926, 12-20-1926, 12-22-1926, 12-23-1926, 12-24, 1926, 12-31-1926, 1-

12-1927, 2-10-1927, 2-28-1927, 3-18-1927, 5-5-1927, 5-16-1927, 12-24-1955, 1-10-1956, 1-4-1991, 5-17-2003, 3-31-2014,

Court Documents

The State of Ohio vs Nick Scaccuto, Case # 3271 Court of Common Pleas, Columbiana County

The State of Ohio vs Rocco Carbicello- Bennie Carbicello, Case # 3332 Court of Common Pleas

Columbiana County

Interview

Robert "Brassy" Beresford, Ex. Sheriff of Columbiana County, October 13, 2012

Chap. 11 *"Chlorine Gas!,"* The Water Filtration Plant Fire, April 3, 1958

Newspaper

The Review, East Liverpool, Oh. 4-4-1958

Records of the East Liverpool Fire Department

Fire Alarm Book #6, Jan. 1942- Nov. 1960, Entry for April 3, 1958 Run #70

Central Station Daily Logbook, March 10, 1958- June 2, 1960, Entry for April 3, 1958 Pg. 16-17

Chap. 12 *"The Deadly Chain,"* The Accidental Death of George Morley, June 5, 1898

Newspapers

The Daily Crisis, East Liverpool, Oh. 6-6-1898, 6-7-1898

The Review, East Liverpool, Oh. 6-6-1898

Chap. 13 *"Tragedies on the Mainline,"* Railroad Disasters, 1893-1948

Newspapers

"Out of the Fog!"

The Review, East Liverpool, Oh. 10-17-1893, 10-18-1893, 2-4-1895

The Tribune, East Liverpool, Oh. 10-21-1893

The Daily Crisis, East Liverpool, Oh. 10-17-1893, 10-18-1893

"A Close Call!"

The Review, East Liverpool, Oh. 7-7-1902

"The Collapse of Bridge #55"

The Review, East Liverpool, Oh. 3-3-1904, 3-4-1904, 3-5-1904, 3-7-1904, 4-11-1904, 6-7, 1905

The Tribune, East Liverpool, Oh. 3-7-1904

The Daily Crisis, East Liverpool, Oh. 4-11-1904

"The Riverside Jumble"

The Review, East Liverpool, Oh. 8-11-1948, 8-12-1948, 8-13-1948, 8-14-1948

Chap. 14 *"Conflagration,"* The Great Diamond Fire, February 28, 1905

Newspapers

The Review, East Liverpool, Oh. 3-1-1905, 3-2-1905, 3-3-1905, 3-4-1905, 3-07-1905, 3-9-1905, 3-10-1905, 3-11-1905, 3-14-1905,

3-16-1905, 3-18-1905, 10-20-1905, 1-24-1906, 2-15-1907, 3-23-1907, 9-3-1907, 2-13-1927, 5-1-1965

The Tribune, East Liverpool, Oh. 3-1-1905, 3-2-1905, 3-4-1905, 3-6-1905, 3-7-1905, 3-9-1905, 3-10-1905, 3-11-1905, 3-14-1905, 3-16-1905,

The Buckeye State, Lisbon, Oh. 3-2-1905

The Daily Herald, Steubenville, Oh. 3-2-1905

Records of the East Liverpool Fire Department

Fire Alarm Book #1, April 1899- May 1912 Entry for February 28, 1905 Run #61

Website

Wikipedia   George P. Ikert

Chap. 15 *"In-Flu-Enza,"* The Spanish Flu Pandemic, 1918

Newspapers

The Review, East Liverpool, Oh. 10-11-1918, 10-12-1918, 10-16-1918, 10-17-1918, 10-19-1918, 10-21-1918, 10-25-1918, 10-28-1918, 10-29-1918, 11-4-1918, 11-8-1918, 11-12-1918, 11-15-1918, 11-16-1918, 11-18-1918, 11-19-1918, 11-20-1918, 11-21-1918, 11-22-1918, 1123-1918, 11-25-1918, 11-26-1918, 11-27-1918, 11-29-1918, 11-30-1918, 12-3-1918, 12-5-1918, 12-6-1918, 12-9-1918, 12-10-1918, 12-11-1918, 12-12-1918, 12-14-1918, 12-16-1918, 12-21-1918, 12-27-1918, 12-28-1918, 1-6-1919, 1-24-1919

Website

Wikipedia   The 1918 Flu Pandemic

Chap. 16 *"Morning of Mayhem,"* Samuel Mann's Insane Rampage, Nov. 16, 1902

Newspapers

The Review, East Liverpool, Oh. 11-17-1902, 11-18-1902, 11-20-1902

The Daily Crisis, East Liverpool, Oh. 11-20-1902

Chap. 17 *"I'm not Drunk, I'm Crazy,"* The Murder of Letha Barrett, May 23, 1946

Newspapers

The Review, East Liverpool, Oh. 5-27-1946, 5-29-1946, 5-31-1946, 6-10-1946, 6-11-1946, 8-8-1946, 9-5-1946, 9-16-1946, 11-13-1946, 11-19-1946, 11-20-1946, 11-21-1946, 11-22-1946, 11-23-1946, 11-25-1946, 11-26-1946, 11-27-1946, 12-6-1946, 6-28-1960

Columbiana County Court Records

Bill of Particulars Case # 5944 Filed 9-4-1946

Marriage Records 1963, Hancock County W. V.

Death Records 1996, Hancock County W. V.

Chap. 18 *"Fields of Flame,"* Oil and Gas Accidents, 1877-1899

Newspapers

The Island Run Disaster

The Potter's Gazette, East Liverpool, Oh. 8-16-1877

The Tribune, East Liverpool, Oh. 8-18-1877, 8-25-1877

The Commercial Gazette, Pittsburgh, Pa. 8-14-1877, 8-15-1877

The Rayl-Karns Oil Well Disaster

The Review, East Liverpool, Oh. 9-25-1899

The Daily Crisis, East Liverpool, Oh. 9-25-1899

Chap. 19 *"The Old Mill is on Fire!,"* The Rocks Springs Park Tragedy, June 5, 1915

Newspapers

The Review, East Liverpool, Oh. 1-6-1914, 6-7-1915, 6-8-1915, 6-9-1915, 6-15-1915, 6-17-1915, 6-18-1915, 6-19-1915, 6-21-1915, 7-1-1915, 7-15-1915, 7-21-1915, 10-19-1915, 1-1-1916, 3-9-1916, 3-27-1916, 4-3-1916, 7-5-1916, 7-7-1916, 7-12-1916, 8-2-1916, 12-5-1916

The Tribune, East Liverpool, Oh. 6-7-1915, 6-8-1915, 7-2-1915

Records of the East Liverpool Fire Department

Central Station Log Book, 1-1-1915 – 10-28-1915, Entry for June 5, 1915 Page 236

Fire Alarm Book # 2, May 1912- Dec. 1922, Entry for June 5, 1915 Run # 76

Souvenir Program 3rd Annual Rock Springs Park Festival, July 22-27 1985, Hancock County

Courier Printing Company, New Cumberland, WV.

Website

East Liverpool Historical Society, Rock Springs Park

Chap. 20 *"Poison for Medicine,"* The Strange Life of Laura Christy, 1879-1937

Newspapers

The Review, East Liverpool, Ohio 1-14-1926, 1-15-1926, 1-16-

1926, 1-18-1926, 1-19-1926, 1-20-1926, 1-21-1926, 10-21- 1926

Websites

www. unknownmisandry.blogspot.com The Unknown History of Misandry, Black Widow Serial Killers, Laura Christy

www.findagrave.com / Lima State Hospital

Burial Records of the Spring Grove Cemetery, City Hall East Liverpool, Oh.

Chap. 21 *"East Liverpool is Burning!,"* Major Downtown Fires

"The Walls Came Tumbling Down!"

Newspapers

The Review, East Liverpool, Oh. 2-23-1925, 2-24-1925, 2-25-1925, 2-26-1925, 2-27-1925, 2-28-1925, 6-3-1925

Records of the East Liverpool Fire Department

Fire Alarm Book # 3, Jan. 1923- Dec. 1930, Entry for February 22, 1925 Run # 30

"A Long Cold Sunday"

Newspapers

The Review, East Liverpool, Oh. 3-4-1968, 3-5-1968, 3-8-1968, 3-25-1968

Records of the East Liverpool Fire Department

Fire Alarm Book # 7, Jan. 1961-Dec. 1978, Entry for March 3, 1968 Run # 41

Central Station Log Book July 1967- Dec. 1970, Entry for March 3, 1968 Page 69

Polk City Directory for East Liverpool, Oh., for the year of 1968

"Fire and Ice"

Newspapers

The Review, East Liverpool, Oh. 1-8-1974, 1-9-1974, 1-12-1974, 1-25-1974

Records of the East Liverpool Fire Department

Fire Alarm Book #7, Jan. 1961- Dec. 1978, Entry for January 8, 1974 Run #4

Central Station Log Book, June 1973-July 1977, Entry for January 8, 1974 Page 72

Polk City Directory for East Liverpool, Oh., for the year of 1974

Chap. 22 *"A Wild and Treacherous Man,"* The Life and Death of "Crip" Cain

Newspapers

The Review, East Liverpool Oh. 5-7-1895, 6-17-1895, 6-19-1895, 7-16-1895, 5-21-1898, 7-25-1898, 10-7-1899, 12-26-1899, 2-5-1900, 7-29-1901, 10-29- 1901, 1-5-1903, 1-6-1903, 1-23-1903, 4-1-1903, 9-1-1903, 10-26-1903, 4-1-1904, 10-20-1905

The Daily Crisis, East Liverpool, Oh. 1-5-1903, 1-6-1903

The Tribune, East Liverpool, Oh.   10-20-1905, 10-24-1905

The Intelligencer, Wheeling, W.V. 10-19-1905, 10-20-1905

Records of the East Liverpool Fire Department

Patrol Department Log Book, Apr. 1899- Dec. 1910, 10- 17-1899, 8-19-1900, 2-28-1901, 7-29-1901, 1-21-1902, 4-14-1902, 9-20-1902, 9-21-1902, 1-3-1903, 3-31-1903, 4-1-1903, 4-5-1903, 8-23-1903, 8-24- 1903, 8-31-1903, 10-20-1903, 3-15-1904,

Chap. 23 "*The Exploding Lamp,*" The Hazlett House Fire of 1905

Newspapers

The Review, East Liverpool, Oh. 6-4-1905, 6-5-1905

The Tribune, East Liverpool, Oh. 6-4-1905, 6-5-1905

Records of the East Liverpool Fire Department

Fire Alarm Book # 1, Apr. 1899- May 1912, entry for June 4, 1905 Run # 9

Chap. 24 "*Did They Get the Wrong Man?,*" The Murder of William Hyatt, February-March 1923

Newspapers

The News, Salem, Oh.   2-26-1923, 3-3-1923, 3-5-1923, 3-26-1923, 3-27-1923, 3-28-1923, 3-29-1923, 3-30-1923, 4-2-1923, 4-3-1923, 4-5-1923

The Herald Star, Steubenville, Oh. 2-26-1923

The Vindicator, Youngstown, Oh. 2-26-1923

Court Records of Columbiana County

State of Ohio vs Edward Johnson Case # 2759

Chap. 25 "*Pursued by Misfortune,*" The Laird Family 1903-1911

Newspapers

The Review, East Liverpool, Oh. 10-24-1898, 10-26-1898, 5-21-1900, 5-22-1900, 3-7-1903, 3-9-1903, 5-11-1907, 5-16-1907, 11-16-1937, 3-25-1968, 9-15-1973

The Daily Crisis, East Liverpool, Oh. 3-7-1903, 3-9-1903

The Tribune, East Liverpool, Oh. 8-28-1911

The Press, Pittsburgh, Pa. 8-27-1911, 8-28-1911, 8-29-1911

Records of the East Liverpool Fire Department

Fire Alarm Book # 1, Apr. 1899- May 1912, Entry for May 11, 1907 Run # 39

Chap. 26 *"A Mighty Deluge,"* The Reservoir Collapse, Oct. 13, 1901

Newspapers

The Review, East Liverpool, Oh. 11-8-1879, 6-30-1893, 7-1-1893, 7-3-1893, 5-26-1899, 11-23-1899, 11-24-1900, 5-1-1901, 10-10-1901, 10-14-1901, 10-15-1901, 10-16-1901, 10-18-1901, 11-12-1901, 11-27-1901, 12-7-1901, 12-18-1901, 1-13-1902, 1-22-1902, 3-22-1902, 4-25-1902, 5-19-1902, 5-31-1902

The Daily Crisis, East Liverpool, Oh. 10-14-1901, 10-15-1901, 10-16-1901, 10-17-1901, 11-12-1901, 1-13-1902, 1-22-1902

Interview

Robert Disch East Liverpool Water Superintendent August 1, 2013

Chap. 27 *"The Death Badge,"* The Death of James McCullough, May 13, 1913

Newspapers

The Review, East Liverpool, Oh. 2-12-1912, 2-13-1912, 2-14-1912, 2-26-1912, 5-12-1913, 5-13-1913, 5-14-1913, 5-15-1913, 5-16-1913, 5-19-1913

Records of the East Liverpool Fire Department

Central Station Daily Log Book , Entrees for May 13, 1913, May 14, 1913, May 15, 1913

Chap. 28 "*A Degenerate!*," The Adamant Porcelain Murders and Arson, February 7, 1918

Newspapers

The Review, East Liverpool, Oh. 2-7-1918, 2-9-1918, 2-11-1918, 2-12-1918, 2-13-1918, 2-14-1918, 2-16-1918, 2-18-1918, 2-19-1918, 4-26-1918, 5-3-1918

The Tribune, East Liverpool, Oh. 2-8-1918, 2-9-1918, 2-12-1918, 2-13-1918, 2-14-1918, 2-15-1918, 2-16-1918, 2-18-1918

Records of the East Liverpool Fire Department

Fire Alarm Book # 2, May 1912 – Dec. 1922, Entry for February 7, 1918, Run # 15 & February 8, 1918, Run # 16

Probate Court Records

Lunacy Inquest Case # 23480 Docket Book #19 Pg. 559 April 25, 1918

Photo Credits

A special thanks to these organizations for the generous use of these photographs.

AC Author's Collection   WHS   Wellsville Historical Society
FM Fire Museum   VIN   Youngstown Vindicator
PRS Pittsburgh Press   DCR   East Liverpool Daily Crisis
SN Salem News   REV   East Liverpool Review
            ELHS   East Liverpool Historical Society

Chapter 1   p.17, Michael Wain
Chapter 2   p.34 WHS
Chapter 4   p. 51 WHS; p. 57 DCR; p. 59 AC; p.60 ELHS
Chapter 5   p. 73 VIN; p. 74 REV; p. 80 VIN
Chapter 6   p. 92 AC; p. 93 AC
Chapter 7   p. 102 AC; p. 103 REV; p. 104 REV; p. 105 AC
Chapter 8   p. 109 FM
Chapter 9   p. 114 REV; p. 116 FM; p. 117 FM; p. 119 REV
Chapter 10 p. 124 WHS; p. 127 AC; p. 134 AC
Chapter 11 p. 140 FM
Chapter 13 p. 154 WHS; p.157 WHS

Chapter 14 p. 160 ELHS; p. 162 AC; p. 164 FM; p.165 AC;
p. 167 REV; p. 169 AC; p. 170 REV; p. 171 FM;
p. 172 AC; p. 173 FM; p. 174 FM; p. 175 REV

Chapter 17 p. 195 REV; p. 196 AC

Chapter 18 p. 208 WHS

Chapter 19 p. 211 Rock Springs Park Festival Souvenir Booklet 1984

p. 213 AC; p. 214 AC; p. 217 Arner Funeral Home

Chapter 20 p. 223 REV; p. 226 REV

Chapter 21 p. 239 FM; p. 242 FM; p. 243 FM; p. 244 FM; p. 246 FM

p. 247 FM; p. 248 FM; p. 249 FM

Chapter 22 p. 257 FM; p. 258 AC

Chapter 24 p. 269 SN; p. 270 REV

Chapter 25 p. 280 PPR

Chapter 26 p. 289 ELHS

Chapter 27 p. 293 FM; p. 299; p. 301 FM

Chapter 28 p. 305 FM; p. 306 ELHS; p. 307 ELHS; p. 310 ELHS

Bibliography

Books

City of Hills and Kilns   William C. Gates   1984

Ghost Rails III Electric   Wayne A. Cole   2007

Way's Packet Directory 1848-1894 Frederick Way Jr., 1983/Revised Edition 1997

Crimetown USA, The History of the Mahoning Valley Mafia, Allan May 2013

Before the Memory Fades 1795-1950 (Wellsville History), Edgar S. Davidson, 1950

"Hit EM Out" The History of the East Liverpool Fire Department, Gary J. Cornell (Unpublished)

Newspapers

The Review et al	East Liverpool, Ohio
The Tribune	East Liverpool, Ohio
The Daily Crisis	East Liverpool, Ohio
The Potter's Gazette	East Liverpool, Ohio
The Union	Wellsville, Ohio
The Journal	Salem, Ohio
The News	Salem, Ohio
The Vindicator	Youngstown, Ohio
The Ohio Patriot	Lisbon, Ohio
The Buckeye State	Lisbon, Ohio
The Herald	Steubenville, Ohio

The Daily Star	Steubenville, Ohio
The Intelligencer	Wheeling, West Virginia
The Press	Pittsburgh, Pennsylvania
The Gazette	Pittsburgh, Pennsylvania
The Commercial	Pittsburgh, Pennsylvania

Newspapers (cont.)

Palm Beach Post	Palm Beach, Florida
Miami News	Miami, Florida

Websites

ReviewOnline.com/
eastliverpoolhistoricalsociety.org
news. google.com/newspapers?
findagrave. com/
genealogypitstop.com/Columbianalinks
postgazette.com
unknownmisandry.blogspot.com

Government Records

Official Records of the East Liverpool Fire Department
Columbiana County, Ohio Court Records

Sources

A special thanks to the staff members of these organizations that always went above and beyond to assist in this project.

Columbiana County Archives & Research Center, Lisbon, Ohio

Museum of Ceramics, East Liverpool, Ohio

The Fire Museum, Central Fire Station, East Liverpool, Ohio

East Liverpool Historical Society, East Liverpool, Ohio

Wellsville Historical Society, Wellsville, Ohio

Tri-State Genealogical Society, Newell, West Virginia

The East Liverpool Review, East Liverpool, Ohio

Libraries

The Carnegie Library, East Liverpool, Ohio

The Carnegie Library, Wellsville, Ohio

The Lepper Library, Lisbon, Ohio

Salem Public Library, Salem, Ohio

Mahoning County Library, Youngstown, Ohio

The Public Library of Steubenville & Jefferson County, Steubenville, Ohio

Ohio County Library, Wheeling, West Virginia

The Lynn Murray Library, Chester, West Virginia

Made in the USA
Middletown, DE
16 October 2022